RECIPROCAL INFLUENCES

RECIPROCAL INFLUENCES

Literary Production, Distribution, and Consumption in America

Edited by
Steven Fink and Susan S. Williams

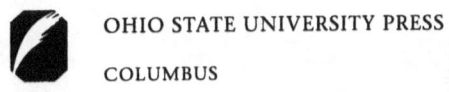

OHIO STATE UNIVERSITY PRESS
COLUMBUS

Copyright © 1999 by The Ohio State University.
All rights reserved.

Library of Congress Cataloging-in-Publication Data

Reciprocal influences : literary production, distribution, and consumption in
  America / edited by Steven Fink and Susan S. Williams.
    p.   cm.
  "The genesis for this book was a colloquium on "The profession of authorship in America: the legacy of William Charvat," which was presented by the English Department of the Ohio State University in April 1996"—P. 5.
  Includes bibliographical references (p.   ) and index.
  ISBN 0-8142-0829-0 (cloth : alk. paper).—ISBN 0-8142-5031-9 (pkb. : alk. paper)
  1. American literature—19th century—History and criticism Congresses. 2. Literature publishing—United States—History Congresses. 3. Books and reading—United States—History Congresses. 4. Authorship—History Congresses.   I. Fink, Steven, 1952- . II. Williams, Susan S.
PS201.R375   1999
810.9′003—dc21   99-25133
                                                                            CIP

Text and cover design by Paula Newcomb.
Cover illustration from *The Knickerbocker*, volume 1, 1833.
Type set in New Baskerville and Stone Serif by Graphic Composition, Inc.

The paper used in this publication meets the minimum requirements of the American National Standard for Information Sciences—Permanence of Paper for Printed Library Materials. ANSI Z39.48-1992.

9 8 7 6 5 4 3 2 1

CONTENTS

Acknowledgments / vii

Introduction
   Steven Fink and Susan S. Williams / 1

Cognitive Patterns and Aesthetic Deformations in Post-Revolutionary American Writing: A Preliminary Inquiry
   Grantland S. Rice / 13

African Americans, Literature, and the Nineteenth-Century Afro-Protestant Press
   Frances Smith Foster / 24

The Problem of Hawthorne's Popularity
   Meredith L. McGill / 36

Margaret Fuller: The Evolution of a Woman of Letters
   Steven Fink / 55

Rereading Emerson/Whitman
   Jay Grossman / 75

The Transatlantic Book Trade and Anglo-American Literary Culture in the Nineteenth Century
   Michael Winship / 98

American Civil War Poetry and the Meaning of Literary Commodification: Whitman, Melville, and Others
   Lawrence Buell / 123

Negotiating an Audience for American Exceptionalism:
Redburn and *Roughing It*
  Julian Markels / 139

Writing with an Ethical Purpose: The Case of Elizabeth Stuart Phelps
  Susan S. Williams / 151

Periodicals Back (Advertisers) to Front (Editors): Whose National Values Market Best?
  Martha Banta / 173

Politics and the Writer's Career: Two Cases
  Michael T. Gilmore / 199

Contributors / 213

Index / 215

ACKNOWLEDGMENTS

The genesis for this book was a colloquium on "The Profession of Authorship in America: The Legacy of William Charvat," which was presented by the English department of The Ohio State University in April 1996. The editors would like to thank Murray Beja, former chair of the department, for initially agreeing to fund the colloquium, and Jim Phelan, current chair, for his support of the actual event and of our subsequent work on this volume. For additional assistance with the colloquium, we would also like to thank the members of our English 900/901 seminar, who provided a sounding board for our own work and for the ideas presented by the visiting speakers; Mary Kelley of Dartmouth College and Martha Woodmansee of Case Western Reserve University, who enhanced the colloquium through their participation; and the Wexner Center for the Arts, which hosted the entire event. We are particularly grateful to Irmgard Schopen, our graduate assistant for the colloquium, who handled a myriad of details with great efficiency and good humor.

As this book has gone to press, we have been assisted by a number of other people as well. We especially want to acknowledge Lucy Caswell of the Ohio State University Cartoon, Graphic and Photographic Arts Research Library, who helped with illustrations, and the Ohio State College of Humanities, which provided both of the editors with leave time as we were bringing this volume to completion. Barbara Hanrahan, the director of the Ohio State University Press, has supported this project from its inception, and we are grateful for her encouragement. Finally, we would like to thank all of the contributors to the volume, who have patiently answered our queries and have been exemplary collaborators on this project. They are our own best reciprocal influences.

Introduction
Steven Fink and Susan S. Williams

The essays collected here were originally presented as part of a colloquium on "The Profession of Authorship in America: The Legacy of William Charvat," sponsored by the English department of The Ohio State University. William Charvat was a member of the Ohio State English department faculty from 1944 until his death in 1966; the great project of his career was "to write the history of American literature in terms of the profession of writing and the business of publishing."[1] Though his work was respected, Charvat himself recognized that it went against the grain of prevailing critical trends, and he died before his most ambitious project could be completed. Nevertheless, his work on the culture of professional authorship included *The Origin of American Critical Thought, 1810–1835; The Cost Books of Ticknor & Fields and Their Predecessors, 1832–1858*, co-edited with Warren S. Tryon; and *Literary Publishing in America, 1790–1850*. Most important, Charvat's previously published as well as unpublished essays intended for his projected work, *The Profession of Authorship in America, 1800–1870*, were compiled by Matthew J. Bruccoli and published posthumously under that title by Ohio State University Press. If at first Charvat's works languished on the library shelves, by the early 1980s they were beginning to be eagerly rediscovered;

in the wake of the emergent French *histoire du livre* and the German *Geschichte des Buchwesens,* the "History of the Book" took shape as a discipline among English and American scholars as well, and Americanists discovered, as Cathy Davidson has put it, that William Charvat was "a book historian before there was such a field."[2] Scholars working in American book history (including almost all of the contributors to this volume) invariably acknowledged their debt to Charvat's seminal work, and by the 1990s, new editions of Charvat's major works were back in print.

An impressive body of sophisticated scholarship in the History of the Book has been, and continues to be, produced, in many respects far outstripping Charvat's early achievement; but there is little to add to Charvat's impressively concise conception of the premises of this discipline:

> It has been recognized often enough that the relation between the writer and society is reciprocal. But ... the tendency is to assign a dynamic role in this relationship to the author only, and a merely passive one to society as represented by the reader. Still worse, most scholars assume that literary history can be adequately represented by a line—with the writer at one end and the reader at the other. Actually, instead of being merely linear, the pattern is triangular. Opposite both the writer and the reader stands the whole complex organism of the book and magazine trade—a trade which for the last two centuries, at least, has had a positive and dynamic function in the world of literature. The book trade is acted upon by both writer and reader, and in receiving their influence the book trade interprets it and therefore transmutes it. Correspondingly, writer and reader dictate to, and are dictated to by, the book trade.
>
> These reciprocal influences are complex.... The critic and historian both need instruments: publishers' records; the correspondence of authors and editors ...; facts about the circulation of magazines and sales of books; and—most difficult of all to find—reliable evidence of reader response.[3]

Among the most important and influential of contemporary History of the Book scholars, Robert Darnton has offered his own formulation of "a general model for analyzing the way books come into being and spread through society," using the image of a "communications circuit" rather than Charvat's triangulation model: Darnton describes the "life cycle" of printed books as a communications circuit that runs from the author to the publisher (if the bookseller does not assume that role), the printer, the shipper, the bookseller, and the reader. The reader completes the circuit, because he influences the author before and after the act of composition. Authors are readers themselves. . . . Book history concerns each phase of this process and the process as a whole, in all its variations over space and time, and in all its relations with other systems, economic, social, political, and cultural, in the surrounding environment.[4]

What is perhaps most notable is that Charvat fully anticipates not only the various components but also the dynamism of Darnton's model; and it might be argued that Charvat's triangulation model actually better captures the dynamic reciprocity of all the components than the essentially one-way circuit constructed by Darnton.

But whether we find a triangle or a circle a more useful and accurate image, scholars engaged in studying literature as it is shaped by and shapes the complex web of literary production, distribution, and consumption agree that the field as a whole draws upon a wide range of disciplines and methodologies; that material culture, intellectual history, economic history, technology, geography, social history, all constitute disciplinary contexts that facilitate our understanding of the cultural work of literature. This does not mean that such scholarship is preoccupied with contexts at the expense of the texts themselves; on the contrary, such scholarship is, at its core, profoundly interested in the aesthetic experience of reading—but it insists (contrary to the presumption of a self-contained literary universe held by the archetypal and New Criticism against which Charvat was reacting) that the aesthetic experience of reading—how one reads and understands a literary text—is conditioned by the complex organic web of factors that shape how that text is produced, distributed, and consumed at any particular cultural moment. Further, the presumption is that the relation between text and context is a reciprocal one: That is, if the various cultural contexts illuminate literary texts, it is also true that literary texts constitute points of access to understanding the larger culture in which they participated.

The essays in this volume share these fundamental assumptions, then, even as they draw upon many and varied cultural contexts and critical methodologies. Each essay has its own, discrete value and makes its own contribution to the critical study of its subject; but it is our hope, too, that the whole of this volume is greater than the sum of its parts—that, collectively, the essays here also function as case studies illustrating a wide range of critical and methodological possibilities for scholarship in the history of literary production and consumption.

While several different organizational principles suggested themselves for this volume, we have chosen to arrange the essays in a more or less chronological order as the most usable and least intrusive design. The collection begins, then, with Grantland Rice's "Cognitive Patterns and Aesthetic Deformations in Post-Revolutionary American Writing: A Preliminary Inquiry." In Robert Darnton's terms, Rice might be said to be most interested in exploring the communication circuit in "its relations with other systems, economic, social, political, and cultural, in the surrounding environment," by examining what Rice describes as the "growing association between the practice of authorship and that of the emerging science of political economy." Using J. Hector St. John de Crèvecoeur's 1782 *Letters from an American Farmer* as his exemplary text, Rice argues that by engaging "a specific pattern of cognition common to both post-Enlightenment political economy and post-Revolutionary aesthetic theory," which he labels "metonymic reasoning," post-Revolutionary writers were able to negotiate contradictory critical injunctions in post-Revolutionary America (as previously delineated by William Charvat): that writing should be "social" rather than "egocentric," but that writing should not be tolerated that "tended to disrupt the political, economic, and moral status quo." By examining the nature and use of "metonymic reasoning," Rice provides not only a subtly nuanced reading of Crèvecoeur's *Letters* but also a way of understanding a major shift in the aims of literary activity in general in post-Revolutionary America.

In the early nineteenth century, the parameters of this literary activity significantly expanded, especially with the increased popularity of—and availability of—newspapers, magazines, and journals. The proliferation of printed materials, along with advances in the publishing industry, led to increased literary access for a number of Americans, including African Americans, Native Americans, and European-American women. In "African Americans, Literature, and the Nineteenth-Century Afro-Protestant Press," Frances Smith Foster shows the ways in which African American publishing was supported by religious institutions. The Afro-Protestant press published political and literary pieces as well as religious ones, and these publications provided important opportunities for aspiring African American writers to get into print. Frederick Douglass's literary skills, for instance, were cultivated by the AME Zion Church well before William Lloyd Garrison (Douglass's well-known mentor) ever heard him speak, and Martin Delany established a newspaper, the *Mystery*, that eventually was bought by AME church officials, who renamed it the *Christian Recorder*. Using these and other examples, Foster invites us to undertake what she terms "a revised analysis of the texts and contexts of early African American literature," as well as of the interconnection between religious institutions and literary production.

In "The Problem of Hawthorne's Popularity," Meredith McGill considers antebellum publishing history through a different kind of case study, this one focusing on the literary career of Nathaniel Hawthorne. Although Hawthorne is now famous for having been neglected at the beginning of his career, McGill shows that this obscurity was part of an authorial persona that Hawthorne himself created in order to renegotiate a relationship to his reading public. This renegotiation was made necessary, in turn, by the way in which his (often anonymous) tales were circulated and reprinted in the antebellum literary marketplace. Ultimately, then, Hawthorne's "fiction of obscurity" was less a reaction against popular literary convention than a strategy for controlling the terms of his own reception. In order to explain this strategy, McGill examines Edgar Allan Poe's reviews of Hawthorne's early fiction. These reviews help uncover the reasons for Hawthorne's success, which Poe both envies and respects. At the same time, they show Poe's understanding of the contingent nature of this success, since it depends on a literary marketplace that "can make forms of literary value both appear and disappear." In this sense, McGill argues, publishing history helps us understand "the historicity of literary value" as well as the terms of Hawthorne's early career.

Not all antebellum writers were as self-effacing as Hawthorne, of course, a fact explored in some detail in Steven Fink's "Margaret Fuller: The Evolution of a Woman of Letters." Like McGill, Fink traces the course of an author's career as it responded to and was shaped by the literary marketplace. But in Fuller's case, the authorial career was marked not by obscurity but rather by an evolving sense of herself as a woman writer, as a Romantic idealist, and as a social reformer. Fink suggests that, over the course of her career, Fuller moved through all four stages of Raymond Williams's typology of literary production—from the unmediated contact with her audience in her series of Conversations to placing essays in magazines to negotiating contracts for book publication and, finally, to her status as "corporate professional," working on salary as a columnist for Horace Greeley's New York *Tribune*. By examining the various market conditions Fuller faced and the particular choices she made over the course of her career, Fink explores the instabilities and tensions, the limitations and opportunities, that she confronted in defining herself as a woman of letters in antebellum America.

Another famously self-reflexive writer, Walt Whitman, is the subject of Jay Grossman's essay, "Rereading Emerson/Whitman." Grossman reconsiders Emerson's famous response to Whitman upon receiving a complimentary copy of *Leaves of Grass,* and Whitman's subsequent use of that letter for promotional purposes, in order to expose the indeterminate nature of poetry itself in the nineteenth century. "Returning to the material text reminds us of the possibilities, exigencies, and possibly the dangers, of the market and of circulation, and what appeared to be static (Emerson and Whitman are poets and agree about what poetry is and should be) now appears to be dynamic." In particular, Grossman argues that the class positions of Emerson and Whitman led them to adopt markedly different assumptions about the relation between poet and audience, assumptions "that both reflect and reproduce contrasting antebellum conceptions about the relations between . . . the representative man and the constituencies to whom and for whom he speaks."

Michael Winship reminds us that, while much book history has been constructed in national terms (including, it must be confessed, this collection), "Books—those international agents of intellectual and cultural exchange—are no respecters of national borders." In his essay "The Transatlantic Book Trade and Anglo-American Literary Culture in the Nineteenth Century," Winship documents and analyzes American involvement in the international book trade by studying customs statistics and tariff and copyright practices during the period 1828 to 1868. After surveying the conditions of the international book trade in general, Winship provides a closer analysis of the import practices of the prominent Boston publishing firm of Ticknor and Fields, focusing on a particular transaction made in 1858. He shows that as Ticknor and Fields engaged in international trade, they utilized three separate communication networks: information, merchandise, and credit. Winship convincingly insists that while Ticknor and Fields played a central role in the publication and promotion of American belles lettres, a full and balanced understanding of their role requires that we also acknowledge the nature and importance of their transatlantic trade.

Although the book trade was a fundamental component of the growing commodification of literature in the mid-nineteenth century, Lawrence Buell uses the example of Civil War verse to remind us that our understanding of literary commodification must be pried loose "from the image of cash value per se . . . [and] from the image of sheer entrepreneurial self-interest." In "American Civil War Poetry and the Meaning of Literary Commodification: Whitman, Melville, and Others," Buell first situates Whitman's *Drum-Taps* and Melville's *Battle Pieces* within the wide array of market niches for American Civil War verse as they are implied by the publisher, the physical production qualities of the texts, and the promotion and distribution efforts. He then goes on to suggest that the extended value of this verse can be fully understood only when we look beyond direct sales. In Whitman's case, for example, we should recognize that while Whitman was virtually unable to place his poetry in newspapers and magazines through the 1850s, after *Drum-Taps* he "was able to place 60 percent of his new poems in newspapers and magazines before their book publication." Buell argues that Whitman's Civil War verse not only yielded both direct and indirect financial benefits, but also "helped advance him to the threshold of canonicity." In this sense, commodification need not be seen as necessarily antagonistic to creativity, since in some cases, "'commodification' may unleash creative energies as well as impose self-censorship."

In "Negotiating an Audience for American Exceptionalism: *Redburn* and *Roughing It*," Julian Markels offers a different perspective on literary creativity through his subtly nuanced rhetorical analysis of the implied author-reader relationship in apprentice novels by Melville and Twain. *Redburn* and *Roughing It*, Markels points out, both begin as initiation stories that turn into picaresque miscellanies as their youthful protagonists travel in opposite directions; and fundamental to both narratives, he argues, is a cultural conflict figured in terms of the opposition between vernacular and genteel discourse. In both of these apprentice novels, however, the narrators waver inconsistently in their identification with vernacular or genteel culture, which results in "some highly self-conscious passages confusedly addressed to disparate audiences." At stake are the terms of American exceptionalism. While Markels discerns in these early novels a strikingly similar ambivalence on the part of the authors, he suggests that "the different paths they finally took can perhaps tell us not only about personal differences but about rhetorical and generational 'reader-response conditions' for the American exceptionalisms later embodied by *Moby-Dick* and *Huckleberry Finn*."

Elizabeth Stuart Phelps's conflicted sense of her literary vocation—the question of what is the proper work of the writer (and particularly the American woman writer)—is the subject of Susan S. Williams's essay, "Writing with an Ethical Purpose: The Case of Elizabeth Stuart Phelps." As a writer, Phelps was a "moral realist," committed to recording the "truth" of experience even while enlisting that truth to serve a clear "ethical purpose." This moral realism, in turn, enabled Phelps to address the conflict she experienced between observation and action, between working on her art and working to effect social change. Her art ultimately enabled her to develop a particular kind of individualism, one defined through intellectual labor and the ability of the self to mediate the "truth." Williams focuses her analysis on Phelps's temperance novel, *A Singular Life*, seeing Phelps addressing her own vocational concerns through those of the novel's protagonist—a clergyman committed to missionary work in a bowery district even as he longs for the comforts and aesthetic pleasures of middle-class life. Yet she also situates Phelps's vocational concerns within the larger context of American realism, showing how Phelps defined her moral realism against the realist project associated with William Dean Howells.

Several of the essays introduced so far have addressed, at least in passing, the significance of texts as material artifacts: Did they appear in books or periodicals? Were they signed or anonymous (or pseudonymous)? Bound in expensive or cheap editions? What is signified by the layout on the page? In "Periodicals Back (Advertisers) to Front (Editors): Whose National Values Market Best?" Martha Banta pays primary attention to the matter of how the "meaning" of texts is profoundly shaped by the material context through a case study of *Life Magazine* between 1883 and 1918. The editorials and political cartoons of this social-satire magazine insistently established the periodical as pacifist and anti-imperialist, which contrasted sharply with the "expansionist implications of items put up for sale in the back of the book by advertisers who had quite different views on war, weaponry, and the patriotic call to extend the nation's global reach." Banta demonstrates that the commercial and editorial interests of the magazine were so at odds that the result was essentially "two magazines," ideologically in conflict, during this period.

In the final essay of this collection, Michael T. Gilmore ("Politics and the Writer's Career: Two Cases") argues that it is not merely the marketplace, cultural ideology, and the institutionalized culture of letters but the political environment as well that acts as a shaping influence on literary production and the course of a writer's career (politics as one of the "other systems" in the "surrounding environment," as Robert Darnton put it). Gilmore offers as case studies assessments of the careers of James Weldon Johnson and William Charvat himself. Gilmore points out that Johnson completed his novel, *The Autobiography of an Ex-Coloured Man,* while serving as U.S. Consul in Nicaragua during Teddy Roosevelt's administration. Gilmore argues that Johnson's beliefs in color-blind meritocracy and social mobility over race, implicit in the novel, were enabled by the climate of the Roosevelt administration; but that these views were unsustainable when the Republicans were defeated by Democrat Woodrow Wilson in 1912, resulting in the resegregation of government. Johnson resigned his post, returned to the United States, never wrote fiction again, and "never again entertained the illusion of being an ex-African American"—turning instead to political activism and racial advocacy. In Charvat's case, Gilmore notes that the "critical fashion" of the 1950s and 1960s "had moved away from Charvat's interest in the commercial side of art, the unglamorous details of literary manufacture, promotion, and distribution," and he argues that "this change in cultural emphasis cannot be understood apart from the political mutations that accompanied and produced it." It is in the context of the Cold War recoil from the radicalism of the 1930s and 1940s that we can understand both the course of literary critical fashion and the course of—and intellectual isolation that finally characterized—Charvat's career.

The essays in this collection tend to be brief, and none presumes to have the final word on its topic; collectively, as well, they do not presume to exemplify all the multiple and complex dimensions of literary production, distribution, and reception. Nevertheless, we do think that they touch on some of the most important critical concerns in current American book history. For instance, readers particularly interested in the material conditions of production and reception may want to begin with the essays by Frances Smith Foster,

Michael Winship, Lawrence Buell, and Martha Banta. Those looking for exemplary case studies of authorial careers—as well as of the gendered construction of authorship—may want to focus on the essays by Meredith McGill, Steven Fink, and Susan S. Williams. Those interested in the relation between politics and authorship will want to consult the essays by Grantland Rice and Michael Gilmore. And those wishing to explore the specific dynamics of reader reception and interpretation may want to begin with the essays by Jay Grossman and Julian Markels. In whatever order one reads these essays, we do hope, certainly, that both individually and collectively they are found to contribute to the body of scholarship built upon the foundation laid by William Charvat and subsequent scholars, and that, in turn, they stimulate interest in further research and scholarship.

Notes

1. William Charvat, Introduction to *The Profession of Authorship in America, 1800–1870: The Papers of William Charvat*, ed. Matthew J. Bruccoli (Columbus: Ohio State University Press, 1968), 3.
2. Cathy N. Davidson, "Toward a History of Books and Readers," in Davidson, ed. *Reading in America: Literature and Social History* (Baltimore: Johns Hopkins University Press, 1989), 20.
3. William Charvat, "Literary Economics and Literary History," 1950; rpt. in *The Profession of Authorship in America*, 284–85.
4. Robert Darnton, "What Is the History of Books?" in Davidson, *Reading in America*, 30. Interestingly, Darnton does not acknowledge Charvat's earlier work at all in this essay.

Suggestions for Further Reading

Barnes, James J. *Authors, Publishers and Politicians: The Quest for an Anglo-American Copyright Agreement, 1815–1854*. London: Routledge and Kegan Paul; Columbus: Ohio State University Press, 1974.

Baym, Nina. *Novels, Readers and Reviewers: Responses to Fiction in Antebellum America*. Ithaca, N.Y.: Cornell University Press, 1984.

Brodhead, Richard H. *Cultures of Letters: Scenes of Reading and Writing in Nineteenth-Century America*. Chicago: University of Chicago Press, 1993.

Buell, Lawrence. *New England Literary Culture: From Revolution through Renaissance*. New York: Cambridge University Press, 1986.

Charvat, William. *Literary Publishing in America, 1790–1850*. Philadelphia: University of Pennsylvania Press, 1959; rpt. Amherst: University of Massachusetts Press, 1993.

———. *The Origins of American Critical Thought, 1810–1835*. Philadelphia: University of Pennsylvania Press, 1936.

———. *The Profession of Authorship in America, 1800–1870: The Papers of William Charvat*, ed. Matthew J. Bruccoli. Columbus: Ohio State University Press, 1968; rpt. New York: Columbia University Press, 1992.

Coultrap-McQuin, Susan. *Doing Literary Business: American Women Writers in the Nineteenth Century*. Chapel Hill: University of North Carolina Press, 1990.

Davidson, Cathy, ed. *Reading in America: Literature and Social History*. Baltimore: Johns Hopkins University Press, 1989.

Foster, Frances Smith. *Written by Herself: Literary Production by African American Women, 1746–1892*. Bloomington: Indiana University Press, 1993.

Gilmore, Michael T. *American Romanticism and the Marketplace*. Chicago: University of Chicago Press, 1985.

Hackenberg, Michael, ed. *Getting the Books Out: Papers of the Chicago Conference on the Book in 19th-Century America.* Washington, D.C.: Library of Congress, Center for the Book, 1987.

Hall, David D. *Cultures of Print: Essays in the History of the Book.* Amherst: University of Massachusetts Press, 1996.

Joyce, William L., et al., eds. *Printing and Society in Early America.* Worcester, Mass.: American Antiquarian Society, 1983.

Kelley, Mary. *Private Woman, Public Stage: Literary Domesticity in Nineteenth-Century America.* New York: Oxford University Press, 1984.

Mott, Frank Luther. *A History of American Magazines, 1741–1850.* New York: D. Appleton, 1930.

Moylan, Michele, and Lane Stiles, eds. *Reading Books: Essays on the Material Text and Literature in America.* Amherst: University of Massachusetts Press, 1996.

Peterson, Carla L. *'Doers of the Word': African-American Women Speakers and Writers in the North (1830–1880).* New York: Oxford University Press, 1995.

Price, Kenneth M., and Susan Belasco Smith, eds. *Periodical Literature in Nineteenth-Century America.* Charlottesville: University Press of Virginia, 1995.

Tebbel, John. *A History of Book Publishing in the United States.* 3 vols. New York: Bowker, 1972.

Weber, Ronald. *Hired Pens: Professional Writers in America's Golden Age of Print.* Athens: Ohio University Press, 1997.

West, James L. W., III. *American Authors and the Literary Marketplace since 1900.* Philadelphia: University of Pennsylvania Press, 1988.

Wilson, Christopher P. *The Labor of Words: Literary Professionalism in the Progressive Era.* Athens: University of Georgia Press, 1985.

Winship, Michael. *American Literary Publishing in the Mid-Nineteenth Century: The Business of Ticknor and Fields.* Cambridge: Cambridge University Press, 1995.

Zboray, Ronald J. *A Fictive People: Antebellum Economic Development and the American Reading Public.* New York: Oxford University Press, 1993.

Cognitive Patterns and Aesthetic Deformations in Post-Revolutionary American Writing: A Preliminary Inquiry

Grantland S. Rice

In *The Origins of American Critical Thought,* perhaps his most forgotten work and about arguably one of the most neglected periods in American literary history, William Charvat set out to describe a dramatic transformation in the sociology of literary reception in post-Revolutionary America.[1] Working inductively and thematically from an array of newspaper and magazine criticism in the years between 1810 and 1835, Charvat typologized five underlying principles that framed contemporary discourse about the aims of literary activity. These basic critical axioms comprised the claim that literature be "optimistic" and not "condone philosophical pessimism or skepticism," the idea that "literature must not advocate rebellion of any kind against the existing social and economic order," the injunction that critics "repress any writer who tended to disrupt the political, economic, and moral status quo," and, most odd given these former principles, the assertion that fiction take a "social" rather than "egocentric" point of view. Although Charvat acknowledged the circularity engendered by this last principle—that literature should underwrite a social rather than self-indulgent point of view at the same time it elided criticism or skepticism of that social order—he stopped short of exploring how this tautology might have been worked out in the aesthetic practices of writers.

I would like to use Charvat's observation as a starting point to get at a series of provisional arguments that have developed out of my current research on the fate of political discourse in post-Revolutionary America. I want to float the idea that the moral injunctions observed by Charvat were ideological epiphenomena underlying three structural transformations in the conditions of late eighteenth-century authorship: a move by early nineteenth-century cultural spokesmen to sublimate a long and continuous tradition of sociopolitical critique, founded in a curious amalgam of Protestant political theory, civic republicanism, and revolutionary dissent, into a stable and authorizing cultural practice; the birth of the autonomous category of the "literary" in American culture, together with the attendant realm of literary aesthetics that served to isolate, standardize, and regulate public rhetoric; and, finally, the specific topic I want to focus on here: a growing association between the practice of authorship and that of the emerging science of political economy. I have argued elsewhere how this last development found material expression in the debates over copyright and literary property after 1790.[2] In this short essay I want to explore a different and more abstract association based on a specific pattern of cognition common to both post-Enlightenment political economy and post-Revolutionary aesthetic theory: something I'll term metonymic reasoning. I want to speculate that it was by this mode of cognition, particularly in its aesthetic manifestation—literary symbolism—that post-Revolutionary writers negotiated the circular critical injunction to avoid egotism without engaging critically with the social or political.

By metonymic reasoning I mean a cognitive disposition that, to paraphrase the linguist George Lakoff, tacitly derives a broader, more integral category—presupposed as an ideal case—from a term understood to be its representative embodiment.[3] If, beginning with Locke, political philosophy turned to metonymic patterns of thought to instantiate concepts as broad and abstract as citizens and civil government from the singular but representative bearer of property, in the same way Adam Smith was to theorize the universal principle of an "invisible hand" by telescoping the actions of an anonymous pin maker, late eighteenth-century aesthetics turned to metonymy as an innovative means to derive the universal or general from the particular. This turn was signaled in literary practice by the emergence of symbolism, an ascendant mode of figurative meaning making that was being separated from political allegory by Goethe and Coleridge during this very period and that shared with the nascent science of political economy a courtship with metonymy. Whereas traditional modes of allegory sought to place a part or piece into a broader, sociohistorical whole to which it gave meaning, symbolism, like the emerging tropes of political economy, rejected the idea of any transhistorical order or design governing human affairs in favor of an empirical methodology that sought to get at the universal through the representative particular itself. Walter Benjamin argued for this aesthetic distinction in *Origin of German Tragic Drama*, claiming that while allegorical representation signified "a general concept [or structure], ... symbolic representation [was] the very incarnation and embodiment of the idea. In the former a process of substitution [took] place ... [while] in the latter the concept itself [had] descended into our physical world, and we see it directly in the image."[4]

The triumph of metonymic reasoning at the end of the eighteenth century was a radical development in both aesthetics and political philosophy, in which the belief that it was possible to discern some general scheme or design, some all-encompassing purpose or pattern in the world that was distinguishable from the observable particular, went back to the ancients.[5] Scholars such as Myra Jehlen, Michael Lienesch, and Sacvan Bercovitch have even gone so far as to link the triumph of metonymic reasoning to the victory of modern millennialism over classical republicanism, claiming that republican notions of time and history as cyclical and recurrent were supplanted with a millennial fascination with particularity, linearity, and teleological progress.[6]

In this speculative piece I want to call attention to one late eighteenth-century narrative that I think signaled the dramatic change in literary sociology described by Charvat and that, not coincidentally, thematized and critiqued what I'm calling the triumph of metonymic reasoning. Looking forward to (rather than backward from) nineteenth-century romanticism, the question I ultimately hope to pose but leave unanswered here is if we can view much of what was innovative about American prose fiction in the years after the Revolution, not in terms of a rise of an American literature, but in terms of a consolidating set of aesthetic deformations, unanticipated effects of a rhetorical and communicative tradition struggling to survive in a culture that was recasting the unpredictable political practice of eighteenth-century public writing into a clearly demarcated and governable category of economic production.

It is more than one of the greatest ironies of American literary history that what is probably the most thoroughgoing critique of the cognitive scaffolding of economic liberalism in late eighteenth-century letters has been seen as a manifesto for the *homo economicus* of American exceptionalism. I am talking about J. Hector St. John de Crèvecoeur's 1782 *Letters from an American Farmer*, the story of a self-classified "humble American planter" who reveals at the end of his narrative that his innovative and optimistic focus on the "exceptional" microcosmic aspects of American labor has blinded him to far more sinister macrocosmic social realities—namely the persistence and expansion of the exploitative relationships of slavery and wage capitalism.[7] As scholarship has gradually come to recognize, *Letters from an American Farmer* is less an account of facts than it is of knowing, less an assessment of the economic conditions of late eighteenth-century America than it is critique of the way in which writers go about accounting for and validating those conditions through observation and theory.

Much of the confusion about *Letters from an American Farmer* has stemmed from a failure to take into account Crèvecoeur's dedication to the French intellectual Abbé Raynal, whose 1770 *Philosophical and Political History of the Settlements and Trade of the Europeans in the East and West Indies* went through countless editions and consistently made the list of the top five most sought-after forbidden best-sellers in pre-Revolutionary France.[8] Historian Robert Darnton quotes one bookseller as claiming in 1774 that the market was so saturated with editions of the *Philosophical and Political History* that "one can consider its sales potential as destroyed," a situation that was rectified after 1781 when the public hangman burned the book in front of the Parliament of Paris.[9] Raynal's history was so popular that writers like the Abbé Roubaud and the philosopher Hornot plagiarized from it freely, and one historian claims that up to 1789 "hardly a year went by but an imitation of Raynal appeared."[10] In the preface to *Letters*, Crèvecoeur admits to reading *Philosophical and Political History* and reflecting "on the relative state of nations" and on "the extended ramifications of a commerce which ought to unite but now convulses the world." Proclaiming Raynal's "genius to be at the head of [his] study," Crèvecoeur admits that he "prosecutes" [Raynal's] labors under [his book's] "invisible but powerful guidance" and expresses his wish to "sanctify [*Letters*] under the auspices of [Raynal's] name." *Letters*, in Crèvecoeur's own words, constitutes a study of the American scene within the matrix of Raynal's theories on slavery and degeneracy.

The concept of Raynal's book was one that was self-consciously original: he claimed that he was seeking to theorize how structural economic patterns dominated the history of nations. Raynal's materialistic thesis, reflected in the title of his work, allowed him to critique the course of European nation building over nearly three centuries, and it afforded him the opportunity to use the settlement of the new world as a backdrop to continue on in the *philosophes'* attack against intolerance and servitude. In the tradition of the great French historian Bossuet, Raynal sought above all to reach truths of a general nature, and he saw the meticulous accumulation of discrete and accurate details, the Enlightenment preoccupation with empiricism, as relatively unimportant to a thinker who possessed the key to the mysteries of the world: a philosophic soul. In fact, when he was confronted with the myriad of factual errors in his *Philosophical and Political History*, Raynal reportedly responded to critics that the lessons and predictions of his survey more than made up for any factual inaccuracies.

Central to Raynal's theory of American history was its turn from agrarianism to commerce. Since in Raynal's definition commerce produced "nothing of itself for it is of a plastic nature ... its business consists in exchanges," he considered agricultural production, particularly by means of independent husbandmen, as the benchmark of a nation's wealth. Invoking an analogous course of civilization in the history of the Roman Empire, Raynal suggested that the ubiquity of civilizational decline was linked to an insidious distancing of the means and modes of agricultural production. Through avarice and sloth, he noted, citizens of Rome "contracted the habit of trusting the care of their subsistence to their slaves," and "proud of the spoils of the universe, [they] held in contempt the rural occupations of [their] founders." Raynal concluded that "the contempt which Romans had for agriculture, in the intoxication of those conquests which had given them the whole world without cultivating it" brought the empire to starvation and finally "to ruin, destroyed rather by its internal vices, than by the barbarians who tore it to pieces" (8:216–17).

Raynal's history of the New World up until the American Revolution followed the same trajectory as his history of Rome. In the original founding of settlements in the New World, victims of the intolerance and despotism of Europe sought asylum in an environment where they could flourish by subsistence farming. As population increased, inevitable class divisions surfaced to subvert the agrarian ideal of equality (7:281–82). In order to produce agricultural products in an environment with rapidly diminishing returns due to population increases, poor climate, and increasing demands on the land, planters not unwillingly forfeited their ideal of subsistence and turned to bound wage labor and slaves. Raynal saw indentureship as a nefarious trade whereby "America acquires its supplies of men for husbandry, as princes do for war, by [artifice]" (7:408–15). The introduction and persistence of slavery Raynal condemned as the harbinger of the collapse of the promise of the New World.

If for Raynal, as it was to be for Marx, "the history of all hitherto existing society was the history of class struggle," Crèvecoeur created in his literary adaptation of Raynal an aspiring philosophical writer who attempts to free himself from such overarching theories of historical necessity. James (Crèvecoeur's American farmer) will focus metonymically on the progress of singular representative individuals rather than synthetically on underlying structural economic conditions. In the first epistle of *Letters,* where James gives a long account of his rationale for writing, a local minister explains why in America a humble farmer, with little knowledge of world history or political philosophy, could aspire to account for the American experience:

> In [Europe], all the objects of contemplation . . . must have a reference to ancient generations and to very distant periods, clouded with the mist of ages. . . . [In America a writer's] imagination, instead of submitting to the painful and useless retrospect of revolutions, desolations, and plagues would, on the contrary, wisely spring forward to the anticipated fields of future cultivation and improvement. . . . [In Europe] the half-ruined amphitheaters . . . must fill the mind with the most melancholy reflections whilst he is seeking for the origin and the intention of those structures with which he is surrounded and the cause for so great a decay. Here he might contemplate the very beginnings and outlines of human society.

James concludes, "I had rather *record* the progressive steps of [an] industrious farmer throughout all the stages of his labours ... than *examine* how modern Italian convents can be supported" (42–43).

In this formulation, knowledge of the part (or of the representative individual) takes precedence over that of the whole at the same time that an individualistic concern with process and procedure supplants that of collective concern with common history. James, too, celebrates the limited nature and scope of his experience, turning to a Lockean celebration of microeconomic potentialities. "I [have] ceased to ramble in imagination through the wide world," he asserts at one point. "My excursions since have not exceeded the bounds of my farm, and all my principal pleasures are now centered within its scanty limits. The instant I enter on my own land, the bright idea of property, of exclusive right, of independence, exalts my mind" (54).

It should come as no surprise that such a self-satisfied James, a would-be theorist of the micropolitical and microeconomic, has little interest in confronting either the needs of collective government or the plight of others, except when they serve to validate or accommodate his own view of the world. He asserts at one point, "Why should I not find myself happy? Where is that situation which can confer more ... felicity than that of an American farmer, possessing freedom of action, freedom of thoughts, [and] ruled by a mode of government which requires little from us? I owe nothing but a pepper corn to my country" (52). At another point, after hearing of the distresses of Russian and Hungarian peasants, James replies, "I am happier now than I thought myself before. It is strange that misery, when viewed in others, should become to us a sort of real good. ... Hard is their fate to be condemned to a slavery worse than our negroes" (52). Thus, like the institution of American slavery, history and experience drop out of James's "empirical" account of America, largely as a result of the particular metonymic reasoning that underwrites much of James's political philosophy. James's self-professed authorial method is to account for America by extrapolating the general from the particular, eschewing structural patterns, and designating general states of affairs from their microscopic material embodiment.

This authorial method speaks, I think, to dramatic changes in the sociology of communication. By appealing to no ostensible theoretical apparatus or organizing argument, James can claim that his observations are merely reflections or amplifications of a concrete but generalizable state of affairs. Thus he can proclaim his innocent objectivity at the same time that he absolves himself of all responsibility (or culpability) for the outcome of his observations. This means that the task of divining authorial intention will fall on anonymous readers. "Remember that you have laid the foundation of this correspondence," he informs his European correspondent. "You well know that I am neither a philosopher, politician, divine, or naturalist, but a simple farmer. I flatter myself, therefore, that you'll receive my letters as conceived, not according to scientific rules, to which I am a perfect stranger, but agreeable to the spontaneous impressions which each subject may inspire" (49–50).

The problem, of course, is James's unexamined point of reference, and the plot of Crèvecoeur's *Letters from an American Farmer* sets out the story of a naive political philosopher whose supposedly atheoretical focus on concrete particulars and more generally on what he terms the underlying "nature" of all industry and labor—self-interest—makes him blind to larger historical forces, particularly those relating to the formation of exploitable social classes. For instance, although James wants to find on Nantucket a perfect geography of self-sufficiency and pastoral timelessness, an island without annals and without "ancient monuments, spacious halls, [or] elegant dwellings," he has difficulty projecting such idealizations on the landscape he describes (110). James finds the island to be as emblematic of the mercantilist forces of colonization and empire as Europe's fallen citadels. Nantucket, the reader comes to realize, is as much a decadent society of idle consumers as it is an enlightened community of hard-scrabble egalitarians, and is complete with women who take opium to alleviate boredom, aristocrats who import extravagant horse chairs, and a wealthy heiress who saves the settlement from the "emoluments" of the island's lawyer by marrying him.[11]

These observations are paired throughout the text of *Letters* with meticulous descriptions of the natural world, descriptions rendered so painstakingly detailed and objective that their telling metaphorical or theoretical implications are completely lost on the narrator. James describes a Mandevillian phalanx of bees with the comment "I am astonished to see that nothing exists but what has its enemy; one species pursues and lives upon the other" (55). He notes how cheap and plentiful the soon to be extinct carrier pigeon is at the market. And when he observes how a wren attacks a swallow sitting meekly "like the passive Quaker," he responds innocently, "Where did this little bird learn that spirit of injustice? It [is] not endowed with what we term reason" (63).

It is only when history breaks into his empirical account with the onslaught of the political factionalism of the American Revolution that James recognizes how his disconnected "empirical" writing has veiled underlying socioeconomic structures. Reversing his early and optimistic assertion of American economic exceptionalism, James notes how "the innocent class are always the victim of the few; they are in all countries and at all times the inferior agents, on which the popular phantom is erected" (204). James concludes by asking his readers to acknowledge the "unreserved manner in which [he] has written" and, in looking over the text, to mourn "with [him] over that load of physical and moral evil with which [they] are all oppressed" (227). Admitting that he has overlooked his "own share" of this evil in his epistemological method of deriving the whole from the part, James confesses his collaboration in mythmaking and asks readers to transform him from his role as author of the text to that of its subject, refiguring in several sentences the entire form of *Letters*. In doing so, he recasts *Letters,* not as an empirical description of America, but as a literary account of the disillusionment of a naive political philosopher who would eschew the idea of history and historical necessity.

If Crèvecoeur's 1782 narrative constituted a sophisticated critique of an emergent epistemological methodology that sought to replace political philosophy with political science, macroeconomics with microeconomics, structural theory with empirical description, and, ultimately, political discourse with literary metonymy, why has it been read as an embodiment of American economic exceptionalism, a reading that has been orthodox almost since its publication? This is to ask the sociological question why *Letters* has been read metonymically rather than rhetorically: anthologists, historians, and critics excerpting and telescoping the whole of *Letters* from a "representative" part entitled "What Is an American?" And to ask this question, finally, is to ask another: Why was the intent of Crèvecoeur's narrative rendered so painstakingly ambiguous that its message has continually frustrated readers?

My tentative answer to both these questions speaks, I think, to the horizon of possible authorship delineated in Charvat's *Origins of American Critical Thought.* Moreover, it speaks to the consequences of such a horizon for a long tradition of sociopolitical critique in early America. Crèvecoeur's mystification of the rhetorical aim of the 1782 *Letters,* achieved in large part by his meticulous failure to make clear the precise relationship between himself and his fictional protagonist James, protected the dislocated son of a French aristocrat (living in Revolutionary New York under an assumed name) from suffering the consequences of making firm political commitments in an unstable Atlantic world. James's concluding statements that "he who governs himself according to what he calls his principles may be punished either by one [political] party or the other for those very principles," that "any kind of opposition to . . . now prevailing sentiments immediately begets hatred," and that "extremes appear equally dangerous to a person of so little weight and consequence" speak, I think, to the pressing framing conditions of Crèvecoeur's sociopolitical narrative (203–5).

But if Crèvecoeur's use of "preromantic" ambiguity protected him from political persecution and guaranteed him a safe haven in the revolutionary politics of the Atlantic world (and, I might add, an enduring place in an emerging American literary canon), it also signaled a profound transformation in traditional modes of authorship in that it encouraged readers to divine—or construct—the writer Crèvecoeur metonymically from his text. We might conclude by speculating that Crèvecoeur's narrative ultimately forfeited its rhetorical, communicative, and even didactic intentions for its metonymic representativeness. Consequently, at the very beginnings of what Charvat termed a new sociology of literacy, we are delivered with the kind of text we would expect given Charvat's assessment of the emergence of American critical thought: an ambiguous and therefore politically transcendent narrative that skirts the Scylla and Charybdis of self-reflexive authorial egotism and potentially destabilizing sociopolitical critique.

Notes

1. William Charvat, *The Origins of American Critical Thought, 1810–1835* (New York: Barnes, 1936).

2. Grantland S. Rice, *The Transformation of Authorship in America* (Chicago: University of Chicago Press, 1997). My discussion of Crèvecoeur in this essay comes from research for this book. Portions excerpted are reprinted with permission.

3. George Lakoff, *Women, Fire, and Dangerous Things: What Categories Re-*

veal about the Mind (Chicago: University of Chicago Press, 1987). See also essays by Wai Chee Dimock and Mary Poovey, in Wai Chee Dimock and Michael T. Gilmore, eds., *Rethinking Class: Literary Studies and Social Formations* (New York: Columbia University Press, 1994), and Myra Jehlen's *American Incarnation* (Cambridge: Harvard University Press, 1986).

4. Walter Benjamin, *Origin of German Tragic Drama* (Berlin, 1922), 3.

5. Albert O. Hirschman, *The Passions and the Interests: Political Arguments for Capitalism before Its Triumph* (Princeton: Princeton University Press, 1977).

6. Myra Jehlen, *American Incarnation;* Michael Lienesch, *New Order of the Ages: Time, the Constitution, and the Making of Modern American Political Thought* (Princeton: Princeton University Press, 1988); Sacvan Bercovitch, *The American Jeremiad* (Madison: University of Wisconsin Press, 1978).

7. J. Hector St. John de Crèvecoeur, *Letters from an American Farmer,* ed. Albert E. Stone (New York, 1963), 37. References hereafter cited in the text.

8. Guillaume Thomas François Raynal, *A Philosophical and Political History of the Settlements and Trade of the Europeans in the East and West Indies* (London, 1783; first French ed. 1770). Raynal's *Histoire philosophique et politique des établissements et du commerce des Européens dans les deux Indes* was the collaborative work of many writers including Diderot. I am following convention by referring to Raynal—as Crèvecoeur does—as principal author. Page references in the text are to 1783 English edition.

9. Robert Darnton, *The Forbidden Best-Sellers of Pre-Revolutionary France* (New York: Norton, 1995).

10. Bernard Fay, *Revolutionary Spirit in France and America* (New York: Harcourt, Brace, 1927).

11. Evidence of the historical passing of James's agrarian idyll insists its way into his narrative from the second letter, in which he notes the impending extinction of the carrier pigeon and the wasteful extermination of quail. Regarding the difference between what James *says* and what he *observes*, Nathaniel Philbrick has argued that on Nantucket James the farmer "sounds like Gulliver describing the Houyhnhnms: he is unwilling to draw appropriate conclusions from the evidence arrayed before him." See "The Nantucket Sequence in Crèvecoeur's *Letters from an American Farmer,*" *New England Quarterly* 64 (1991): 414–32.

African Americans, Literature, and the Nineteenth-Century Afro-Protestant Press

Frances Smith Foster

In the first trimester of the nineteenth century, the number of newspapers in the United States increased from 200 to more than 1,200.[1] The rapid growth of newspapers was in concert with the emergence of commercial publishing firms and was within the context of an equally impressive increase in the number of journals and magazines, circulating libraries, and literary societies. The increased literacy that organized public schools and coeducational colleges were beginning to foster made authorship both a pastime and a profession for more men and women than ever before in the history of this nation. Those whose reading skills or economic status did not permit them to freely participate in the expansion of the literate and the literati were not entirely excluded. Reading aloud was a favorite entertainment in many homes, and the burgeoning lyceum movement begun in 1826 soon made the words and wisdom of writers and scholars accessible in virtually every state, practically all major urban areas, and a good many rural ones.

African Americans also became public intellectuals. The percentage was small. Law, custom, and circumstance made reading and writing forbidden pleasures or impossible dreams for all but a most fortunate few, and generally African Americans with the time and talent to take advantage of such opportunities were barred from the auditoriums and salons where popular writers and speakers performed. But as early as 1780, organizations such as the African Union Society of Newport, Rhode Island, had been founded to establish free schools "for any person of colour in this town."[2] By the 1820s Philadelphia boasted of sixteen schools for African Americans, and eleven of these schools were taught by African American teachers. Nor were Southern and rural areas entirely without African American educational institutions. Bishop Daniel Payne started his school in Charleston, South Carolina, in 1829, and Reverend William Watkins founded the Watkins Academy for Negro Youth in Baltimore, Maryland, not long afterward. None of these institutions operated without opposition and many were destroyed or outlawed, but, like phoenixes, still they rose.

The literate few formed lending libraries, such as the Colored Reading Society of Philadelphia (1828), and literary societies, including Boston's Afric-American Female Intelligence Society (1831), which promoted literacy and literary production. They were small but intrepid bands, but long before slavery was abolished and at the time the public-school systems were beginning to have significant effect upon the literacy rates of the country in general, African Americans organized to promote the "Word" in African American communities. Those few were sufficient to institutionalize the African American literary tradition begun in the eighteenth century with scattered publications by Phillis Wheatley, Jupiter Hammon, Benjamin Banneker, Prince Hall, Absalom Jones, the Friendly Society of St. Thomas's African Church, and many others.

Thus, in the beginning of the nineteenth century when print media were popularized, African Americans, like other Americans (including Native Americans, Mexican Americans, and European American women),[3] began to visualize the possibilities in newspapers and publishing companies that would meet their special needs and interests. That they knew these needs and interests combined the physical and metaphysical is all the more expected when one recalls that the beginning of the nineteenth century was shaped by the Second Great Awakening. During this period, many tried to make "the Word" flesh, and words of poets and novelists as well as preachers and journalists were promoted by revived Protestants. Their words generally informed readers and hearers that every human being regardless of race, class, or gender could—indeed was expected to—

dedicate her or himself to living and sharing "the Word." For a significant number, this meant learning to read the Bible—and other "good books"—for themselves. Many felt commissioned to work to bring God's kingdom into being on this earth. Some of the "Christian Soldier" writings that spewed from the presses argued for slavery and patriarchal authority on biblical bases, but many presses were formed by antislavery societies, temperance organizations, and radically democratic evangelical Christians who understood, as Phillis Wheatley had declared some fifty years earlier, that "*Negroes,* black as *Cain /* May be refin'd, and join th' angelic train."[4] Afro-Protestants were especially partial to the liberation theology of the latter groups and to the part that literacy played.[5] They, like most United States Americans, used the Bible and its didactic offspring, Webster's Blue-Backed Speller and McGuffey's Reader, in their Sunday schools, literary societies, and such. But Afro-Protestants were keenly aware that their circumstances often produced perspectives and imperatives that differed somewhat from those of Euro-Protestants. Afro-Protestants supplemented these texts with their own hymnals, sermons, spiritual narratives, autobiographies, and interpretative histories.

At first, they, like most United States Americans, contracted out their publications, paying printers and hiring booksellers for each individual project. The seventh edition of Lemuel Haynes's 1805 sermon *Universal Salvation, . . . with Some Account of the Life and Character of Its Author* was "printed for Cornelius Davis" in 1810. The *Confession of John Joyce* was "Printed at No. 12 Walnut-Street, for the Benefit of Bethel Church. 1808" and Bishop Richard Allen held the copyright. William Hamilton's "Hymn" was, along with Joseph Sidney's *An Oration, Commemorative of the Abolition of the Slave Trade,* "Printed for the Author" in 1814. By 1817 the increased need for "educational materials," along with the realization of the professional and financial opportunities of the emerging publishing industry, compelled Bishop Allen and leaders of the Bethel African Methodist Episcopal Church in Philadelphia to establish a "Book Concern." The AME Book Concern, the earliest known African American publishing company, was followed by the AME Zion Church's Publishing House in 1841. After the Civil War, other Afro-Protestant denominations formed their own publishing houses.[6] These Afro-Protestant presses stimulated African American literary production by providing venues for African American authors, publishing literature for African American readers and articulating standards within which they were to read and to write.

While not every African American publishing venture was directly associated with an Afro-Protestant denomination or congregation, Clint Wilson's observation that "the roots of America's Black press are planted firmly in the soil of the church"[7] is valid. To begin with, as Wilson points out, the earliest publishing companies were founded and funded by the Afro-Protestant Press. It was in Afro-Protestant soil that a significantly large number of editors and contributors whom twentieth-century minds identify as "secular" or "political" were first cultivated. Many of the schools, fraternities, and literary societies that sponsored their own periodicals grew out of, or were nurtured by, Afro-Protestant churches. More often than not, groups founded for and dedicated to distinctly fraternal, political, or aesthetic issues used Afro-Protestant facilities for printing their literature and for holding their meetings. It is the business of this essay to examine more closely the roles of Afro-Protestantism in the production of African American literature, and by this example to suggest that other scholarship in the history of the book might benefit from closer analyses of the relationships between religious institutions and literary production.

What is generally overlooked or misunderstood by contemporary readers and sometimes misrepresented in decontextualized reprints and secularized summaries is that in the early nineteenth century, most people did not make grand distinctions between the church and the state. Afro-Protestants, in particular, preached a theology in which the Word was to be made Flesh, again and again. All who believed were commissioned, if not compelled, not only to proclaim the Word but to become Doers of the Word.

Even those Afro-Protestant presses that focused primarily upon providing their congregations with doctrinal tomes and disciplines, hymnals, and church histories generally published nondenominational texts also. They promoted literacy and literature as part of their evangelical missions, and sometimes, as with the National Baptist Convention, they placed the Home Missions Board under the authority of its Publishing Board. A pamphlet written in 1857 by Mary Still to the "Females of the African Methodist Episcopal Church" exemplifies a prevalent philosophy of the first two-thirds of the nineteenth century. Still writes that "being deeply impressed with the utility of a Periodical, devoted to Religion, Morality, Science and Literature, for the dissemination of useful knowledge among a downtrodden and an oppressed race, and for promoting a more general interest in our ranks, the ecclesiastical power in the A.M.E. Church, have provided for publishing an organ devoted to those principles made sacred by the God of nature." She asserts that "the great difficulty among us arises mainly from the want of a stronger literary force" and that the proposed periodical "will in some measure unite again the national chain which has long been broken by slavery, prejudice, and oppression, and bind us together in love and respect for each other's welfare"; therefore, she says, it is the "great moral duty" of the women to take "immediate action in the literary department of the A.M.E. Church."[8]

In nineteenth-century Afro-Protestant newspapers, especially, conference reports and church business shared space with politics and poetry. Denominational presses published volumes of meditations, essays, sermons and commentaries, books on African American history and culture, autobiographies, novels, poetry, and plays. They served as distributors for privately published texts, offered books as bonuses for subscribing to their periodicals, printed book reviews and literary criticism, and explicitly encouraged readers to become published writers.

Consider, for example, the July 13, 1854, issue of the AME *Christian Recorder.* Under a column entitled "Our Expectation," the editor wrote, "We expect that all of our preachers and people, our friends and well-wishers, will send in their communications for our columns. We wish to be benefitted by all the possible light that we can gather from them upon such subjects as come under our notice, as a *religious, literary, and scientific* journal" (emphasis mine).

Sometimes, encouragement had to be tempered with what a later *Christian Recorder* editor headlined as "Some Editorial Plain Talk": After reminding would-be contributors of several policies regarding length, originality, and manuscript form, the frustrated editor warned

> Finally, unless practice has already attained perfection with you, don't expect the *Recorder* to encourage your experiments in poetry-making. . . . if you can't express yourself creditably in the language of the Muses, stick to plain English and do your best at that. . . . If the gift is within you neglect it not, but until you are certain that you can "pass muster" we will be forced to see you later in this respect. The rule may be asserted as an ironclad one, that no one who writes bad English can write good poetry.[9]

While editors tried to convince aspiring contributors to hone their literary skills before they tried to publish their efforts, most did not require them to belong to the denomination that sponsored a particular periodical. Frances E. W. Harper, a Unitarian, published in the *Christian Recorder*, the *A.M.E. Review*, and several others for more than fifty years. Ida B. Wells-Barnett, a member of the African Methodist Episcopal Church, edited two Baptist newspapers, *The Evening Star* and *The Living Way*.

Martin R. Delany provides a salient example of individuals influential in the Afro-Protestant press whose primary historical identification is not with the religious communities. Delany studied medicine in 1836 and practiced that profession intermittently throughout his career. *The Oxford Companion to African American Literature*, like most reference works which include Delany, identifies him as a "political activist, early Afrocentric ideologue, explorer, lecturer, newspaper editor and correspondent, U.S. Army major, and author of several tracts and a novel." If Martin R. Delany had any religious affiliation, it is not generally known. In 1843 in Pittsburgh, Delany began publishing the *Mystery*, "a weekly newspaper that promoted civil rights, provoked blacks and whites by its challenges to old-fashioned understandings of race, and defended black writing and called for more."[10] Before joining Frederick Douglass as co-editor of the *North Star*, Delany sold the *Mystery* to AME Church officials, who renamed the paper *The Christian Herald*. In 1852 the former *Mystery* was again renamed, when it was relocated to Philadelphia. Now known as the *Christian Recorder*, the newspaper, under the leadership of several editors, sometimes focused more on official AME Church business than at other times, but it continued to promote civil rights, to challenge racism, and to promote African American literature. The full name of the paper shows its *Mystery* origins had not been forgotten, for the masthead proclaims *The Christian Recorder, published by the African Methodist Episcopal Church in the United States, for the Dissemination of Religion, Morality, Literature and Science*.

The *Repository of Religion and Literature and Science and Art*, a quarterly begun in Indianapolis, Indiana, in 1858, is a prime example of how the Afro-Protestant Church produced literature via affiliates. The *Repository* was not an official Church organ, but it was created by the "Literary Societies of the Baltimore, Indiana and Missouri Conferences of the African M. E. Church." The cover page of each issue reminded readers that "the object of this periodical is, first, to diffuse useful knowledge among our people. Second, to cultivate and develop their talents and elevate their intellectual, moral and religious characters." In the July 1858 issue of the *Repository* are five entries under "Religion," nine under "Literature" (including one called "Woman— her True Sphere"), and eight under "Science." "Poetry" and "Children" are the final two sections. The *Repository* was one of many such nineteenth-century periodicals established by African American literary societies, debating clubs, fraternal and professional groups, schools and colleges which began under the auspices of Afro-Protestantism.

Among those publishing ventures that were neither founded by nor affiliated with the Afro-Protestant Church but that were, nonetheless, products of that institution are those by Frederick Douglass, a "sexton, steward, class leader, clerk and local preacher" of the AME Zion Church in New Bedford, Massachusetts, and by Douglass's pastor, Thomas James, former slave, militant abolitionist and editor of *The Rights of Man*. The popular notion perpetuated by Garrison's introduction to Douglass's 1845 *Narrative* and by virtually every biographical sketch of Douglass since then is that William Lloyd Garrison discovered the fugitive slave, mentored his oratorical career, and as editor of the *Liberator*, modeled Douglass's subsequent career in publishing. According to Thomas James and Afro-Protestant records, however, the AME Zion church had begun cultivating Douglass's leadership, oratory, and probably his editorial skills before Garrison had ever heard Douglass speak. In his *Autobiography*, Thomas James writes that when Reverend James arrived in New Bedford, Douglass was

> right out of slavery, but had already begun to talk in public, though not before white people. He had been given authority to act as an exhorter . . . and I . . . licensed him to preach. He was then a member of my church. On one occasion, after I had addressed a white audience on the slavery question, I called upon Fred. Douglass, . . . to relate his story. He did so, and in a year from that time he was in the lecture field with Parker Pillsbury and other leading abolitionist orators.[11]

The objective here is not to disavow William Lloyd Garrison's influence upon Douglass and others. Indeed, Garrison's influence, at least for a brief time, supplanted that of Douglass's minister, Thomas James. Shortly after joining the professional abolitionist ranks, Douglass wrote his congregation that "he had cut loose from the church; he had found that the American church was the bulwark of American slavery." This did not mean, Thomas James cryptically noted, "that Mr. Douglass had repudiated the Christian religion at the same time that he bade good-by to the churches." Two of the published objectives in Douglass's "Prospectus" for the *North Star*—to "exalt the stand of *Public Morality*" and to "promote the Moral and Intellectual Improvement of the COLORED PEOPLE" (emphasis his)[12]—in fact echo those common to Afro-Protestant periodicals.

The religious and literary odysseys of Frederick Douglass and Thomas James, of the literary societies of the AME Church, and of other affiliated Afro-Protestant groups are similar to those of many other individuals, including Reverend Alexander Crummell, Reverend Henry Highland Garnet, Reverend Thomas Detter, and the seven ministers among the eleven members of the Committee on a National Press whose influence upon the development of African American writing is well documented. They invite our revised analysis of the texts and contexts of early African American literature. They also require our careful consideration of how contemporary publishing—especially twentieth-century anthologies, reprints, and scholarly articles—"shapes" African American literary history by ignoring or understating its roots in the Afro-Protestant press and the religious affiliations of some of our best-known writers and editors.

Take, for example, the history of *Freedom's Journal*, the earliest extant African American newspaper. Virtually every twentieth-century comprehensive anthology or historical study of African American literature mentions *Freedom's Journal*, frequently quoting, from the first issue on March 16, 1827, these words: "We wish to plead our own cause. Too long have others spoken for us. Too long has the publick been deceived by misrepresentations, in things which concern us dearly." Scholars regularly identify *Freedom's Journal* as marking "the beginning of a national movement among the colored masses and usher[ing] in the Negro Renaissance ... [and as] a race-paper, created for the express purpose of fighting slavery, and of voicing the thoughts and hopes of the free people of color."[13] And this is true. *Freedom's Journal* was established with "authorized agents" in New York, Maine, Massachusetts, Rhode Island, Connecticut, Pennsylvania, Maryland, Washington, D.C., and New Jersey. Within a year, it was international—with agents in Canada, Haiti, and England. *Freedom's Journal* was highly political and uncompromisingly abolitionist. But the group of African American men who founded this paper included Richard Allen and other Afro-Protestant ministers. They chose as senior editor of this "race-paper" Samuel Cornish, a Presbyterian minister. And so a paper that purported to speak to and on behalf of 500,000 African Americans had as its motto a quotation from Proverbs: "Righteousness Exalteth a Nation," a motto that Cornish subsequently used for other editorial projects, including *Rights of All* (1829), *The Weekly Advocate* (1837), and *The Colored American* (1837–41).

Freedom's Journal was founded, in part, because of a series of virulently racist articles in the New York newspapers and the refusal of those papers to print the rebuttals and perspectives of African Americans. The founders did indeed "wish to plead" their own cause, to speak for themselves to a public "deceived by misrepresentations." But this goal is not the first one articulated.

The first paragraph states the paper's "noble objectives" of being "a paper devoted to the dissemination of useful knowledge among our brethren, and to their *moral and religious* improvement" (emphasis mine). In that same issue, the African Americans who founded and financed this paper emphasize their intention to help shape African American literature, saying, "We deem it expedient to establish a paper, and bring into operation all the means with which our benevolent CREATOR has endowed us, for the moral, religious, civil and literary improvement of our injured race." The intention to publish words designed for "moral, religious, civil and literary improvement" was prominently reprinted in subsequent editions. Content analysis shows *Freedom's Journal* took its "religious" and "literary" mandates seriously. On the front page (along with those well-rehearsed words about "pleading our own cause") is the first installment of the "Memoirs of Capt. Paul Cuffee." The premier issue includes a biographical sketch of the Reverend Abraham Thompson; an appeal for African American missionaries to go to Africa; a report concerning poet Gilbert Horton's imprisonment in Washington, D.C.; a poem called "The African Chief"; an advertisement for B. F. Hughes's school "for Coloured Children of Both sexes" (which, the ad notes, is under the sponsorship of St. Philip's church); and several items of local and international news, including an article on the Irish egg trade and one on Chinese footbinding.

Freedom's Journal announced in its first issue also that it intended to be "a medium of intercourse between our brethren in the different states of this great confederacy: that through its columns an expression of our sentiments, on many interesting subjects which concern us, may be offered to the publick," and it "respectfully invite[d] our numerous friends to assist by their communications." The journal encouraged readers to write for publication, and its issues regularly included letters, essays, and poems by "Arion," "Toilus," "Rosa," and other aspiring writers. *Freedom's Journal* reprinted works by prominent African American writers such as Phillis Wheatley. (In fact, it initiated a campaign to establish a memorial to Wheatley.) It urged "the necessity of reading," but also warned readers "to be judicious in the selection of the works they peruse" and to beware, especially, of "works of fiction which might mislead the mind not previously fortified: and so far from imparting solid advantage, they lead the reader to make calculations which are slender as the spider's web, deceptive as the ignis fatuus, retarding the mind from making substantial progress, and obstructing the prosperity of our race." *Freedom's Journal* also reprinted literature by Euro-American writers when it was appropriate. An intriguing item in the October 31, 1828, issue announces that "Don Juan is received. We cannot admit it into our columns, as the last communication from the same pen, has been considered by some of our female readers, as rather too personal."

Among this newspaper's financial backers, distribution agents, and contributing authors was David Walker of Boston, who the *Norton Anthology of African American Literature* introduces as "the most militant voice among the early African American protest writers."[14] "Militant" Walker certainly was, and his published opinions are allegedly the reason he met a mysterious death not long after publishing his *Appeal . . . to the Colored Citizens of the World* in 1829.

David Walker's relationship with *Freedom's Journal* provides another compelling example of the interplay between Afro-Protestantism and African American literature. David Walker was a mentor of author/orator/activist Maria W. Stewart, who in 1831 published "Religion and the Pure Principles of Morality" and in 1832 a book of meditations and prayers. Walker was also a leader in the *Journal*'s campaign to free George Moses Horton, the slave-poet of Chapel Hill, North Carolina. A year before David Walker published his *Appeal* in pamphlet form, *Freedom's Journal* printed its prototype essay. After his death, Walker's story and his *Appeal* were kept in print for several years by Reverend Henry Highland Garnet. And as William Andrews has pointed out, David Walker's *Appeal* served as an "enabling text and a touchstone by which its successors, from Garnet's own 'Call to Rebellion' speech in 1843 to Eldridge Cleaver's *Soul on Ice* (1967) can be measured, valued, and preserved" (*Norton Anthology*, 178).

The intricate connection between religion and literature and science and art and Afro-Protestantism's commitment to a gospel of social reform lessened as the century progressed. Yet as late as 1873 the *Missionary Record* of Charleston, South Carolina, was still subtitled "A Superior Weekly Family Newspaper devoted to Christian Graces, Literature, Arts, Science, Politics and the Progress of Civilization." Its July 7 issue included articles on "Wilberforce University," "The Depth of the Ocean," "Eating with an Appetite," "Punctuality," "Physiognomy," "American Morals," and "The [Susan B.] Anthony Verdict." It included ads for *Scientific American*, Martin R. Delany's *History of the African Race in America*, and the Georgetown *Planet*. To ignore or to underestimate the intricate and persistent relationship among African Americans, their literature, and the Afro-Protestant Press is to misunderstand, misrepresent, mistake, or maybe just "miss seeing" significant sources and defining characteristics of African American, and American, culture.

Notes

1. James D. Hart, *The Popular Book: A History of America's Literary Tastes* (Berkeley: University of California Press, 1963), 67.

2. Dorothy Porter, *Early Negro Writing, 1760–1837* (Boston: Beacon Press, 1971), 80.

3. *The Cherokee Phoenix* was founded in Georgia in 1828. *El Crespusculo de la Libertad* was founded in 1834.

4. "On Being Brought from Africa to America" (1767). Reprinted in Julian D. Mason, Jr., ed., *The Poems of Phillis Wheatley* (Chapel Hill: University of North Carolina Press, 1989), 53.

5. The term "Afro-Protestant" assumes differences between or within "Protestantism" which relate to theological, institutional, and cultural influences sufficient to modify or reconstruct adherents' practices and rituals. In this context the term includes institutions such as the AME Church, the AME Zion Church, the CME Church, the National Baptist Convention, and

other congregations and congregants founded by and dominated by African Americans and African American cultural imperatives.

6. For example, the Colored Methodist Episcopal Church established the CME Publishing House in Memphis, Tennessee, in 1870; the African Methodist Episcopal Church expanded its operations by forming the AME Sunday School Union and Publishing House in Nashville, Tennessee, in 1881; and the National Baptist Publishing Board consolidated various local entities in 1896.

7. *Black Journalists in Paradox* (New York: Greenwood Press, 1991), 17.

8. Mary Still, *An Appeal to the Females of the African Methodist Episcopal Church* (Philadelphia, 1857), 7–9.

9. July 7, 1892.

10. Allan D. Austin, "Martin R. Delany." In William R. Andrews, Frances Smith Foster, and Trudier Harris, eds., *The Oxford Companion to African American Literature* (New York: Oxford University Press, 1997), 205.

11. *The Autobiography of Rev. Thomas James* (1886). Reprinted in *Rochester History* 37 (October 1975): 1–32, quotation on 7–8.

12. *Prospectus for an Anti-Slavery Paper to be Entitled North Star* (1847).

13. Bella Gross, "*Freedom's Journal* and *The Rights of All*," *Journal of Negro History* 17 (July 1932): 245.

14. "David Walker," in Henry Louis Gates, Jr., Nellie Y. McKay, et al., eds., *The Norton Anthology of African American Literature* (New York: W. W. Norton, 1997), 178.

The Problem of Hawthorne's Popularity
Meredith L. McGill

> *I had hoped to add a new dimension to literary history, but the dimension turned out to be too narrow. Literary history, no matter what the historian's approach, must be primarily concerned with literature. If the approach is wholly extrinsic, as mine was at the beginning, the product is likely to be sterile. Facts and figures about sales of books and incomes of authors are interesting—but not interesting enough, unless they specifically reveal something about the ways in which writers and their writings function in a culture. Similarly, the history of publishing, with which I became deeply involved, tended, like most specialties, to become an end in itself. Publishing is relevant to literary history only in so far as it can be shown to be, ultimately, a shaping influence on literature.*
> —William Charvat, Preface to *Literary Publishing in America, 1790–1850*

William Charvat's partial disavowal of his ground-breaking scholarship in the published version of his Rosenbach lectures is striking both for its poignancy and for its prescient understanding of a disciplinary divide that continues to trouble the relation of literary study to the history of the book. Discussing the critical impasse that kept his major study, *The Profession of Authorship in America*, unfinished and out of print until after his death, Charvat imagines it first as a problem of ambition ("the dimension turned out to be too narrow"), then as a failure of relation (the history of publishing considered as "wholly extrinsic" to literary study), and finally as a question of the proper subordination of publishing history to literature ("relevant

... only in so far as it can be shown to be, ultimately, a shaping influence"). Though publishing history first appears under the sign of diminishment—it is "narrow," "sterile," and "not interesting enough" —it exerts a surprising power, soliciting a deep involvement and threatening to become "an end in itself." Despite his derogation of mere "facts and figures," what Charvat seems most worried about is the tendency of literature to slip from his grasp.

Charvat offers two strategies for stabilizing the relation between these two disciplines: limiting his study to the profession of authorship, where, he imagines, financial exigencies constrain creative ambition, suggesting that it is through privation that the material conditions of authorship most reliably leave their mark; and forcibly relegating publishing history to a position that is decidedly exterior (if not "wholly extrinsic") to literary study: "in order to keep literature at the center of my investigations, I began working from the inside out—that is, from what the literary work itself could tell me about the writer's relation to society, out toward the reading public and the publishing economy which conditioned that relation."[1]

The persuasiveness of Charvat's model—his arrangement of the literary work, society, the public, and the economy into ever larger (and more distant) concentric circles—is substantially undercut by his suggestion that it is only by banishing publishing history to the periphery that he could keep literature at the center of his study. In the essay that follows, I want to suggest another solution to the problem that Charvat outlines, one that responds more to his insight about the elusiveness of the literary under publishing history's gaze than to his desire to use "the publishing economy" to secure a literary subject with which he already has begun. I will argue that publishing history is most valuable to literary history when it dislocates its subject—when it redraws the boundary between the literary and what lies outside of it. The first section of the essay outlines some of the ways in which attending to the publication history of Nathaniel Hawthorne's early fiction alters our understanding of the contours of his reputation and disrupts the critical conventions that have tied the murky period of Hawthorne's literary apprenticeship to his much-heralded later writings. Publishing history here exposes an instability in our concept of the literary, a dislocation that is not easily set to rights either by acts of critical generosity (expanding the canon to include this overlooked fiction) or by acts of ever-greater critical discrimination (recalibrating our sense of Hawthorne's achievements in the major novels with a renewed appreciation of the sophistication of the minor fiction). In establishing the popularity of Hawthorne's early fiction, publishing history jarringly reminds us of the historicity of literary value and calls for a criticism supple enough to recognize and to describe a shifting target. In the second section of the essay, I turn to Edgar Allan Poe's well-known reviews of Hawthorne as an exemplary instance of such critical recognition. Poe's struggle to understand the popularity of Hawthorne's early fiction alerts us to the ways in which the tone of ease and inconsequence that has seemed the hallmark of its insignificance can be seen as a successful, if precarious, engagement with the problem of literary value. Turning Charvat's concentric circles outside in, Poe's reviews will remind us that the question of the cultural status of the literary is internal to the workings of literature itself.

1. The Uses of Obscurity

As he was completing the manuscript of *The House of the Seven Gables* in January 1851, Nathaniel Hawthorne sent his publisher, James T. Fields, a short preface for a new edition of his first collection of tales and sketches. Republishing *Twice-Told Tales* (1837; 1842) was part of Fields's aggressive campaign to keep Hawthorne's name before the public following the extraordinary success of *The Scarlet Letter* in the spring of 1850. Taking the opportunity to reflect on his writing, Hawthorne begins this gently ironic description of his early literary failures with some comically exaggerated claims. Pressing the modesty topos to the point of inversion, Hawthorne claims to have been "for a good many years, the obscurest man of letters in America" and credits this "distinction" to the conditions of his tales' publication: "These stories were published in magazines and annuals, extending over a period of ten or twelve years, and comprising the whole of the writer's young manhood, without making (so far as he has ever been aware) the slightest impression on the Public."[2]

One needn't be familiar with Hawthorne's penchant for self-deprecatory prefaces to be suspicious of this series of superlatives. Although he goes on to admit that "one or two" of these tales "had a pretty wide newspaper circulation," Hawthorne is too interested in drawing connections between aesthetic failure and readerly neglect to qualify the claim substantially, crediting the slightness of his early literary production to a "total lack of sympathy at the age when his mind would naturally have been most effervescent" (1150). Alternately accusatory and self-blaming, Hawthorne uses the fiction of readerly neglect to control the terms of his reception, stepping in to criticize his early work for the benefit of his current readers. While for the most part, this self-critique is an exercise in diminished expectations, consisting of warnings as to form and tone ("Instead of passion, there is sentiment"; "In what purport to be pictures of real life, we have allegory" [1152]), Hawthorne concludes the Preface with a sly turn that ought to be taken a good deal more seriously. He remarks that "on the internal evidence of his sketches," readers have confused the author with his authorial persona, regarding him as a "mild, shy, gentle, melancholic, exceedingly sensitive and not very forcible man" (1153). Self-effacing to the last, Hawthorne flatters the reader by suggesting that he has formed his sense of self on the pattern of his reception: "He is by no means certain, that some of his subsequent productions have not been influenced and modified by a natural desire to fill up so amiable an outline and act in consonance with the character assigned to him" (1153). What has too often gone unnoticed or unsaid is that Hawthorne's disclaimer extends to his Preface and to the fiction of obscurity itself. What could be more melancholy than an author who is unable to distinguish himself from his readers' projections and who has come to regard his name as a pseudonym (1153)? What better history of an "exceedingly sensitive and not very forcible man" than one who vacillates in assigning blame between authorial seclusion and readerly neglect?

I dwell on the self-confirming fiction of Hawthorne's obscurity because it has exerted a tenacious and distorting hold on critical accounts of his career. Despite Hawthorne's subtle disclaimer, critics have tended to perform precisely the operation he warns against, taking the Preface as a candid explanation of the motives for his seclusion and as an accurate account of his early reception. Stephen Nissenbaum has long since provided the tools for unpacking what was immediately at stake for Hawthorne in perpetuating this fiction. In his essay "The Firing of Nathaniel Hawthorne," Nissenbaum recounts Hawthorne's struggle to protect his patronage post as a Custom-House surveyor by defining his appointment as literary and apolitical. Turned out by the Whig administration in the summer of 1849, Hawthorne found himself the focal point of a virulent debate on the spoils system. Because much of the success of *The Scarlet Letter* (1850) was initially due to its topical "Custom-House" introduction,

Hawthorne had even more of a stake the following year in perpetuating the fiction of a "young manhood" spent in a shadowy "Dream-Land" (1153), detached from worldly concerns and responsibilities. Like the letters and newspaper articles written in his defense, in which Hawthorne was described as a "retired, quiet and inoffensive" man who strived to live "above the prejudices of the time," Hawthorne's Preface seeks to write the prehistory of an author too timid and withdrawn to have engaged in the petty political maneuvering with which he had been publicly charged.[3]

Nina Baym, too, has done much to explode the fiction of Hawthorne's writerly isolation, arguing that far from "the productions of a person in retirement" (1152), much of Hawthorne's early fiction was composed with practical assistance from and intellectual exchange with his mother, uncle, and sisters in the midst of the busy Manning household.[4] Certainly, Hawthorne's short stint as editor and chief writer for the Boston eclectic, *The American Magazine of Useful and Entertaining Knowledge* (March–September 1836), was in every sense collaborative. His letters from the time are full of pleas to his sister Elizabeth to send extracts and "concoctions" to him in Boston, along with his laundry, by the family stagecoach line.[5] So, too, Hawthorne's careful angling for a succession of political appointments following the first publication of *Twice-Told Tales* suggests both the possession of and a willingness to exploit his considerable political and literary connections. Hawthorne's failed attempts to be named historiographer of Charles Wilkins's expedition to the South Seas (1837) and postmaster of Salem (1840; 1843–44), and his successful appointments as a measurer of salt and coal in the Boston Custom House (1839–40) and surveyor in Salem (1846–49), suggest not a writer in self-defeating, melancholy withdrawal from the world, but one actively engaged in the pursuit of a sinecure that would allow him to write without forcing him to depend on a literary career for sustenance. Indeed, the biographical and bibliographical evidence suggests that Hawthorne's problem was not that his tales and sketches failed to make "the slightest impression on the Public," but that the form of their circulation in newspapers, periodicals, and annuals left him possessed of a reputation that he could not easily turn to profit. As Hawthorne wrote to Horatio Bridge in 1843, "It is rather singular that I should need an office, for nobody's scribblings seem to be more acceptable to the public than mine, and yet I shall find it a tough scratch to gain a respectable support by my pen."[6]

Nevertheless, the fiction of Hawthorne's obscurity has proved too useful, both to Hawthorne and to his critics, to be easily dislodged. Despite ample evidence of the broad circulation of his early tales and sketches in a variety of periodicals, modern critics, who by and large share Hawthorne's bias toward the form of the book, have tended to take his depiction of his neglect at face value, regarding the twenty-year period in which he wrote more than seventy works of short fiction as a prolonged and unheralded apprenticeship for his "Major Phase,"[7] the concentrated three-year period in which he achieved national fame as the writer of novel-length romances. I have suggested above some of the reasons why Hawthorne himself might have eagerly, if ironically, claimed the distinction of early obscurity: the still-pressing need to position himself as detached from the world of politics in the wake of the Custom House firing; the desire to distance himself from his participation in mass-cultural and feminized forms such as the eclectic magazine, the gift book, the children's book, and the women's periodical; and the remarkable opportunity for self-fashioning provided by his newfound alliance with Ticknor and Fields's increasingly national and high-cultural publishing juggernaut.[8] Republication allows Hawthorne imaginatively to withdraw these tales and sketches from prior circulation. The absolutism of his insistence on their wholesale rejection by the public gives the clue to his ambition: if Hawthorne can succeed in identifying this fiction with the admittedly distended but suddenly remote period of his minority ("the whole of the writer's young manhood"), this minor fiction can be superseded and redeemed by the success of his later work.[9]

It is less clear, however, why modern critics should concur with Hawthorne's self-deprecatory assessment. Most broadly, the presumption of Hawthorne's rejection by the public has enabled critics to regard his early fiction through a highly selective lens. Critics have tended to value selected tales for their historical irony, a hallmark of literary value that places Hawthorne at a critical remove from both his Puritan heritage and his immediate cultural context. When his writing from the 1830s and 1840s has been evaluated more comprehensively, it has most often been made sense of by being retrospectively assembled into the novel-like structures that Hawthorne projected, then abandoned, as the tales and sketches were published in various periodicals. Perhaps overly comfortable in the role of rescuer and restorer of the author's intention, literary critics have paid significantly more attention to authorial wish than to cultural fact, focusing on the failure of Hawthorne's ambitions—the collapse of his narrative designs—rather than evaluating the forms in which these fictions circulated and were read. For instance, while there has been a great deal of speculation about the precise makeup of the unpublished sequences "Seven Tales of My Native Land," "Provincial Tales," and "The Story-Teller," there exists no treatment of the early tales that groups them according to pseudonym, the elaborate naming system that establishes networks of affinity across tales and periodicals, distinguishing the stories "By the author of the Gray Champion," from those "By the author of Sights from a Steeple" and "By the author of the Gentle Boy."

Contributing to the occlusion of much of Hawthorne's early work has been the presumption of a consensus as to the aesthetic value of individual tales and sketches. One of the most careful readers of Hawthorne's historical tales, Michael Colacurcio, frankly asserts what is simply implicit in most major studies—that there is a radical drop-off in quality in much of this writing, that only a select group of tales are properly Hawthorne's: "For though it has been possible to fold [a number of sketches] into a pseudo-historical recipe for 'the Hawthornesque,' no one (I think) should want to whip up a counterformula out of ingredients mixed equally from 'Sir William Pepperell,' 'Little Annie's Ramble,' 'A Rill from the Town Pump,' 'The Toll-Gatherer's Day,' 'Mrs. Bullfrog,' and 'The Lily's Quest.'"[10] And yet, many of the tales that Colacurcio would place beyond the pale of the "Hawthornesque" circulated more widely in Hawthorne's day than the historical tales that critics have justly come to value. To give but a very few examples, "The Wives of the Dead," which was initially published anonymously ("by F. . . . . ") in the popular Boston gift book *The Token* (1832), was reprinted with Hawthorne's name attached in the New York mammoth weekly *Brother Jonathan* in December of 1839, and with a change of title (as "The Two Widows") in the partisan monthly *The United States Magazine and Democratic Review* in July 1843, from which it was copied into the temperance newspaper *The Hampden Washingtonian* (August 10, 1843), and the Philadelphia literary weekly, *Alexander's Messenger* (July 22, 1846)— all while the tale remained uncollected in book form.[11] "David Swan," which was anonymously printed in *The Token and Atlantic Souvenir* for 1837, saw its circulation take off after it was printed in the small edition of one thousand copies of *Twice-Told Tales* in the spring of that year: it was reprinted in Boston and Salem newspapers, in the Philadelphia monthly *Atkinson's Casket* (November 1837), in miscellanies of pirated fiction published in Boston, New York, and London, and as a representative example of Hawthorne's writing in Rufus Wilmot Griswold's important anthology *The Prose Writers of America* (Philadelphia, 1847).[12] If scholars have struggled to understand why Hawthorne failed to include "My Kinsman, Major Molineaux" and "Alice Doane's Appeal" in his early collections, what are we to make of the London piracy of *Twice-Told Tales* (1849), which reprinted "Footprints on the Sea-Shore," "Sunday at Home," "David Swan," and "Sights from a Steeple," but *omitted* "The Minister's Black Veil," "The May Pole of Merry Mount," "The Gentle Boy," and "Endicott and the Red Cross"?[13] The evidence of the wide reprinting of these sketches, combined with early reviewers' enthusiastic embrace of Hawthorne's "sedate, quiet dignity," his "easy grace and delicacy," his "calm, meditative fancy," and his lack of "dramatic pretension," suggests that we have been overlooking a literary phenomenon of substantial, if baffling, significance.[14]

The enthusiastic reprinting of much of Hawthorne's early work suggests that he was in possession of a significant, if uneven and unpredictable, reputation—a reputation from which he could not be assured to profit and which neither he nor his critics could confidently measure or describe. The uncontrolled circulation of Hawthorne's early fiction raises questions about authorial and critical mastery and suggests a final rationale for the collusion of literary critics in the fiction of his obscurity. Taking their cue from Hawthorne's self-characterizations, critics have come to read Hawthorne's novels of the early 1850s as allegories of this neglect. Michael Gilmore in particular has examined *The Scarlet Letter* and *The House of the Seven Gables* across a thematic axis that opposes the artist and the marketplace, an opposition that draws its interpretive charge from Hawthorne's early failure to be recognized and remunerated by the reading public. Gilmore ratifies Hawthorne's desire for detachment when he reads *The House of the Seven Gables* as dramatizing both its author's estrangement from and complicity with the market. According to Gilmore, in this novel Hawthorne was "unable to suppress his misgivings that in bowing to the marketplace he was compromising his artistic independence and integrity."[15] What becomes invisible to a critical narrative that presumes a history of neglect is that the fiction of obscurity itself is one of the means by which

Hawthorne, who is thoroughly and in many ways successfully embedded in the literary marketplace, *renegotiates* a relation to the reading public.

If the tendency of recent criticism has been to trade on Hawthorne's investment in his obscurity, imagining that his early failure in the market is at least partially redeemed by the sophistication of his later thematizations, Poe's approach to Hawthorne's early fiction is decidedly less heroic. In the three reviews he published in *Graham's Magazine* and *Godey's Lady's Book* between 1842 and 1847, Poe is determined to uncover the reasons for the success of Hawthorne's tales and sketches and to trace the precise limits of his popularity. For Poe, however, the limit to Hawthorne's success does not simply lie either inside or outside of his fiction—it is neither a question of his abilities as a writer nor a matter of injustice in the history of his reception. Rather than positing literature as the site at which market conditions are confronted and potentially mastered, Poe suggests that what is exhilarating and frightening about the literary marketplace is the way in which it can make forms of literary value both appear and disappear. For Poe, it is a shift in the conditions of writing and reading that threatens radically to recast what readers most value about Hawthorne's sketches

2. "Sleeping Beauty in the Waxworks": Monotony and Repose in Early Hawthorne

Poe's reviews of Hawthorne are important not only because they helped to forge a critical consensus on Hawthorne's first two collections of short fiction, *Twice-Told Tales* (1837; 1842) and *Mosses from an Old Manse* (1846) but because the problem of Hawthorne's popularity so troubled Poe that it proved the catalyst for the theory that has made these reviews famous—Poe's elaboration of his poetics of effect. What interests me is the interpretive problem that provokes Poe's fantasy of absolute authorial control and the terms of analysis he derives from his study of Hawthorne. In these reviews, Poe struggles to define precisely what is distinctive about Hawthorne's fiction and why it is that Hawthorne's originality has left him with a curiously uneven reputation, "the example, *par excellence,* in this country, of the privately-admired and publicly-unappreciated man of genius" (578).[16] Poe begins to theorize his own writing practice while speculating on the relation between success in the literary marketplace and subtle tonal differences, generating his poetics of effect from his perception of the disarmingly short distance between the narrative quality he associates with commercial and aesthetic failure—monotony—and the tone he ascribes to Hawthorne—that of repose.

Hawthorne's early fiction raises for Poe the question of the relation of style to sales in part because Poe had initially assumed that in Hawthorne's case there was no relation whatsoever between the two. Poe remarks that before he undertook to write his reviews he had assumed that Hawthorne owed his literary success to "one of the impudent *cliques*"—that is, a regional coterie of publishers and literati who promoted each other's work regardless of quality.[17] Poe's elaboration of the precise nature of Hawthorne's originality, then, is hedged about with anxiety over what it takes to succeed in the literary marketplace *without* the intervention of the coteries.

Poe's concern about the suitability of Hawthorne's characteristic, intimate mode of address to conditions of mass production is evident from his opening gambit, which, typical of Poe, appears at first to be nothing more than a strange sort of pedantry: "In the first place, they should not have been called 'Twice Told Tales'—for this is a title that will not bear *repetition*. If in the first collected edition they were twice-told, of course now they are thrice-told" (568). Poe calls attention to the discrepancy between the oral context invoked by Hawthorne's title, in which "telling twice" is potentially a ground of value,[18] and the printed form of the collected tales, the fact of their publication and republication, which, in Poe's eyes, threatens to undermine Hawthorne's claim to uniqueness. Why this is so becomes apparent as Poe struggles to define the tonal distinctiveness on which Hawthorne's claim to originality rests. Poe insists that Hawthorne's "essays"—what we would call his "sketches"—are significantly different both from the "Rosa-Matilda effusions" (568) that filled the gift books and magazines in which many of Hawthorne's early tales were first printed and from the sketches of his nearest high-culture precursors: Washington Irving, Charles Lamb, Leigh Hunt, and William Hazlitt. As Poe explains,

> A painter would at once notice [the] leading or predominant feature [of Hawthorne's sketches] and style it *repose*. There is no attempt at effect. All is quiet, thoughtful, subdued. Yet this repose may exist simultaneously with high originality of thought.... At every turn we meet with novel combinations, yet these combinations never surpass

the limits of the quiet. We are soothed as we read; and withal is a calm astonishment that ideas so apparently obvious have never occurred or been presented to us before. (570)

Hawthorne's ability continually to produce novel combinations distinguishes his sketches from those of *The Spectator* and Washington Irving, in which, Poe claims, "repose is attained rather by the absence of novel combination, or of originality, than otherwise" (570). Repose, then, is a tricky stylistic marker, in that it can signal both a high degree of originality and its lack, a notable authorial achievement or a kind of generic, unremarkable writing (what Poe refers to as "the calm, quiet, unostentatious expression of commonplace thoughts"; 571).

It is, in fact, the all too easy collapse of this difference, the transformation of the admirable tone of repose into its unremarkable double that concerns Poe in his final review of Hawthorne. The publication of *Mosses from an Old Manse* gave Poe yet another opportunity to consider the effect of republication on the reception of Hawthorne's tales, an opportunity to reflect on the peculiar resistance they offer to mass acceptance. In this review Poe is tougher on Hawthorne, arguing that the novelty of combination that distinguished his writing has all but disappeared under the force of repetition. In part through the republication of his tales, Hawthorne has reached that point at which "novelty becomes nothing novel," a point of no return in this system, since, as Poe remarks, "the artist, to preserve his originality, will subside into the common-place" (580). Hawthorne's ultimate failure, then, is a product of his success: his persistent reassertion of his powers of novel combination only serves "to deaden in the reader all capacity for their appreciation" (580).

Toward the end of this review Poe comes up with a figure for the kind of artistic failure he has been describing all along: the collapse of repose into monotony, the transformation of the "natural ease" that he has associated with Hawthorne's style into conspicuous artificiality. Describing what he considers to be the unfortunate, unchanging manner of the majority of American writing, Poe remarks, "The author who ... is merely at *all* times *quiet,* is, of course, upon *most* occasions, merely silly or stupid, and has no more right to be thought 'easy' or 'natural' than has a cockney exquisite or the sleeping beauty in the waxworks" (582). Poe's first figure for this writing, the "cockney exquisite," aligns it with artificiality, excess, and an unconsciousness of its absurdity. His second attempt to represent the relentless dullness of generic American prose, the "sleeping beauty in the waxworks," more subtly performs the collapse of difference it seeks to represent. What initially registers as a distinction between the object of representation (the sleeping beauty) and its location (the waxworks), and, by way of a quick metonymic slide, its medium (wax), starts to look like repetition or refiguration. If at first we are disillusioned to find that the sleeping beauty is an artificial, man-made thing, we are doubly disillusioned to find a reflection of this disillusionment in the subject of the wax statue itself. After all, should we be lulled by the excellence of the artist into suspending our disbelief, the sleeping beauty would still be unconscious. This is a figure for a difference that, ultimately, makes no difference at all, the meaningless slide of novelty into predictable readerly expectation, the collapse of a distinction between the suspension of activity that is characteristic of repose and the lifelessness of sheer materiality.

Poe's exasperation with the inability of Hawthornian novelty to *stay* novel prompts him to speculate on the difference between "absolute" or "metaphysical" originality and what he terms "true originality"—an originality that could survive under conditions of mass production. "Absolute novelty," Poe argues,

> tasks and startles the intellect, and so brings into undue action the faculties to which, in the lighter literature, we least appeal. And thus understood, it cannot fail to prove unpopular with the masses, who, seeking in this literature amusement, are positively offended by instruction. But the true originality—true in respect of its purposes—is that which, in bringing out the half-formed, the reluctant, or the unexpressed fancies of mankind . . . thus combines with the pleasurable effect of *apparent* novelty, a real egoistic delight. (580)

According to Poe, fiction that aims at absolute originality runs the risk of introducing a sense of inadequacy and cultural hierarchy into the experience of reading. "True originality," on the other hand, is marked by the readerly delusion of a unique form of intimacy with the author, in effect, the mass production of an unconsciousness of the conditions of mass production:

> [In the case of absolute novelty] the reader . . . is excited, but embarrassed, disturbed, in some degree even pained at his own want of perception, at his own folly in not having himself hit upon the idea.

> In the [case of true originality], his pleasure is doubled. He feels and intensely enjoys the seeming novelty of the thought, enjoys it as really novel, as absolutely original with the writer—*and* himself. They two, he fancies, have, alone of all men, thought thus. They two have, together, created this thing. Henceforward there is a bond of sympathy between them, a sympathy which irradiates every subsequent page of the book. (581)

Poe scholars commonly read this passage as a precursor of his more fully developed account of his writing practice in "The Philosophy of Composition." And yet it is useful to ask what Poe's definition of "true originality" suggests about the writing against which it is measured and from which it borrows many of its concerns. Just as we have come to understand Poe's poetics of effect as a market aesthetic—one that takes the problem of mass reception as a point of departure for composition—so too do we need to attend to the "poetics of repose" as a series of aesthetic choices that, rather than being made negligible by their mass-market appeal, are important by virtue of a self-conscious relation to the market.

A full treatment of the antebellum "poetics of repose" would need to examine Hawthorne's work in relation to his numerous contemporaries who wrote "Tales and Sketches," including Theodore S. Fay, Lydia Sigourney, Sarah Josepha Hale, and Catharine Maria Sedgwick.[19] In closing, however, I'd like to hazard a few generalizations about the cultural value of repose, based on Poe's insights into Hawthorne's tone and on some of the common characteristics of Hawthorne's most popularly reprinted sketches. In thinking about the "poetics of repose," it helps to remember that Hawthorne's tone bothered Poe insofar as it attained a high level of originality, or distinctiveness, without meeting any of his other criteria for excellent prose writing. As he noted, "There is no attempt at effect" (570). And yet Poe's admiration of and patience with Hawthornian repose dramatically lessened across the space of the reviews, so that he concludes the series with the exhortation: "Let him mend his pen, get a bottle of visible ink, come out from the Old Manse, cut Mr. Alcott, hang (if possible) the editor of 'The Dial,' and throw out of the window to the pigs all his odd numbers of 'The North American Review' (588). Despite its tendency, through repetition, to collapse into mere monotony, the tone of repose, which Poe also associates with "conservatives, hackneys, and cultivated old clergymen" (579), was clearly a cultural force that a poetics of effect would have to contend with.

The outlines of some of Hawthorne's sketches begin to suggest why. True to the eschewal of effect, they are either eventless or are built around narratives that are pared to the bare minimum. "Sights from a Steeple" and "Foot-prints on the Sea-Shore" feature speakers who move quietly through the landscape, choosing a series of objects to subject to aesthetic attention. In "The Wives of the Dead," the action is limited to the staggered delivery of the news that the premise of the tale—the tragic deaths of the husbands of two sisters—is entirely mistaken. In a move that must have exasperated Poe, Hawthorne draws the sketch to a close before either sister tells the other what she exclusively knows. The narrative point of this story, which dramatizes the sisters' isolate, interior dramas of consciousness restored, is that nothing changes. So, too, for what can only be called the center of unconsciousness in "David Swan," a story of what might have happened had its protagonist not slept through the entire story. Like Poe's sleeping beauty in the waxworks, David Swan remains wholly closed off to the series of romance possibilities, the fragments of aborted stories, that pass by him while he's sleeping. To take liberties with a phrase of W. H. Auden's, Hawthorne's sketches make nothing happen. Which may, indeed, be a clue to their cultural value. In one of the most overwrought sections of his review, Poe works hard to distinguish Hawthornian repose from the idleness that characterizes the light writing of *The Spectator* and Washington Irving, arguing that in these sketches, "by strong effort, we are made to conceive the absence of all" (571). Addison's and Irving's is a tone of studied idleness that works to reinscribe the difference between labor and leisure. Poe suggests by contrast that Hawthorne's sketches function as a kind of metacommentary on this process: in Hawthorne "the absence of effort is too obvious to be mistaken" (571). The too-conspicuous effortlessness of Hawthorne's tales suggest that they no longer perform the aristocratic transaction by which the labor of reading works to confirm the idleness of authors. Poe suggests that by making his sketches accessible and commonplace, Hawthorne produces a tone of "ease" that is really easy—that the "cultural work" of these sketches is to perform no work at all.[20] Perhaps, then, these sketches are popular because they do the work of legitimating fiction by allowing, but not requiring, that it be either moral or useful.

Poe's fascination with the characteristic tone of Hawthorne's sketches recasts their very insignificance as the product of careful calculations about the cultural place of the literary in the 1830s and

1840s. Indeed, when successful, Hawthornian repose seems to approach perilously close to Poe's definition of "true originality," establishing a "bond of sympathy" between author and reader while appearing maddeningly free of the dynamics of domination and control that will be a hallmark of Poe's elaboration of his poetic method in "The Raven" and "The Philosophy of Composition." If Hawthorne's sketches avoid, in their structure, tone, and scale, the problem of an aspiration toward "absolute novelty" that is implicitly self-destructive, they are, nevertheless, exceedingly fragile—subject to erasure under the force of repetition and unable to withstand sustained critical attention.

Hawthorne's Preface to the Ticknor and Fields edition of *Twice-Told Tales* bears witness to the seriousness with which he read Poe's characterization of his predominant tone and his implicit warnings about literary ambition. Tucked away between an invitation to precisely the biographical speculation that Hawthorne disclaims[21] and a dreary passage that proposes to compensate for readerly neglect through nostalgia, is a self-description of his early fiction in startlingly Poe-esque terms. This passage is suddenly legible as genuinely analytic once we've shaken off our melancholy conviction of Hawthorne's neglect. Indeed, given the terms of Poe's begrudging praise, it can actually seem like boasting:

> The sketches are not, it is hardly necessary to say, profound; but it is rather more remarkable that they so seldom, if ever, show any design on the writer's part to make them so. They have none of the abstruseness of idea, or obscurity of expression, which mark the written communications of a solitary mind with itself. They never need translation. It is in fact, the style of a man of society. Every sentence, so far as it embodies thought or sensibility, may be understood and felt by anybody, who will give himself the trouble to read it, and will take up the book in a proper mood. (1152)

The "proper mood," however, is precisely what the Preface discourages, tempting us with fantasies of obscurity, not clarity; seclusion, not society; and the spontaneous disappearance of the tales and sketches, instead of their ready accessibility.

William Charvat, who, like the young Hawthorne, struggled to combine his scattered essays into the form of a book, understood much about the power of partial disavowals to provoke a shifting of the critical terrain. In refusing to be self-congratulatory about the prospects of the interdisciplinary field he was to have such an important hand in creating, Charvat has provoked decades of attempts to move beyond the critical impasse he described. As Hawthorne suggests rather more self-pityingly, it is the "imperfectly successful" attempts at communication that, through their very imperfections, "open an intercourse with the world" (1152).

Notes

I am extremely grateful to both the audience and the organizers of the Charvat conference at Ohio State University and to the Newberry Library Fellows seminar at which I presented earlier versions of this essay.

1. *Literary Publishing in America, 1790–1850* (Amherst: University of Massachusetts Press, 1993), 7–8.
2. Nathaniel Hawthorne, *Tales and Sketches* (New York: Literary Classics of the United States, 1982), 1150.
3. "The Firing of Nathaniel Hawthorne," *Essex Institute Historical Collections* 114 (April 1978): 64, 66. Many of Hawthorne's defenders alluded to his national reputation as a means of lifting him above the concerns of local politicians (in Hawthorne's words, the "slang-whangers—the vote distributors—the Jack Cades"; 61) who reaped the benefits of patronage after a change of administration. *The Albany Atlas,* for example, referred to Hawthorne as "the gentle Elia of our American literature" (65) while the *Philadelphia Evening Bulletin* made the case that, as a literary man and *not* a political appointee, Hawthorne should be "saved from the pinch of poverty" by "the bestowal of the government patronage" (66). Perhaps in recoil from what was ultimately a losing strategy, Hawthorne suggests in the Preface that his actual reputation was intensely local. Referring only to the dissemination of his tales in book form, Hawthorne writes: "The circulation of the two volumes was chiefly confined to New England; nor was it until long after this period, if it even yet be the case, that the Author could regard himself as addressing the American Public, or indeed, any Public at all. He was merely writing to his known or unknown friends" (1151). If in the wake of the Custom House firing it had served Hawthorne's local, political purposes to be known as a national literary figure, the occasion of Fields's republication of the *Twice-Told Tales* offered Hawthorne a spectacular form of erasure: the national production of the Hawthorne persona as a local and apolitical figure.

4. "Nathaniel Hawthorne and His Mother," *Feminism and American Literary History* (New Brunswick: Rutgers University Press, 1992), 36–56. This essay was first published in *American Literature* 54 (1982): 1–27.

5. See letters 59–72 in Thomas Woodson et al., *The Letters, 1813–1843*, vol. 15 of *The Centenary Edition of the Works of Nathaniel Hawthorne* (Columbus: Ohio State University Press, 1984), 228–47.

6. Quoted in Horatio Bridge, *Personal Recollections of Nathaniel Hawthorne* (New York: Harper and Brothers, 1893), 94. Hawthorne's letters to Bridge concerning his editorial rewriting and promotion of Bridge's *Journal of an African Cruiser* (1845) suggest an author who is confident of his abilities, proud of his publishing connections, and known to be possessed of a good reputation. For example, while Hawthorne later complained that the publisher, Evert Duyckinck, had left Bridge's name off the title page in lieu of his own, he had earlier suggested to Bridge something approximating this arrangement: "My name shall appear as editor, in order to give it what little vogue may derived from thence—and its own merits will do the rest" (*Letters 1843–1853*, 94; 26).

7. The phrase is Nina Baym's, whose *The Shape of Hawthorne's Career* (Ithaca: Cornell University Press, 1976) remains the most influential account of the career as a whole.

8. For an account of the literary benefits of Hawthorne's cultivation of obscurity, see John McWilliams, "The Politics of Isolation," *The Nathaniel Hawthorne Review* (Spring, 1989): 2–7. Richard Brodhead provides an excellent account of Fields's innovative publication and distribution strategies in his chapter "Manufacturing You into a Personage: Hawthorne, The Canon, and the Institutionalization of American Literature," *The School of Hawthorne* (New York: Oxford University Press, 1986), 48–66. Brodhead argues convincingly that Fields's most significant achievement was the identification and marketing of specific writers as a cultural elite—a group that included Longfellow, Emerson, Hawthorne, Holmes, Lowell, and Whittier. The groundbreaking essay on Fields's merchandising tactics is William Charvat, "James T. Fields and the Beginnings of Book Promotion, 1840–1855," *Huntington Library Quarterly* 8 (November 1944): 75–94, reprinted in *The Profession of Authorship in America 1800–1870* (New York: Columbia University Press, 1992), 168–89.

9. Hawthorne's ironic disregard for minor writing in the Preface to *Twice-Told Tales* contrasts sharply with his early enthusiasm for writing children's books, by definition a minor genre. In a letter to Longfellow concerning a possible collaboration, Hawthorne writes expansively about "entirely [revolutionizing] the whole system of juvenile writing," acknowledging that minor writing is not incompatible with literary ambition: "Seriously, I think that a very pleasant and peculiar kind of reputation may be acquired in this way—we will twine for ourselves a wreath of tender shoots and dewy buds,

instead of such withered and dusty leaves as other people crown themselves with; and what is of more importance to me, though of none to a Cambridge Professor, we may perchance put money in our purses" *The Letters, 1813–1843*, 266–67.

10. Michael J. Colacurcio, *The Province of Piety: Moral History in Hawthorne's Early Tales* (Durham: Duke University Press, 1995), 485.

11. See C. E. Frazer Clark, Jr.'s invaluable *Nathaniel Hawthorne: A Descriptive Bibliography* (Pittsburgh: University of Pittsburgh Press, 1978), A 2.28, A 2.48, A 19.1.a, C 2. Clark's work, while not a comprehensive list of the reprinting of Hawthorne's tales—a bibliographic feat which is as yet impossible owing to the inadequately indexed state of nineteenth-century periodicals—represents the best information available.

12. See Clark, A 2.1, A 2.4, A 2.39–40, A 2.51, A 19.10, C 8, C 11, C 19. It is striking that Griswold's selections are all what we would consider minor fiction: "A Rill from the Town Pump," "David Swan," "The Celestial Railroad," and a selection from "Buds and Bird Voices" (Clark, C 19).

13. See Clark, A 2.4.

14. All of these remarks are taken from reviews found in John L. Idol, Jr., and Buford Jones, eds., *Nathaniel Hawthorne: The Contemporary Reviews* (New York: Cambridge University Press, 1994), 20, 21, 27, 30.

15. *American Romanticism and the Marketplace* (Chicago: University of Chicago Press, 1985). Brook Thomas's *Cross Examination of Law and Literature* (New York: Cambridge University Press, 1987) and Walter Michaels's *The Gold Standard and the Logic of Naturalism* (Berkeley: University of California Press, 1987) differently position their accounts of *The House of the Seven Gables* in relation to the fiction of Hawthorne's withdrawal from the market.

16. Review of *Twice-Told Tales* and *Mosses from an Old Manse*, *Godey's Lady's Book* (November 1847), in G. R. Thompson, ed., *Edgar Allan Poe: Essays and Reviews* (New York: Literary Classics of the United States, 1984), 578.

17. Review of *Twice-Told Tales*, *Graham's Magazine* (May 1842) in Thompson, *Edgar Allan Poe*, 574. Poe comments that he "had good reason for so supposing"; his evidence is most probably, the laudatory reviews of *Twice-Told Tales* published by Longfellow in the *North American Review* immediately in the wake of both the 1837 and 1842 editions.

18. Hawthorne self-deprecatingly refers to the volume as "twice-told tediousness" in a letter to Longfellow (*Letters 1843–1853*, 249), alluding to Shakespeare's *King John* III.iv.108: "Life is as tedious as a twice-told tale." Nevertheless, his title seems designed to provoke critics to revalue the already printed tales and sketches by transposing them into an imaginary oral context, a critical response exemplified by Park Benjamin's and Elizabeth Palmer Peabody's reviews of the volume. See Idol and Jones, *Nathaniel Hawthorne*, 27–34.

19. It would also need to grapple with John Bryant's *Melville and Repose:*

The Rhetoric of Humor in the American Renaissance (New York: Oxford University Press, 1993). Bryant's strong interest in linking the tone of repose to the comic kept his work on the periphery of my analysis, but Bryant has done a remarkable job of tracing the genealogy of this posture toward the reader from eighteenth-century British writing through the novels of Herman Melville.

20. See Sandra Tomc, "An Idle Industry: Nathaniel Parker Willis and the Workings of Literary Leisure," *American Quarterly* 49, no. 4 (December 1997): 780–805, for a provocative analysis of the importance of literary idleness to the articulation of entrepreneurial professionalism.

21. Note the parenthetical, accidental correspondence between the conditions of composition and Hawthorne's narrative persona. Hawthorne nominally refuses to identify the two but also courts such an identification through resemblance: "With the foregoing characteristics, proper to the productions of a person in retirement (which happened to be the Author's category, at the time), the book is devoid of others that we should quite as naturally look for" (1152).

Margaret Fuller: The Evolution of a Woman of Letters
Steven Fink

In Margaret Fuller, we have an example of a writer who explicitly, and even vehemently, rejected the model of the emerging professional woman writer of the type described by Mary Kelley as the "literary domestic";[1] Fuller declared that she wanted to "write like a man of the world of intellect and action" and not "like a woman of love and hope, and disappointment."[2] And yet, because she was a woman in nineteenth-century America, Fuller could not really define herself on any model provided by any of her male contemporaries. Precisely because of her anomalous position, then, Fuller's career brings into high relief for us some of the instabilities and tensions of that cultural moment—fraught possibilities that lurked just beneath the surface of any writer's career.

Furthermore, the nature of literary production and consumption was undergoing dramatic changes, so that defining oneself as a professional writer was something like shooting at a moving target. In *New England Literary Culture,* Lawrence Buell effectively draws upon Raymond Williams's "typology of artistic production," describing four basic market situations that evolved from the late eighteenth century through the mid nineteenth century and applying them to American literary culture:[3] Williams designates the first phase as the "artisanal," in which an "independent producer ... offers his own work for direct sale" (Buell illustrates this phase with the example of Joel Barlow selling his own poetry by subscription). The second phase is the "post-artisanal," in which "the producer sells his work not directly but to a *distributive* intermediary, who then becomes, in a majority of cases, his factual if often occasional employer" (Buell's example here is Nathaniel Hawthorne's producing stories for Samuel Goodrich's gift books). The third phase is the "market professional," wherein "the writer negotiates a contract, involving royalties and copyright, with a publisher" (illustrated by the example of Longfellow's contract negotiations with Ticknor and Fields). And the fourth phase is that of the "corporate professional," in which "the artist becomes the employee of a literary organization"—for example, a magazine or newspaper. Here Buell's example is Margaret Fuller's literary journalism for the New York *Tribune*, which she produced while on an annual salary, with an explicit standard of productivity. As Buell notes, in broad terms we can see the norm for literary production evolving throughout these phases sequentially, but because these phases imply distinct ideologies of authorship that are unstable and contested, we can find manifestations of all four stages not only at a single historical moment but even in the career of a single author. Buell points out that Nathaniel Parker Willis went through all four phases in his career, and I want to indicate that this is also true for Margaret Fuller.

Briefly, we can see the first, or artisanal, phase in the famous "Conversations" Fuller conducted for a select class of educated women in Boston from 1839 to 1844. Fuller herself promoted and sold subscriptions for her courses, often through direct personal correspondence. The second, or post-artisanal phase, is represented by the pieces that Fuller sold to magazines such as the *American Monthly Magazine*, or, in a somewhat more complicated way, by her simultaneously editing and writing for the Transcendentalist journal *The Dial*. The third phase—the market professional—appears in Fuller's negotiation of contracts for *Summer on the Lakes* with Little, Brown; for *Woman in the Nineteenth Century* with Greeley and McElrath; and for *Papers on Literature and Art* with Wiley and Putnam. Finally, the fourth phase, the corporate professional, is, as has already been noted, exemplified by her employment on salary with the New York *Tribune*.

Moreover, each of these authorial positions is further complicated and particularized in Fuller's case by several other factors: First, her relation with both publishers and readers was complicated by the fact that she was a woman who rejected the dominant emerging models of female authorship. Second, her relation to the literary marketplace was further complicated by the fact that Fuller was both a Romantic idealist and a reformer, for whom financial remuneration was not, *in principle*, the chief aim or even an essential consequence of publication; while at the same time Fuller found herself, after her father's sudden death in 1835, virtually always in rather desperate economic straits and so *in fact* always needing to consider her literary work as a potential source of income. I would therefore like to examine more closely particular moments in the course of Fuller's career to illustrate some of the conceptual and material tensions that emerged as she explored the various market conditions accessible to her as a writer.

Fuller's first appearance in print was an insignificant piece except that it is richly suggestive of the ideological conception of authorship to which she was educated. She was given a rigorous classical education by her father, a Jeffersonian republican who served four terms in Congress before retiring to fulfill his dream of becoming a gentleman farmer. Margaret was reading Latin at six, and she later recalled "the influence of those great Romans, whose thoughts and lives were my daily food during those plastic years."[4] Thus, when in 1834 historian and Jacksonian democrat George Bancroft attacked the Roman aristocracy and Brutus in particular in a *North American Review* essay on "The Influence of Slavery on the Political Revolutions of Rome," Fuller's father asked twenty-four-year-old Margaret to write a reply.[5] Her "Defense of Brutus" was printed, without identifying its author (it was signed only "J."), in the *Boston Daily Advertiser* for November 24, 1834. When a reader replied to her essay in print, disagreeing but treating her argument very seriously and respectfully, Fuller revealingly reported her success to a friend, writing that, "as he remarked that I wrote with 'ability' and seemed to *consider me* as an elderly gentleman *I considered* the affair as highly flattering."[6]

What we find here is a conception of authorship and public discourse that prevailed in the late colonial and early national period but that was already fast disappearing in Jacksonian America. This idea of authorship has nothing to do with professionalism or the commodification of literature; rather, it assumes a situation in which writing is conducted in the public sphere by the best-educated classes as an expression of civic duty and participation in a republican ideal of citizenship. Given the disfranchisement of women, however, this was an ironic role, at best, for Margaret Fuller. As much as she might wish to "*write like* a man of the world of intellect and action" (emphasis mine), Fuller was not and could not *be* such a man—in spite of her apparent pleasure at being mistaken, on this occasion, for an "elderly gentleman."

Still, the conception of authorship as an amateur vocation, independent of and resistant to the commodification of literature and to the emerging literary marketplace, persisted with considerable tenacity for Fuller and many of her contemporaries—both male and female. Under the influence of German Romanticism and her Transcendentalist Unitarian friends, Fuller evolved from republican citizen to Romantic idealist, who wrote, not as a matter of civic duty, but, as she now put it, "to vent my inner life."[7] This involved a dramatic shift from public to private conception of authorship and so actually comported more easily with conventional conceptions of women's role, yet it retained and even reinforced the resistance to professional, commercial writing.

Margaret was also profoundly ambitious, however. Moreover, after her father's death in 1835, Fuller desperately needed to earn an income to contribute to her own and her family's support. The result was a deeply conflicted sense of her role as a writer and of her relation to the marketplace. In the spring of 1836, for example, Elizabeth Peabody reported that Park Benjamin, who had recently become co-editor of the *American Monthly Magazine*, "seems really desirous to help along Margaret Fuller & me—in making our thoughts known."[8] Fuller seems to have responded almost immediately, submitting substantive review essays based on her recent reading, which were duly printed (unsigned) in the June and July 1836 numbers of the *American Monthly*.[9] When she submitted a more ambitious essay on "Modern British Poets," however, the editors apparently balked at her assessment of the Romantics and asked her to revise or delete some portions. Already sensitive about marketing her writing, she wrote to Elizabeth Peabody, "With regard to what you say about the American Monthly, my answer is, I would gladly sell some part of my mind for lucre, to get command of time; but I will not sell my soul: that is, I am perfectly willing to take the trouble of writing for money to pay the seamstress; but I am *not* willing to have what I write mutilated, or, what I ought to say, dictated to suit the public taste" (*MFL* VI: 274).

In the end, the editors agreed to publish her essay (which appeared in two parts, in the September and October 1836 numbers), but they now printed it with the signature "M.F." and added a disclaimer noting that "the opinions expressed in this paper must be received as those of the individual writer, and not of the Editors. . . . with the view taken of Lord Byron, for instance, we disagree almost entirely. It however gives us pleasure to present to our readers an article of so much power and beauty, from so bold and original a hand."[10]

Finding that editors and "public taste" could be so sharply censorious only reinforced Fuller's ambivalence about exposing her thoughts and feelings through publication. While Fuller had contributed essays, reviews, and poems to her friend James Freeman Clarke's *Western Messenger* from its beginning in 1835 through 1838, she nevertheless wrote to Clarke in January 1839 declining his request for some poems, explaining,

> Genius seems to me excusable in taking the public for a confidant. Genius is universal, and can appeal to the common heart of man. . . . But for us lesser people, who write verses merely as vents for the overflowings of a personal experience, . . . it seems to me that all the value of this utterance is destroyed by a hasty or indiscriminate publicity. The moment I lay open my heart, and tell the fresh feeling to anyone who chooses to hear, I feel profaned. (*MFL* II: 33–34)

Yet if Fuller felt profaned by publication at times, the alternatives were dismayingly limited. She complained to a friend, "You know we women have no profession except marriage, mantua-making and school-keeping" (*MFL* VI: 279). She did indeed attempt teaching, about which she vacillated between intense enthusiasm and despondent exhaustion. And in spite of her reservations she never really withheld her writing from the public eye—though criticism and translation seemed safer and less profane than poetry or other more personal expression. She envisioned an ambitious life of Goethe, and in 1839 she published a translation of Eckerman's *Conversations with Goethe* as part of George Ripley's Specimens of Foreign Standard Literature series.

While this labor was without pay, the literary marketplace in general was becoming increasingly commercialized (even as it exploited non- or anticommercial conceptions of authorship, as I shall discuss shortly). Combined with her ambition and her real need for an income, the attractions of professionalization thus exerted a more or less constant pressure on Fuller's development as a woman of letters. In the autumn of 1839 (less than a year after she confessed to Clarke that publication seemed a profanity), Fuller turned again to Elizabeth Peabody for help in finding a print outlet for her work: "The Democratic Review is not what I want," she wrote, "yet I might like to put something there occasionally, and should like to be asked. As to what my answer would be I would only ask of you, ... Are they good pay (for I have heard the contrary)—? Will they pay me *unasked*? or torture all my lady like feelings as almost all other persons have with whom I have been concerned—" (*MFL* II: 91–92). Fuller was clearly attracted to the possibility not only of publishing but of selling her work (and the *Democratic Review*, which was publishing the stories of Peabody's brother-in-law, Nathaniel Hawthorne, did pay, though somewhat sporadically and not as well as Hawthorne and others wished);[11] but as a woman, she had—at this point, at least—a strong sense of gender (and class) propriety that made it painful for her to be put in the situation of asking for or negotiating payment.

For the moment, her series of Conversations provided a far more comfortable means of negotiating her status as a public figure and woman of letters. In some ways an extension of her teaching, but now to a class of adults, her Conversations were also an innovative and socially acceptable alternative to the public lecture platform, meeting the specific needs of a class of prosperous and well-educated women who were similarly ambitious but disfranchised. Whereas social conventions did not yet allow women to speak in public to mixed audiences, Fuller's private course of Conversations catered to a female audience in an innovative but entirely respectable way, avoiding the need to work through any mediating institution—whether as lecturer for a society, or as editor, or as school administrator—and so allowing her to market her intellectual wares by direct sale. With the help of friends, Fuller herself recruited participants in her Conversations, who paid her directly—$10 each for the first series of Conversations, $20 each after that.[12] With twenty-five to thirty participants in each series, Fuller was able to earn a quite comfortable income and establish a reputation as a powerful intellectual. The limits of this enterprise were also significant, however. The audience for her Conversations was local and finite, their content not reproducible either for sale or for wider distribution.[13]

Fuller conducted Conversations each year for five years, but she simultaneously agreed to assume the editorship of a new Transcendentalist journal, *The Dial*. Work began in 1839—the year of her first course of Conversations—and the first number was published in July 1840. The *Dial* provided not merely a print outlet for her own writings but one over which she, as editor, had virtually complete control. The editorship gave Fuller an opportunity to define (and so test the viability of) a periodical that, while necessarily subject to the laws of the existing market, was dedicated to providing a vehicle through which individuals might freely "vent the inner life." As she recorded in her private journal, "It is now proposed that I should conduct a magazine which would afford me space and occasion for every thing I may wish to do."[14]

Just what she "wished to do" as editor was still a matter of considerable ambivalence, however. Larry J. Reynolds argues that the *Dial* "grew out of the coterie publishing practices of . . . the Fuller circle . . . who had been sharing 'pacquets' or 'portfolios' of material with one another for several years." That is, he argues that it was not by default but by design that Fuller made the "portfolio" writings of her circle (rather than the Unitarian ministers of the Transcendental Club) the vital center of the *Dial* and shaped it as a coterie journal. Emphasizing Fuller's anxiety about the marketplace, Reynolds argues that Fuller envisioned the *Dial*'s audience as "a large circle of ideal friends. For her, the American public was hopelessly vulgar and ignorant, and she was reluctant to address it at this time."[15] Yet Reynolds understates Fuller's genuine interest in addressing and engaging the American public, which operated as a powerful and complicating counterforce to her coterie ideals and her resistance to the marketplace. Pleading with Frederick Henry Hedge (one of the original members of the Transcendental Club but also an old friend of Fuller's) for a contribution to the *Dial*'s first issue, for example, she explained, "I could make a number myself with the help Mr. E[merson] will give, but the Public, I trow, is too astute a donkey not to look sad at *that*"; and confessing that she found little of her own writing to be relevant, she added, "I would fain do something worthily that belonged to the country where I was born, but most times I fear it may not be" (*MFL* II: 124–25). Making a similar plea to William Henry Channing, she explained, "It is for dear New England that I wanted this review; for myself, if I had wanted to write a few pages now and then, I had ways and means of disposing of them"(*MFL* II: 131).

It was not that Fuller was loath to address the American public, then; on the contrary, she was eager to address it and saw her project as part of a larger agenda of literary nationalism. Rather, the challenge Fuller and the *Dial* faced was how to engage that public without abandoning their commitment to a Romantic aesthetic of private, "portfolio" writing. Fuller was aided in the production of the *Dial* by both Ralph Waldo Emerson and George Ripley, and the profound ambivalence they all shared about the nature of this enterprise, its aims, and its audience, is manifested in the contributions each of them made to the first number of the journal. They all agreed that the journal should be a forum for the freest possible expression of *Ideas*. Ripley, in his "Prospectus" for the *Dial,* indicated that it was to be a sort of hybrid between the popular monthly magazines and the more scholarly quarterly reviews, whereby "it may present something both for those who read for instruction, and those who search for amusement."[16] Emerson, who ended up writing the opening address, "The Editors to the Reader," declared that the journal "has all things to say and no less than all the world for its final audience"; yet these ambitions were to be realized, he insisted, by relying not on "the pens of practised writers," but "from the beautiful resources of private thought.... from the secret confession of genius afraid to trust itself to aught but sympathy" (*Dial* I.i: 3–4). Fuller, who contributed "A Short Essay on Critics" to the *Dial*'s first number, expresses a similar ambivalence about the writer's proper relation to his or her audience. Even while she acknowledges that the role of the critic is to mediate between author and audience, she dismisses contemptuously that species of critical essay that is "got up to order by the literary hack writer, for the literary mart, and the only law is to make them plausible." Rather, critical essays should be "epistles addressed to the public through which the mind of the recluse relieves itself of its impressions" (*Dial* I.i: 5). Yet this model of criticism forces Fuller into some curious paradoxes. The critical essay is "addressed to the public," she concedes, yet she characterizes the critic as a "recluse" who is not thinking of his or her audience but whose mind "relieves itself of its impressions." Criticism, it turns out, does not mediate between the private and public but is merely another means by which the writer gives "vent to the inner life." Criticism is not a response to public demand or inquiry; it does not have pedagogical or rhetorical designs upon its audience; it does not take into account the language, conventions, or values of any particular audience. Fuller says of the critic, "if he adapts his work to us ... we will not talk with him.... We will go to the critic who trusts Genius and trusts us, who knows that all good writing must be spontaneous" (*Dial* I.i: 10). Having adopted a high Romantic conception of the author and of literary expression, Fuller has moved so far from the republican citizen model of authorship and public rhetoric that genius is a matter of "secret confession," and criticism is the work of a recluse relieving himself. Both shun the marketplace and enter the public sphere entirely unself-consciously, almost by accident, or by some coy gesture exposing that which was not really intended to be seen. The *Dial*'s audience was all the world, but the world's access to it is represented as something akin to voyeurism, so that the integrity of the artist might be preserved while her mind is nevertheless exposed.

The *Dial* was a brave and interesting, if occasionally ludicrous, experiment. For Margaret Fuller the writer, it provided a vehicle for publishing critical essays on music, art, and literature, most notably on Goethe and the Germans who so engaged her in this phase of her career. It also gave her an outlet for her landmark feminist essay "The Great Lawsuit" (later revised for book publication as *Woman in the Nineteenth Century*); and it gave her an opportunity to publish several mystical and experimental "flower" sketches that she almost certainly could never have published elsewhere and which are among her most interesting (and neglected) compositions. For Fuller the editor, the *Dial* provided an open field for her to wield her critical and aesthetic judgments in shaping what she hoped would be a coherent and provocative new journal. But it was not commercially viable. Its subscription list never exceeded three hundred,[17] and when, after two years as editor, Fuller discovered that the journal had not done well enough, even without paying any of its contributors, to pay her the modest sum of $200 she had been promised, she realized she needed to resign her position (*MFL* III: 53–54).

Emerson reluctantly took over as editor, and Fuller was both happy and relieved; but she wrote to Emerson of her concern that this change in leadership would mean that "you will sometimes reject pieces that I should not. For you have always had in view to make a good periodical and represent your own tastes, while I have had in view to let all kinds of people have freedom to say their say, for better or worse" (*MFL* III: 58). Fuller's representation of her tenure as editor is certainly consistent with the liberal and disinterested spirit of its inception, but it is not entirely accurate. In fact, Fuller had exercised a considerable degree of editorial control: while she was eager to draw upon the "portfolios" of her circle of intimates (including Samuel Ward, Ellen Hooper, and Caroline Sturgis), she nevertheless exercised her editorial authority to reject Henry Thoreau's submissions pretty consistently (even in the face of Emerson's enthusiastic support, and even after Thoreau dutifully revised and resubmitted his verses in response to her recommendations).[18] She rejected a submission from William Wetmore Story that she found too long and badly written by explaining that there was simply no more room in that issue (which seems to have been true, though at other times Fuller was desperate for material to fill out a number). And she rejected or deferred publishing the poems of William Ellery Channing, another of Emerson's protégés (and subsequently Fuller's own brother-in-law) (*MFL* II: 188–89). Thus, Fuller did not in fact simply provide an open channel for the free expression of all kinds of work, but was, on the contrary, an active, engaged, critical editor who seemed to relish the exercise of her critical powers in the service of a project she believed in. My point here is not so much that Fuller misrepresented her editorship as that we see here one of many examples in Fuller's career and writings of a deep-seated ambivalence about her role and values as she shaped herself as a woman of letters in a complex and evolving literary marketplace. In this case, the position she assumed in her letter to Emerson was consistent both with her Romantic idealism and, in particular, with her sense of female propriety, but it failed to acknowledge the real pleasure she took, and the success she had, in the exercise of literary and professional power.

One further comment about the *Dial:* Thinking again in terms of Raymond Williams's typology of artistic production, we can see that writing for the *Dial* looks as though it belongs to the phase of post-artisanal production, in which (rather than engaging in direct sales) the writer sells his or her work to a distributive intermediary—that is, a magazine—which is in effect the writer's employer and which is then responsible for marketing the work. But the *Dial* did not pay for contributions at all, even though the magazine itself was sold, of course (subscriptions cost $3 per year for the quarterly publication). So the *Dial* (like many periodicals of the day, and especially the quarterly reviews, but unlike the newer popular monthly magazines) operated exactly as a distributive intermediary in a post-artisanal market situation, but could do so only if the artistic producer—the writer—

did not really enter the market economy at all. Under these circumstances, the writer offered his or her works for publication *not as commodities for sale* but on some other basis—either to engage in public discourse in order to fulfill one's sense of civic duty, or in the service of some particular cause (such as social or moral reform), or simply to satisfy one's vanity.

From the point of view of the aspiring professional writer, such an arrangement was of course undesirable, though it might be regarded, in the context of the still-evolving literary marketplace of the day, as a necessary if imperfect vehicle for public exposure (the popular monthly magazines, for example, often paid neophyte authors nothing at all, while paying popular writers quite handsomely). On the other hand, from the publisher or editor's point of view, it was perhaps necessary, in order to market a magazine profitably, to perpetuate a nonprofessional conception of authorship. Thus, for example, in 1842, at the same time the *Dial* was passing from Fuller to Emerson, the New York periodical *Brother Jonathan* was shamelessly justifying its exploitation of writers by cynically appealing to the already anachronistic notion that the *professional* writer was unpatriotic: "The man who would be literary must earn his living first—pursue an honest occupation. . . . His necessities thus provided for, literature may be to him the most delightful and ennobling amusement. . . . We want no . . . purely literary men. . . . There is no room in a republic for any such diploma pedants."[19]

The difficulty here is that from both sides this is an extremely unstable situation. Market forces are such that, if the writing is in fact not marketable, the publication itself will fail, as was the case with the *Dial;* and if the writing is marketable, the publisher will only be able to exploit the artist for so long before a competitor offers the writer more attractive terms for publication. For a while, the pirating of foreign works unprotected by international copyright provided sufficient competition to stave this off, but the exploitation of unpaid writers broke down long before the passage of international copyright laws in 1892. The second quarter of the nineteenth century in the United States was a period of extremely unstable transition in the literary marketplace, in considering which we must recognize some curious hybrid situations that reveal with particular clarity the underlying tensions and conflicts in the ideology of authorship and literary production.

If Fuller and her contemporaries did not grasp all of this, neither was it entirely lost on them. As Fuller retired from the editorship of the *Dial* and began to think of other literary avenues to explore, she wrote to Emerson, "Much, much do I wish for myself I could find a publisher who is honest and has also business talents"(*MFL* III: 58). And it is probably not coincidental that her next literary project after stepping back from the quixotic *Dial* was a narrative account of her travels from Niagara Falls to Michigan Territory, published as *Summer on the Lakes, in 1843*. While Fuller's digressions and interpolations make this a somewhat peculiar and eccentric book (revealing her continuing attachment to the aesthetic of "portfolio" literature), Fuller was aware that there was a substantial market for accounts of the West, and she succeeded, to some extent, in tapping into that market. It is a book full of interest, but here I want merely to sketch out the publishing history of the book to suggest how fully Fuller was embracing a professional identity.

When Fuller was ready to seek out a publisher for her book, she turned to Emerson, who agreed to act as agent on her behalf and subsequently presented her with offers from two Boston publishers—Little, Brown and his own publisher at the time, James Munroe. Little, Brown offered to publish her book on their own account, with a royalty of 10 percent on retail sales after expenses were recouped. Munroe offered to publish it on terms of half profits on sales to booksellers (that is, discounted 20 percent from retail), but "half profits" contracts also committed the author to risking the cost of half the losses should the book fail to recoup expenses. For an edition of one thousand copies, profits were nearly identical if the entire edition sold (about $100), so any apparent advantage of "half profits" was illusory. In spite of this and the fact that Little, Brown had better distribution connections in New York and in the South than Munroe, Emerson recommended his own publisher; but Fuller overrode his advice and decided to publish her book with Little, Brown.[20]

On the eve of its publication, in May 1844, Fuller confessed some of her anxieties to Emerson: "All looks auspicious, except that I feel a little cold at the idea of walking forth alone to meet that staring sneering Pit critic, the Public at large, when I have always been accustomed to confront it from amid a group of 'liberally educated and respectable gentlemen'"(*MFL* III: 196). Again we see in this letter Fuller's sense of female propriety pulling her back from the public sphere, shaping and containing her sense of herself as a writer even as it acts in counterpoint to her more self-assured decision to override the recommendation of her male adviser, Emerson, in making publishing arrangements for the book.

Whatever her anxieties, when *Summer on the Lakes* came out, Fuller was eager to help promote its sale in any way she could, and she was deeply pleased by early favorable responses. She explained the publishing terms to her close friend William Henry Channing, noting that Little, Brown would of course oversee the distribution of the book, but adding that "any effort from my friends helps, of course. Short notices by you, distributed at Phila New York and even Cincinnati would attract attention and buyers!! Outward success in this way is very desirable to me, not so much on account of present profit to be derived, as because it would give me advantage in making future bargains, and open the way to ransom more time for writing" (*MFL* III: 198).

By the beginning of 1845, seven hundred copies of *Summer on the Lakes* had been sold, and Fuller felt encouraged; but by May of 1845, W. H. Graham was advertising, in the New York *Tribune*, the sale of four hundred copies, probably remaindered.[21] It is not clear that Fuller saw any profit at all from the book. Fuller had embraced her professional status and handled the publishing negotiations as shrewdly as possible, but publishing terms were rarely favorable to the authors; and while Little, Brown was a stronger house than Munroe, neither had mastered the more aggressive marketing and distribution strategies of several growing New York houses.

By this time, Horace Greeley had suggested to Fuller that she expand her *Dial* essay "The Great Lawsuit" into a small book, and he also offered her a job as literary editor of his New York *Tribune*. Fuller accepted, and her move to New York, her work on the *Tribune*, and her association with Greeley and other New York publishing figures mark Fuller's full emergence as a professional writer. The book she wrote, retitled *Woman in the Nineteenth Century*, was clearly a more ambitious, more radical, and more inflammatory book than *Summer on the Lakes*. Fuller was anxious about its reception and concerned about its ability to engage an audience. She explained to William Henry Channing that a small edition might be most appropriate: "The writing, though I have tried to make my meaning full and clear, requires, shall I say? too much culture in the reader to be quickly or extensively diffused. I shall be satisfied if it moves a mind here and there"(*MFL* III: 242).[22] Its very notoriety, of course, assured it a certain level of interest, and, published by Greeley and McElrath in an inexpensive edition (priced at fifty cents), aggressively advertised and distributed, it in fact sold out an edition of fifteen hundred copies very quickly, for which Fuller was paid $85.[23]

The publication of *Woman in the Nineteenth Century* solidified Fuller's reputation as a radical. If Fuller's lingering sense of female propriety had caused some private compunctions and constraints upon her career, *Woman in the Nineteenth Century* was certainly her boldest public challenge to the conventions of "women's sphere." Edgar Allan Poe described it as a work of "unmitigated radicalism," "a book which few women in the country could have written, and no woman in the country would have published, with the exception of Miss Fuller."[24]

When Fuller accepted Greeley's offer to join the staff of the *Tribune*, she was of course further challenging the constraints of "women's sphere," in actions as well as word. But if we trace Fuller's career in terms of her relation to the literary marketplace, we also see what looks like an ironic—though perhaps inevitable—shift toward accommodation with market forces, even as she does become ideologically more radical. In Raymond Williams's terms, in joining the *Tribune* Fuller became a "corporate professional," working on salary and (at least to some extent) taking her writing assignments and deadlines from Greeley. Yet this position was clearly Fuller's most effective and influential vehicle for the expression of her strong and provocative views on both social and aesthetic issues. In addition to literary reviews, Fuller wrote frequently on a variety of social issues and institutions, including female prison reform, insane asylums, and immigration.[25] She wrote a total of some 250 columns for the *Tribune*, with a far larger and more widely distributed readership than she could have achieved through any other means. She liked Greeley, and though he occasionally provoked her with short notice and strict deadlines, she liked the work, and she liked New York (as much as all this rather horrified her Concord and Boston acquaintances). To one correspondent she wrote, "I am pleased with your sympathy about the Tribune, for I do not find much among my old friends. They think I ought to produce something excellent, while I am satisfied to aid in the great work of popular education" (*MFL* IV: 39).

This is a dramatic shift from her earlier construction of herself as a writer, but I think it represents not so much a reversal of her earlier position as the evolution of her ideology as it adapted to her increasingly astute understanding of the literary marketplace and the complex dynamics of the triangulation of author-publisher-reader. By defining her aim here as "the great work of popular education," Fuller can imagine the emerging literary marketplace as the tool, not the enemy, of her idealism and as a potentially powerful instrument of reform—though the underlying profit motive that actually drove the market forces would always make this a delicate and strained alliance.

In the autumn of 1846, Fuller left for Europe (a long-postponed dream of hers), and so entered the final period of her career. Greeley had agreed to pay her $10 a column for anything she sent him as a foreign correspondent, and he gave her a $120 advance.[26] Before she left, however, she negotiated for the publication of a collection of some of her essays with the New York firm of Wiley and Putnam. Consisting mostly of collected *Tribune* pieces, but also including essays gleaned from the *American Monthly* and the *Dial*, *Papers on Literature and Art* would be printed in two volumes, as part of the Wiley and Putnam Library of American Books. Initiated in 1845, this was the first series of exclusively American books printed by an American publisher, and it already included works by Poe and Hawthorne, among others. The series thus marks a particularly interesting moment in the history of publishing in America, manifesting a particular kind of literary nationalism.

The brainchild of Evert Duyckinck, who edited the series for Wiley and Putnam, the Library of American Books was closely associated with Duyckinck's whole circle of New York literary nationalists, known as "Young America." Fuller respected Duyckinck and was eager for her collection to appear in this series, but in the end her *Papers on Literature and Art* proved to be a frustrating and unsatisfying venture for her. First of all, the publishing terms were not particularly favorable to her. Each of the two volumes was to be priced at fifty cents, and Fuller was offered a choice between a 12 percent royalty on all copies after expenses were recouped or a half-profits contract. She explained to her brother, "As it takes two thousand copies to pay expenses, I may make nothing or very slowly. Still I shall be content, as it is an object to me to get the pieces in an accessible form" (*MFL* IV: 198–99). Then the publisher Wiley requested that Fuller delete one essay in particular from the collection as well as all other religiously controversial matter. Recalling her reaction to editorial interference from the *American Monthly Magazine* a decade earlier, Fuller bristled sharply at these demands but ultimately agreed to the deletions when Duyckinck put it in terms of needing to reduce each volume by thirty pages in any case (*MFL* IV: 212, 219). At the same time, Fuller either asked or agreed to include, as an appendix to the second volume, extended excerpts from a dramatic work by Cornelius Matthews, a close friend of Duyckinck and a fellow Young American, though much reviled as a writer in the popular press. The result was a collection with which Fuller was dissatisfied and which never yielded her a profit. Three years later, when Fuller was in Rome—in the midst of the revolutionary fervor, secretly married, the mother of a young child, and in desperate financial straits—she wrote to friends, "Go to Wiley and Putnam and ask if all that stuff published as my miscellanies is forever to be unprofitable as well as flat and stale. . . . It is now the third year, and if you could squeeze for me even a very small sum from his publishing mercies, it would be most welcome" (*MFL* V: 296–97).

Among the most interesting of the pieces included in her *Papers on Literature and Art* is an essay entitled "American Literature," the one piece written specifically for this collection. It is a remarkable exercise, in which Fuller strikes nearly all the stops in the rhetoric of literary nationalism, seemingly designed to appeal to Duyckinck and the Young Americans, and so appropriate for the series. Yet her underlying position is that all of our literary glory lies in our future promise, and she is in fact quite critical of the current state of letters in the United States. Moreover, her ultimate target is the literary marketplace itself. American literature is currently

> in this dim and struggling state, and its pecuniary results exceedingly pitiful. From many well known causes it is impossible for ninety-nine out of the hundred, who wish to use the pen, to ransom, by its use, the time they need. This state of things will have to be changed in some way. No man of genius writes for money; but it is essential to the free use of his powers, that he should be able to disembarrass his life from care and perplexity. This is very difficult here; and the state of things gets worse and worse, as less and less is offered in pecuniary meed for works demanding great devotion of time and labour . . . and the publisher, obliged to regard the transaction as a matter of business, demands of the author to give him only what will find an immediate market, for he cannot afford to take anything else. This will not do![27]

Fuller's only hope is that the public taste may eventually be sufficiently educated to create a market for enduring literature, and interestingly she places her highest hopes in the newspapers as the best and most effective vehicle for public education. Here, then, is where, in America, the corporate professional and the literary genius meet.

The last years of Fuller's life were spent in Italy. Her dispatches on the Roman revolution to the *Tribune* were famous, but a variety of difficulties, including the difficulties of transatlantic communication and payments, left her nearly destitute much of the time. Her great work from this period was to be a history of the Roman revolutionary effort, and she determined that she needed to return to America to oversee in person the contract negotiations and publication (*MFL* VI: 51, 55, 64). For some time, her American friends had been urging her to return, but she had said it was not possible; now that she was ready, she needed also to reveal to them that she had married an Italian and had a two-year-old son—with no real evidence that she had actually ever married Giovanni Ossoli and much suspicion of the contrary. Her American friends did not abandon her, but now they were worried that she would not be able to survive the ostracism she would experience in America's "good society." When living in America, Fuller had always been extremely conscious of social conventions and propriety, and she had been careful to remain within acceptable boundaries even as she challenged the status quo. Now, however, her notoriety and radicalism had perhaps exceeded permissible bounds, and both she and her friends were acutely aware of the fact that her professional career would be profoundly affected as well. Fuller's friends therefore now tried to persuade her to stay in Italy. Emerson promised to act as her agent and make the "best terms" for an American publisher for her book, either in Boston or New York, so it was "needless" for her to come all the way to America only to negotiate a contract. Fuller's friend Rebecca Spring was less evasive: "Much as we should love to see you, and strange as it may seem, we, as well as all your friends who have spoken to us about it, believe it will be undesirable for you to return at the present."[28]

Fuller, her husband, and their child all perished in a shipwreck just a few hundred yards off Fire Island, and her book manuscript was lost. Her attempted return was a desperate gesture in many ways. Rome had become her real home, and she intended to return within a few years, but she thought that only by returning to the United States could she find her proper audience and at the same time regain the financial footing she would need to reestablish herself in Rome. Her friends' anxieties may in fact, however, have been well founded, and it is questionable whether she could have succeeded.

The lesson Fuller had learned during her last several years in the United States was that survival in the profession of authorship was a matter of complex and delicate negotiation within the changing terms of the triangulation of writer-publisher-reader; and I suspect that she may have irrevocably upset that balance at last. Fuller's Roman years were probably her most heroic, most liberated, and most fulfilling (even as they brought her poverty and bouts of severe depression); but because the United States was, in the decade before the Civil War, still sufficiently provincial that one's social and professional lives were seen as intimately intertwined, Fuller would certainly have experienced a degree of social disfranchisement here that would have reverberated through, and perhaps finally broken, her professional life as well.

Notes

1. Mary Kelley, *Private Woman, Public Stage: Literary Domesticity in Nineteenth-Century America* (New York: Oxford University Press, 1984), xviii–ix, and *passim*.
2. Fuller journal entry, quoted in Joan Von Mehren, *Minerva and the Muse: A Life of Margaret Fuller* (Amherst: University of Massachusetts Press, 1994), 3.
3. Raymond Williams, *The Sociology of Culture* (New York: Schocken, 1981), 44–53; Lawrence Buell, *New England Literary Culture: From Revolution through Renaissance* (New York: Cambridge University Press, 1986), 57.
4. *Memoirs of Margaret Fuller Ossoli*, ed. R. W. Emerson, W. H. Channing, J. F. Clarke, 2 vols. (Boston: Phillips, Sampson and Co., 1852), I: 18.
5. Charles Capper comments on this, "No doubt Timothy Fuller detected in the incipient young Jacksonian's denigration of Brutus and concomitant glorification of Caesar as a friend of the people something of the populist statism that classical republicans like Fuller had always detested as much as they did the aristocracy." *Margaret Fuller: An American Romantic Life*, vol. 1: *The Private Years* (New York: Oxford, 1992), 144.
6. *The Letters of Margaret Fuller*, ed. Robert N. Hudspeth, 6 vols. (Ithaca: Cornell University Press, 1983–1994), I: 226. Subsequent references to the *Letters* will be abbreviated *MFL* and cited parenthetically in the text.
7. Fuller's inscription for an 1832 journal, quoted in Von Mehren, *Minerva and the Muse*, p. 54. See this echoed in the letter cited below.
8. *Letters of Elizabeth Peabody: American Renaissance Woman*, ed. Bruce A. Ronda (Middletown, Conn.: Wesleyan University Press, 1894), 166.

9. [Margaret Fuller], "The Life of Sir James Mackintosh," *American Monthly Magazine* (June 1836): 570–80; "Present State of German Literature," *American Monthly Magazine* (July 1836): 1–13.

10. M. F.[Margaret Fuller], "Modern British Poets," *American Monthly Magazine* (September 1836): 235–50; (October 1836): 320–33.

11. See, for example, Nathaniel Hawthorne, *The Letters, 1813–1843*, ed. Thomas Woodson et al., vol. 15 of *The Centenary Edition of the Works of Nathaniel Hawthorne* (Columbus: Ohio State University Press, 1984), 681–682; and *The Correspondence of Henry David Thoreau*, ed. Walter Harding and Carl Bode (New York: New York University Press, 1958), 141.

12. See *MFL* II: 86–89; and Capper, *Margaret Fuller*, 293. By 1841, Fuller attempted a course for a mixed audience of men and women, though this was generally deemed less successful than the women-only courses. For a record of this mixed-audience series, see Caroline Healey Dall, *Margaret and Her Friends; or, Ten Conversations with Margaret Fuller* (Boston: Roberts Brothers, 1895).

13. This must be qualified by noting that, half a century after the fact, Caroline Healey Dall did successfully publish her record of the 1841 series of Conversations, cited above.

14. Quoted in Capper, *Margaret Fuller*, 335.

15. Larry J. Reynolds, "From *Dial* Essay to New York Book: The Making of *Woman in the Nineteenth Century*," in *Periodical Literature in Nineteenth-Century America*, ed. Kenneth W. Price and Susan Belasco Smith (Charlottesville: University Press of Virginia, 1995), 17–34; quotations from pp. 20, 22.

16. The "Prospectus" was first published on May 4, 1840, and was subsequently reprinted on the back cover of each number of the *Dial*. On the attribution to Ripley, see Joel Myerson, *The New England Transcendentalists and the* Dial (Cranbury, N.J.: Associated University Presses, 1980), 47 and 236, n. 43.

17. See Joel Myerson, "A Union List of the *Dial* (1840–1844) and Some Information about Its Sales," *Papers of the Bibliographical Society of America* 67 (3rd Quarter 1973): 322–28; and Myerson, *New England Transcendentalists and the* Dial, 48, 74, 88, 90.

18. On Thoreau, see Steven Fink, *Prophet in the Marketplace: Thoreau's Development as a Professional Writer* (Princeton: Princeton University Press, 1992), 24–35. For a complete index of the *Dial*, identifying authors, see the "Appendix" to Myerson's *New England Transcendentalists and the* Dial, 289–315.

19. "Authors and Authorcraft," *Brother Jonathan* I.ii (March 12, 1842): 296–97.

20. On the negotiations for *Summer on the Lakes*, see *The Letters of Ralph Waldo Emerson*, ed. Ralph Rusk, 6 vols. (New York: Columbia University Press, 1939), III: 246–51; and Fink, *Prophet in the Marketplace*, 211–12.

21. Joel Myerson, *Margaret Fuller: A Descriptive Bibliography* (Pittsburgh: University of Pittsburgh Press, 1978), 13.

22. Larry J. Reynolds notes that in revising "The Great Lawsuit" into *Woman in the Nineteenth Century,* Fuller added erudite catalogues and dense literary and historical allusions, making the book seem "addressed to the few, not the multitude," even while she explained that her title change was designed to make her project more readily accessible. "When Fuller's book took on a life of its own," Reynolds suggests, "it contradicted her conscious intention of writing for a new audience of lay readers," thus manifesting her anxiety and ambivalence about her proper audience. See Reynolds, "From *Dial* Essay to New York Book," 27.

23. Myerson, *Margaret Fuller,* 20; and *MFL* IV: 56.

24. Edgar Allan Poe, "The Literati of New York City—No. IV. Sarah Margaret Fuller," *Godey's Magazine and Lady's Book* 33 (August 1846): 72–75; rpt. in Joel Myerson, ed. *Critical Essays on Margaret Fuller* (Boston: G. K. Hall, 1980), 35.

25. A useful introduction to and generous selection from Fuller's *Tribune* career is found in *Margaret Fuller's New York Journalism,* ed. Catherine C. Mitchell (Knoxville: University of Tennessee Press, 1995).

26. Von Mehren, *Minerva and the Muse,* 228.

27. S. Margaret Fuller, "American Literature; Its Position in the Present Time, and Prospects for the Future," *Papers on Literature and Art,* 2 vols. (New York: Wiley and Putnam, 1846), II: 125–26.

28. Emerson and Spring quoted in Von Mehren, *Minerva and the Muse,* 329.

Rereading Emerson/Whitman
Jay Grossman

I want in the following pages to reconsider the literary relation between Emerson and Whitman. My investigation is governed by the assumption that this association is a particularly important site for analyzing how Emerson's position of centrality—"the cow from which the rest drew their milk," as F. O. Matthiessen memorably puts it in *American Renaissance*[1]—not only enables our understanding of certain features of antebellum literary culture, but also (necessarily, perhaps) disables our interrogations into other aspects of that history, particularly with regard to the career and writings of Walt Whitman.

In the special context of this anthology, however, I am also particularly struck by the number of assumptions that I bring to my critical practice that derive in one way or another from the writings of William Charvat. This is especially true because I am interested in reconsidering the version of Whitman and of American literary history that is created through Emerson—a Whitman and a literary history that have been, I would argue, largely "transcendentalized," with the effect of keeping more or less at the margins significant questions pertaining to gender, sexuality, social class, and politics. (I focus mostly on the latter two in the following pages.) I take it as axiomatic that one of Charvat's most significant contributions to the practice of literary history is the healthy dose of skepticism he often brings to precisely this question of the transcendent.[2] In ways that I hope to demonstrate, then, this essay is about estranging Emerson/Whitman, their relation to each other, and their relation to us; it is about replacing the slash in my title that persists in many critical accounts but that sometimes fails to differentiate these two authors sufficiently in relation to some central questions in antebellum literary history. I begin by recontextualizing one of the indisputably central documents exchanged between Emerson and Whitman, a re-examination that has the effect of destabilizing the generic categories that situate their relationship, and much outside these categories as well. In the second section, I sketch in brief some of the consequences of the reading in part 1 pertaining largely to the question of virtual representation, the implied relation between a constituency and the "representative" man who speaks for (or re-presents) it.

1.

I begin with the famous letter of July 21, 1855, that Emerson sent to Whitman upon receiving his complimentary copy of the first edition of *Leaves of Grass,* a complimentary copy that may itself represent Whitman the longtime printer and sometime publisher's intervention in what he knew to be an insufficient system of marketing and promotion under which, as William Charvat noted, American authors often languished.[3] This letter is quite probably the best-known document in the "paper trail" of their relation, and yet I want to suggest that for precisely this reason—for being always already so well known—the letter is rarely read at all (figs. 1 and 2). Yet only by reading the letter closely will we recognize a crucial fact about it: that neither the word "poet" nor "poetry" appears a single time in Emerson's 1855 letter of praise that has ostensibly marked the beginning of a great poetic career.[4] It is a realization of some consequence, given that the Emerson/Whitman relation is said so often to depend upon precisely their conjunction at the central, still point of poetry—what it is, who makes it, how it works.

Indeed, when F. O. Matthiessen reminds us near the end of *American Renaissance* that "Whitman set out more deliberately than any of his contemporaries to create the kind of hero whom Emerson had foreshadowed in his varying guises of the Scholar and the Poet,"[5] he

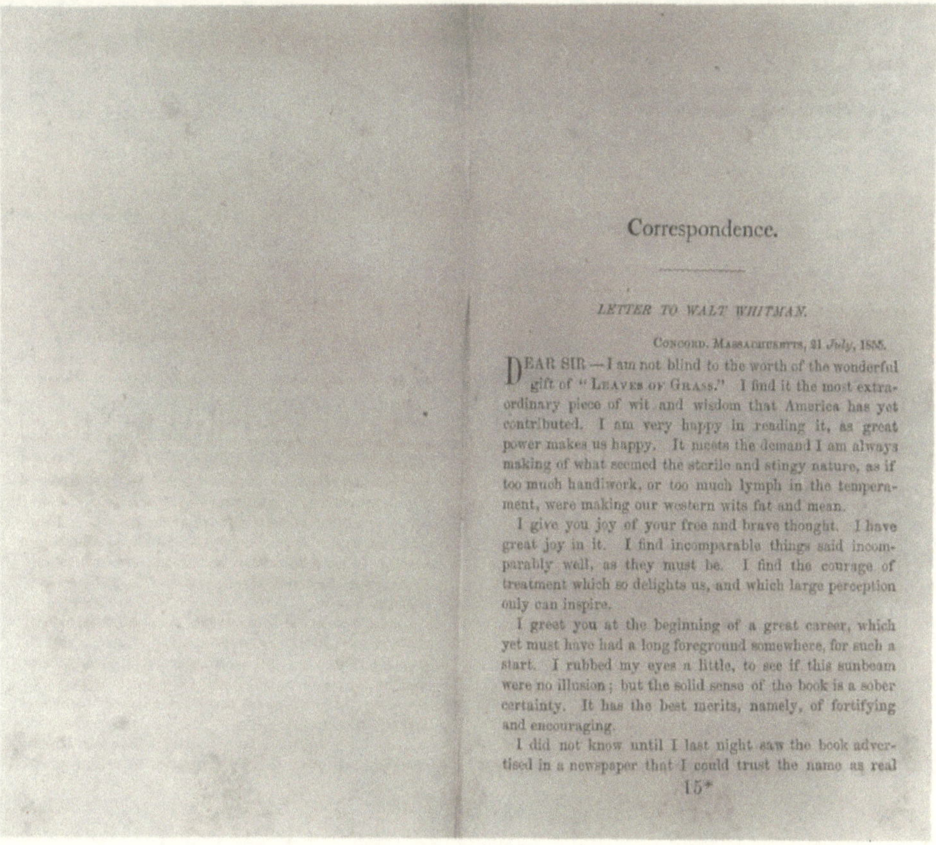

Correspondence.

LETTER TO WALT WHITMAN.

CONCORD, MASSACHUSETTS, 21 *July*, 1855.

DEAR SIR—I am not blind to the worth of the wonderful gift of "LEAVES OF GRASS." I find it the most extraordinary piece of wit and wisdom that America has yet contributed. I am very happy in reading it, as great power makes us happy. It meets the demand I am always making of what seemed the sterile and stingy nature, as if too much handiwork, or too much lymph in the temperament, were making our western wits fat and mean.

I give you joy of your free and brave thought. I have great joy in it. I find incomparable things said incomparably well, as they must be. I find the courage of treatment which so delights us, and which large perception only can inspire.

I greet you at the beginning of a great career, which yet must have had a long foreground somewhere, for such a start. I rubbed my eyes a little, to see if this sunbeam were no illusion; but the solid sense of the book is a sober certainty. It has the best merits, namely, of fortifying and encouraging.

I did not know until I last night saw the book advertised in a newspaper that I could trust the name as real

15*

Figure 1.

is offering us the most canonical version of their relationship, in which Whitman follows Emerson's model for becoming a poet. More recently, David Reynolds has said of Emerson's letter that it "was by far the most glowing and, in terms of Whitman's *poetic* aims, the most appropriate. . . . If Lincoln's Gettysburg Address remade America, . . . Emerson's letter came close to making Whitman."[6] Certainly there is a great deal to say about the uses to which this letter has been put—both by Whitman and by others—in "making" Whitman's literary reputation. But Reynolds's contention here also recapitulates the long-standing critical truism that Emerson did not simply make Whitman's reputation, but rather made, in some not very subtle sense, Whitman himself. Of course one source for this commonplace

> 346   LEAVES-DROPPINGS.
>
> and available for a post-office. I wish to see my benefactor, and have felt much like striking my tasks and visiting New York to pay you my respects.
>
>   R. W. EMERSON.
>
> ---
>
> LETTER TO RALPH WALDO EMERSON.
>
>   BROOKLYN, *August*, 1856.
>
> HERE are thirty-two Poems, which I send you, dear Friend and Master, not having found how I could satisfy myself with sending any usual acknowledgment of your letter. The first edition, on which you mailed me that till now unanswered letter, was twelve poems — I printed a thousand copies, and they readily sold; these thirty-two Poems I stereotype, to print several thousand copies of. I much enjoy making poems. Other work I have set for myself to do, to meet people and The States face to face, to confront them with an American rude tongue; but the work of my life is making poems. I keep on till I make a hundred, and then several hundred — perhaps a thousand. The way is clear to me. A few years, and the average annual call for my Poems is ten or twenty thousand copies — more, quite likely. Why should I hurry or compromise? In poems or in speeches I say the word or two that has got to be said, adhere to the body, step with the countless common footsteps, and remind every man and woman of something.
>
> Master, I am a man who has perfect faith. Master, we have not come through centuries, caste, heroisms, fables, to halt in this land today. Or I think it is to collect a ten-fold impetus that any halt is made. As nature, inexorable, onward, resistless, impassive amid the threats and screams of disputants, so America. Let all defer. Let all
>
>   LEAVES-DROPPINGS.   347
>
> attend respectfully the leisure of These States, their politics, poems, literature, manners, and their free-handed modes of training their own offspring. Their own comes, just matured, certain, numerous and capable enough, with egotistical tongues, with sinewed wrists, seizing openly what belongs to them. They resume Personality, too long left out of mind. Their shadows are projected in employments, in books, in the cities, in trade; their feet are on the flights of the steps of the Capitol; they dilate, a larger, brawnier, more candid, more democratic, lawless, positive native to The States, sweet-bodied, completer, dauntless, flowing, masterful, beard-faced, new race of men.
>
> Swiftly, on limitless foundations, the United States too are founding a literature. It is all as well done, in my opinion, as could be practicable. Each element here is in condition. Every day I go among the people of Manhattan Island, Brooklyn, and other cities, and among the young men, to discover the spirit of them, and to refresh myself. These are to be attended to; I am myself more drawn here than to those authors, publishers, importations, reprints, and so forth. I pass coolly through those, understanding them perfectly well, and that they do the indispensable service, outside of men like me, which nothing else could do. In poems, the young men of The States shall be represented, for they out-rival the best of the rest of the earth.
>
> The lists of ready-made literature which America inherits by the mighty inheritance of the English language — all the rich repertoire of traditions, poems, histories, metaphysics, plays, classics, translations, have made, and still continue, magnificent preparations for that other plainly signified literature, to be our own, to be electric, fresh, lusty, to express the full-sized body, male and female — to give the modern meanings of things, to grow up beautiful, lasting, commensurate with America, with all the passions of home, with the inimitable sympathies of having been

Figure 2.

may be the well-known but, it must be said, highly ambiguous quotation in which Whitman asserts that he had been "simmering, simmering, simmering; Emerson brought me to a boil."[7] What does it signify to be "simmering?" Is "boiling" a metaphor for consensus, as some commentators have assumed? What we have discovered about this letter bears repeating, then: Emerson calls *Leaves of Grass* "the most extraordinary piece of wit and wisdom that America has yet contributed," and he applauds its "large perception." He declares it "free" and "brave," and sings its author's "courage"—but no variant of the word "poet" appears.

What Emerson does write, and what in fact frames all his compliments, is a curious rhetoric of illusion and disbelief. Beginning with its opening phrase—"I am not blind to the worth of the wonderful gift of 'Leaves of Grass'"—an assertion that begins with a negation and sounds very much like a (possibly defensive) response to a question, the letter recapitulates in at least two other places this emphasis upon obscured vision and illusion. Moreover, grammatically speaking, Emerson's praise in this sentence goes to the "wonderful gift" and not to *Leaves of Grass* itself, embedded as is Whitman's volume within the series of prepositional phrases.

The rhetoric of illusion recurs just after the most famous sentence of the letter: "I greet you at the beginning of a great career, which yet must have had a long foreground somewhere for such a start. I rubbed my eyes a little, to see if this sunbeam were no illusion; but the solid sense of the book is a sober certainty." There is an equally solid sense one gets that more than simply Emerson's vision is strained by the book he has in front of him. The notion of "foreground" in the letter signifies Emerson's quest to recover a meaningful genealogy for the book, to position it someplace within the range of knowledges and perhaps institutional affiliations that seem either necessary or perhaps natural to this classically trained Harvard man. (It might be noted parenthetically that the search for a foreground to explain Whitman begins with this sentence; one significant answer to the puzzle emerged in the late 1940s when Malcolm Cowley announced the answer as a mystical experience on a June morning in 1853 or 1854.)[8] The emphasis, then, in this oft-quoted sentence could be upon the "must," not the "foreground," where it has usually been placed. The prose then moves back toward its default images of blindness, of an inability to grasp; the metaphor of the "sunbeam"—"I rubbed my eyes a little, to see if this sunbeam were no illusion"—makes Whitman's book seem both delightful in its organicism and somehow threatening: it possesses a brilliance that almost renders its readers "blind."

This rhetoric of the letter might be taken to record Emerson's surprise or disbelief at the discovery of something that is as alien and yet as familiar as Whitman's book may have seemed—a book that makes Emersonian claims to grandeur but that importantly changes the framework, significance, language, and form of those claims. "It has the best merits, namely, of fortifying and encouraging," Emerson ends the paragraph, but he does not, significantly, tell us who or what is being fortified and encouraged.[9] The book is powerful, but in an unfamiliar, ungraspable way—and the absence of grammatical objects bespeaks Emerson's difficulty of apprehension.

The question of illusion returns a final time in the letter's penultimate sentence: "I did not know until I last night saw the book advertised in a newspaper that I could trust the name as real and available for a post-office." Of course we know what Emerson must mean: he seeks to verify the author's name, since it did not appear on the title page, and it takes two different forms where it does occur in the 1855 volume.[10] Nevertheless the form of this admission augments the undercurrents of disbelief or unbelief that wash through Emerson's response as a whole. This undercurrent rises to the surface, we might say, nearly twenty years later when Emerson can find no place for the writer of *Leaves of Grass* in his 1874 *Parnassus* collection of American poetry.[11]

Clearing our own vision of what it is we "know" to be true about this letter means clearing our vision as well of what we may surmise Whitman wants us most to notice about it. He, it seems safe to say, would have us focus quite literally upon Emerson's best-known endorsement—"I greet you at the beginning of a Great Career," which he subsequently embossed in gold on the spine of the 1856 edition. But it may well be the case that—however much Whitman might wish us to think differently—one cannot judge the 1856 edition by its cover. Indeed, Emerson's letter gains some of its deepest resonances in relation to this specific material context in which, for at least some nineteenth-century readers, the names Emerson and Whitman very likely circulated together for the first time. For while Whitman released Emerson's letter to the New York *Tribune* for publication and also printed copies of the letter that he specified at the top of each page were "for the convenience of private reading only,"[12] the first publication in which Emerson and Whitman's names circulated together was the 1856, second edition of *Leaves of Grass*, and, more precisely, the section of reviews that Whitman reprinted just behind Emerson's letter and his lengthy reply in the appendix called "Leaves-Droppings" at the back of that volume (fig. 3).[13]

To unpack the significance of Emerson's rhetorical recalcitrance in the letter, we might note the last paragraph of another review Whitman reprinted in his edition, on the page facing the advertisement alerting the reader to the booksellers stocking *Leaves:* "[This] book should find no place where humanity urges any claim to re-

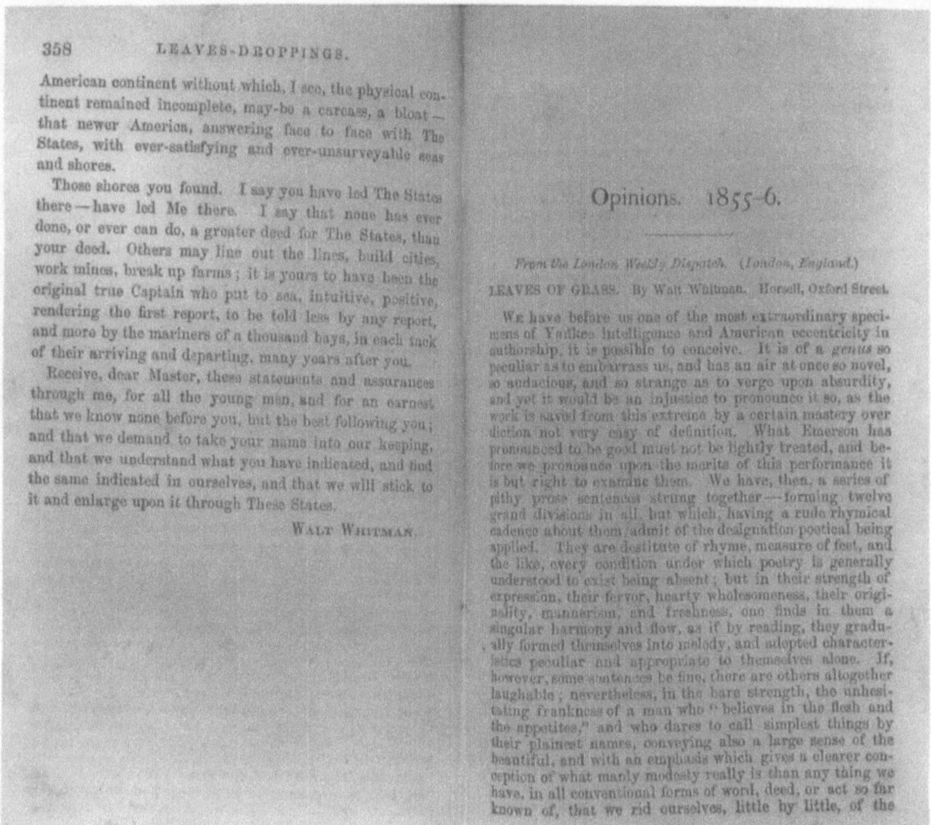

358 LEAVES-DROPPINGS.

American continent without which, I see, the physical continent remained incomplete, may-be a carcass, a bloat—that newer America, answering face to face with The States, with ever-satisfying and ever-unsurveyable seas and shores.

Those shores you found. I say you have led The States there—have led Me there. I say that none has ever done, or ever can do, a greater deed for The States, than your deed. Others may line out the lines, build cities, work mines, break up farms; it is yours to have been the original true Captain who put to sea, intuitive, positive, rendering the first report, to be told less by any report, and more by the mariners of a thousand bays, in each tack of their arriving and departing, many years after you.

Receive, dear Master, these statements and assurances through me, for all the young men, and for an earnest that we know none before you, but the best following you; and that we demand to take your name into our keeping, and that we understand what you have indicated, and find the same indicated in ourselves, and that we will stick to it and enlarge upon it through These States.

WALT WHITMAN.

Opinions. 1855-6.

From the London Weekly Dispatch. (London, England.)

LEAVES OF GRASS. By Walt Whitman. Horsell, Oxford Street.

We have before us one of the most extraordinary specimens of Yankee intelligence and American eccentricity in authorship, it is possible to conceive. It is of a *genus* so peculiar as to embarrass us, and has an air at once so novel, so audacious, and so strange as to verge upon absurdity, and yet it would be an injustice to pronounce it so, as the work is saved from this extreme by a certain mastery over diction not very easy of definition. What Emerson has pronounced to be good must not be lightly treated, and before we pronounce upon the merits of this performance it is but right to examine them. We have, then, a series of pithy prose sentences strung together—forming twelve grand divisions in all, but which, having a rude rhymical cadence about them, admit of the designation poetical being applied. They are destitute of rhyme, measure of feet, and the like, every condition under which poetry is generally understood to exist being absent; but in their strength of expression, their fervor, hearty wholesomeness, their originality, mannerism, and freshness, one finds in them a singular harmony and flow, as if by reading, they gradually formed themselves into melody, and adopted characteristics peculiar and appropriate to themselves alone. If, however, some sentences be fine, there are others altogether laughable; nevertheless, in the bare strength, the unhesitating frankness of a man who "believes in the flesh and the appetites," and who dares to call simplest things by their plainest names, conveying also a large sense of the beautiful, and with an emphasis which gives a clearer conception of what manly modesty really is than any thing we have, in all conventional forms of word, deed, or act so far known of, that we rid ourselves, little by little, of the

Figure 3.

spect, and the author should be kicked from all decent society as below the level of the brute. There is neither wit nor method in his disjointed babbling, and it seems to us he must be some escaped lunatic, raving in pitiable delirium" (384; see fig. 4). Our first response to this review may be simply to recall that, for the poet who would "sound [his] barbaric yawp over the roofs of the world," being "kicked from all decent society" may be very high praise indeed.[14] Still, the word "wit" recalls Emerson's phrase in the 1855 letter—"the most extraordinary piece of wit and wisdom"—and, as I hope to show, the connection is not a spurious one. This review is founded upon the same logic that underwrites Emerson's 1855 letter, in which Emerson praises Whitman's book but withholds from it the

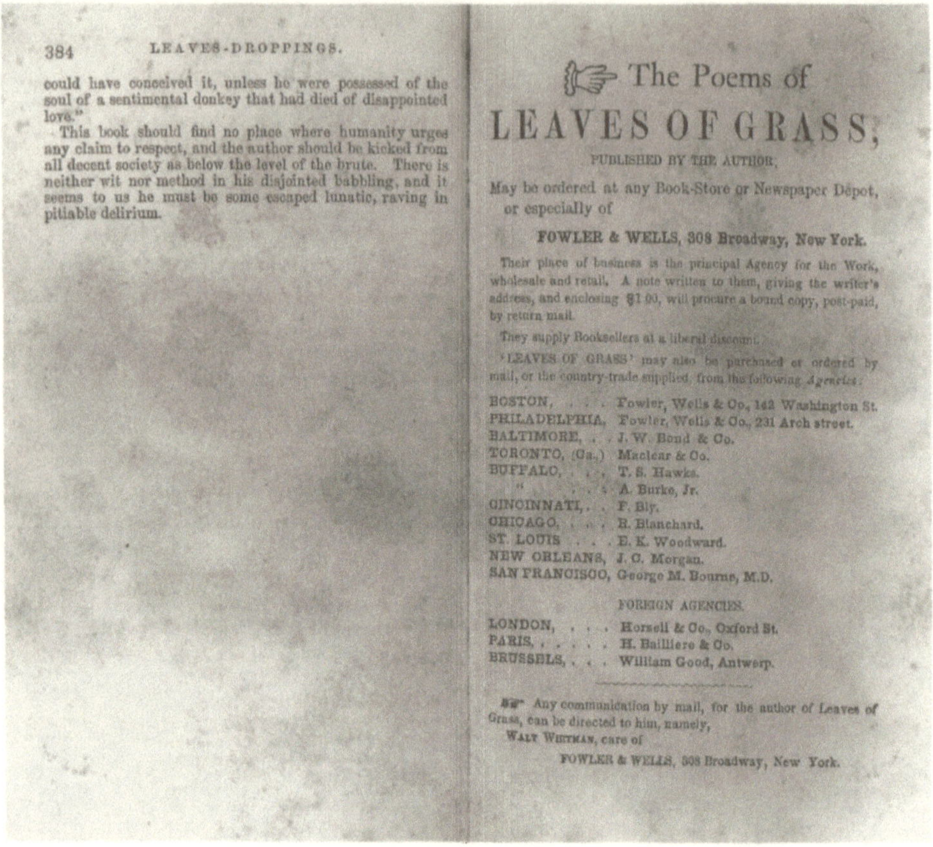
384 LEAVES-DROPPINGS.

could have conceived it, unless he were possessed of the soul of a sentimental donkey that had died of disappointed love."

This book should find no place where humanity urges any claim to respect, and the author should be kicked from all decent society as below the level of the brute. There is neither wit nor method in his disjointed babbling, and it seems to us he must be some escaped lunatic, raving in pitiable delirium.

The Poems of

LEAVES OF GRASS,

PUBLISHED BY THE AUTHOR,

May be ordered at any Book-Store or Newspaper Dépot, or especially of

FOWLER & WELLS, 308 Broadway, New York.

Their place of business is the principal Agency for the Work, wholesale and retail. A note written to them, giving the writer's address, and enclosing $1 00, will procure a bound copy, post-paid, by return mail.

They supply Booksellers at a liberal discount.

'LEAVES OF GRASS' may also be purchased or ordered by mail, or the country-trade supplied from the following *Agencies*:

BOSTON, . . .	Fowler, Wells & Co., 142 Washington St.
PHILADELPHIA,	Fowler, Wells & Co., 231 Arch street.
BALTIMORE, . .	J. W. Bond & Co.
TORONTO, (Ca.)	Maclear & Co.
BUFFALO, . . .	T. S. Hawks.
" . . .	A. Burke, Jr.
CINCINNATI, . .	F. Bly.
CHICAGO, . . .	R. Blanchard.
ST. LOUIS . . .	E. K. Woodward.
NEW ORLEANS,	J. C. Morgan.
SAN FRANCISCO,	George M. Bourne, M.D.

FOREIGN AGENCIES.

LONDON, . . .	Horsell & Co., Oxford St.
PARIS, ...	H. Bailliere & Co.
BRUSSELS, . . .	William Good, Antwerp.

Any communication by mail, for the author of Leaves of Grass, can be directed to him, namely,

WALT WHITMAN, care of

FOWLER & WELLS, 308 Broadway, New York.

Figure 4.

privileged name "poetry." Emerson's calling Whitman's book a "piece of wit and wisdom" (a phrase that makes *Leaves of Grass* sound like a nineteenth-century version of *Poor Richard's Almanac*) *shares* with this review an inability, or unwillingness, to see Whitman's writings as the work of a "poet." And Whitman chose to reprint both the review and Emerson's letter in the edition, which raises a now obvious but perhaps previously unexpected possibility: that Whitman reads Emerson's letter not simply as an endorsement but as a negative review, like the one quoted above. And he seems to delight no less in having it (and reprinting it) for that reason. The 1856 edition wants to have it both ways (at least): to marshal the full marketing potential of Emerson's endorsement even while marking its differences from Emerson and from "traditional" poetry more generally. Rather than signaling some absolute discipleship, then, Whitman's foregrounding Emerson's letter, when reconsidered within the larger context of the other reviews reprinted in the 1856 edition, helps us to reposition their budding relationship within a much broader and more complex range of concerns, not least the question of how to sell a book of the New by drawing upon selective dimensions of its relation to the Old.[15]

The generic slippage around which this argument revolves—poetry is not the unitary figure we thought it was—opens out the possibility of other kinds of slippages that I would suggest are kept in check by the generic category. Suddenly, Emerson's writing to Whitman is not only the extraordinary event that it has seemed to be—though it is also that. It is also now fruitfully seen as another facet in the nineteenth century's ongoing conversation about poetry, and the reviews printed at the back of the second edition of *Leaves of Grass* along with Emerson's letter become pieces of the rich evidence we possess about the competing agendas of these debates. What are the distinctions between mere wit and poetry? Who decides in nineteenth-century America what qualifies as poetry? Returning to the material text reminds us of the possibilities, exigencies, and possibly the dangers of the market and of circulation, and what appeared to be static (Emerson and Whitman are poets and agree about what poetry is and should be) now appears to be dynamic.

Thinking about poetry as a site of contestation also has a more specific explanatory power in relation to Whitman's early revisions of *Leaves of Grass*. Here William Charvat's denominating Whitman's poetry "non-commercial verse" and at one end of a spectrum, the opposite of which, he writes, is "the merely commercial rhymes of an Edgar Guest," might help us understand what Whitman is up to, for that second edition is a curious mix of revision and resemblance; for example, while it is radically smaller than the first edition, it takes its frontispiece and title page virtually unaltered from the original version (fig. 5). If Charvat is correct when he argues that popular poetry "does not challenge the reader on grounds where he does not wish to be met,"[16] then we may have a plausible explanation for the most notable additions to this second edition: the inclusion of both a table of contents and distinct titles for every poem (fig. 6). From a perspective in which the category "poetry" is contested rather than "given," Whitman's use of these titles can be seen as a friendly but no less

Figure 5.

insistent interpellation, or shaping, of his readers, for the word "poem" occurs in every title, and in the majority, "Poem" is the first word ("Poem of The Propositions of Nakedness," "Poem of Faces," and most famously, "Poem of Walt Whitman, an American," eventually entitled "Song of Myself" [in 1881]). Though its lines failed to rhyme or demonstrate fixed meter and often extended virtually from one edge of the page to the other, and though its poems dealt with overtly political and sometimes sexually explicit subjects, the 1856 edition of *Leaves of Grass* insists that it rightly deserves to be included in the generic category "poetry"—an assertion that may carry important consequences for what has been called "The Continuity of American Poetry." Indeed we may now see the way in which that

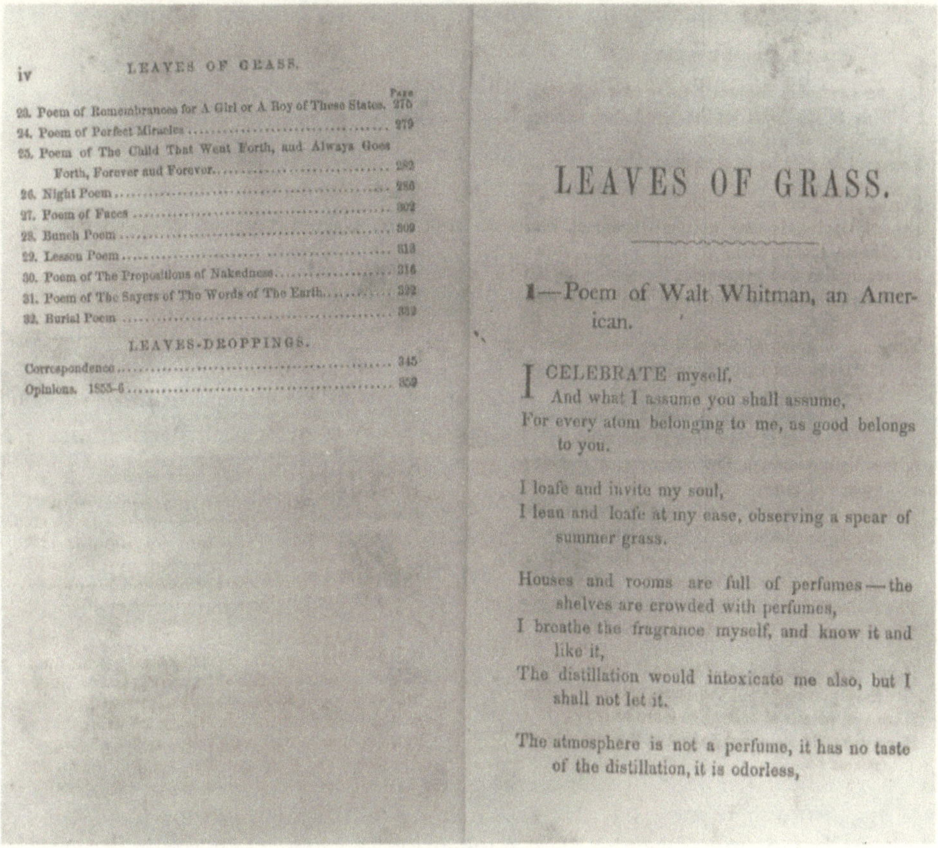
iv LEAVES OF GRASS.

LEAVES OF GRASS.

1—Poem of Walt Whitman, an American.

I CELEBRATE myself,
And what I assume you shall assume,
For every atom belonging to me, as good belongs to you.

I loafe and invite my soul,
I lean and loafe at my ease, observing a spear of summer grass.

Houses and rooms are full of perfumes—the shelves are crowded with perfumes,
I breathe the fragrance myself, and know it and like it,
The distillation would intoxicate me also, but I shall not let it.

The atmosphere is not a perfume, it has no taste of the distillation, it is odorless,

Figure 6.

"continuity" cannot easily be separated out from the material texts in which those *poetries* appear, are read, reviewed, and variously approved or denounced. Nor, as I hope I have suggested, would we want too hastily to insist upon such separations.

2.

Considering these discontinuities places us in a position to examine class-inflected dynamics present in writings by these two central figures that we may previously have missed, partly because the presumed generic equivalence between them at the site of poetry helps hold some of these other questions at bay. I want to offer now some of what I think is gained by conceiving Emerson and Whitman as caught in 1856 mid-step in some dance of mutual misrecognition.

The writings of Emerson and Whitman encode dramatically different dynamics between the writer and the reader that both reflect and reproduce contrasting antebellum conceptions about the relations between the many and the few, between the representative man and the constituencies to whom and for whom he speaks. From a perspective of post-1980s identity politics (but not only from this perspective), we might easily ask, How could this help but be the case? Interpellated by the material practices of their widely different cultural and educational milieux—their lived lives in Cambridge, Concord, Brooklyn, and Manhattan—into quite distinct notions of the relations between leaders and followers, Emerson and Whitman come into the (supposedly) homogenized period of Matthiessen's Renaissance with very different conceptions of the functions and class associations of the (poetic) word in the world.[17]

Many entries in Emerson's early journals, for example, register a fascination with the figure of the powerful speaker standing alone in a vocabulary that we will immediately recognize as having religious, as well as highly charged political connotations. These lines are taken from Emerson's dedication to his 1823 journal:

> Then [God] gave [man] an articulate voice. He gave him an organ exquisitely endowed, which was independent of his grosser parts,— but the minister of his mind & the interpreter of its thoughts. It was designed moreover as a Sceptre of irresistible command, by whose force, the great & wise should still the tumult of the vulgar million, & direct their blind energies to a right operation. (*JMN* II: 104–5)[18]

If we can read past the phallic excess (though it is not by any means unrelated), this passage echoes the familiar exhortation from Genesis giving man dominion over the earth, but rewrites its mandate explicitly in the terms of social class, making "an articulate voice" the divinely endorsed means employed by "the great & wise" for controlling not simply animals, but "the vulgar million." This depiction of the power of the orator would seem to leave little room for either compromise or exchange, and in that respect it resembles structurally the model of the relations between leaders and citizens explained by President John Quincy Adams, for example, in his first address to Congress in 1825, when he openly worried that the "career of public improvements" of which he was in favor would be legislatively derailed because the Congress and his administration had or would become "palsied by the will of our [its] constituents." Such analogizing—from Emerson's journal to Adams's address—may serve to remind us that, as Allen Grossman has argued, "an entailment of any style a person speaks is the structure of a social world that can receive it—a political formation and its kind of conscious life."[19] What then are the parameters and "political formations" of the social worlds Emerson's (and Adams's) writings entail?[20]

Christopher Newfield, in his recent book *The Emerson Effect,* helps us to see an Emerson who "defines freedom as individual movement and personal growth, but accompanies these with the pleasurable loss of self-governance," a writer and theorist for whom "inequality is not simply overlooked but becomes a positive necessary component of the law that binds."[21] In other places, though, Newfield's Emerson cannot abide even these limited negotiations between autonomy and the law: "Emerson's theory of language [Newfield writes] does not either succeed or fail adequately to imagine personal autonomy, for whatever its cultural reception has been, it does not seek autonomy in the first place."[22] Newfield is in part here remarking the subsumption of eloquence and the eloquent man in Emerson's scheme by the Universal Oversoul. Likewise, for Kevin Van Anglen, Emerson speaks "a language of authority that simultaneously affirmed the autonomy and freedom of the self and yet fused that *concession* to antinomian claims with a more imperious and patriarchal conception of the writer's role than that ever envisaged by the critics of Unitarian Boston."[23]

From within this frame, it should hardly be surprising to hear Emerson ventriloquizing Adams in his journal: "The great & wise are the representative governors of the mass of men" (*JMN* II: 401). This is the territory of *Federalist* No. 10, with its arguments in favor of filtered, virtual representation, and Emerson invests this natural aristocracy with an authority that corresponds to the belief of the Founders that mechanisms had to be devised to bypass the presumably rasher judgments of the public at large. A significant journal entry from 1834 likewise demonstrates how Emerson's lectures may be embedded within these political contingencies: "When you come to write Lyceum lectures, remember that you are not to say, What must be said in a Lyceum? but what discoveries or stimulating thoughts have I to impart to a thousand persons? not what they will expect to hear but what is fit for me to say" (*JMN* IV: 372). Here, then, is the Brahman Emerson, perfectly at home within the parameters of reform and instruction from above, as well as with Publius's filtered model that reminds us of the lines drawn between virtual and strict conceptions of political representation.

The question becomes how we are to reckon the differences between Emerson and Whitman around these central issues, though it seems quite clear that Whitman, in his fierce 1856 polemic "The Eighteenth Presidency!"—to take but one salient example—is registering his dissent: "I expect to see the day when the like of the present personnel of the governments ... will be looked upon with derision, and when qualified mechanics and young men will reach Congress and other official stations, sent in their working costumes, fresh from their benches and tools, and returning to them again with dignity" (*LAW* 1308). If Whitman refuses here a theory of virtual political representation, it is as a parallel gesture to the parataxis that structures the verbal representation in much of *Leaves of Grass,* a logic Allen Grossman has described as "a taxonomy of which the sorting index is mere being-at-all," and which promises "the bestowal of presence across time": "Instead of a 'poetic language' (always a mimetic version of the language of one class) Whitman has devised a universal 'conjunctive principle' whose manifest structure is the sequence of end-stopped, nonequivalent, but equipollent lines. . . . The principle of the language . . . is the deletion . . . of centralizing hypotactic grammar. . . . What is obtained is an unprecedented trope of inclusion."[24]

This is inclusivity with high costs, to be sure: Grossman argues that it is in fact a "new slave culture" that Whitman creates, because "the Whitmanian voice, like the slave, is uncanny—a servant of persons."[25] But I want to suggest that it is only from the outside that the Whitmanian voice looks or sounds this way, only if our gaze is directed longingly at our canonized poet, fearing as we may fear that *his* presence is being lost, that his canonical power shall be lost to us—and then where would we be, where would that leave us? Is it possible, however, that Whitman is delighting (at these moments) in exactly such absence, a distant corollary to the mood exhibited in "As I Ebb'd with the Ocean of Life": "Oppress'd with myself that I have dared to open my mouth . . ." (*LG* 254)? In the catalogues, I am suggesting, Whitman's speaker stops speaking and closes his mouth—or at least hides that mouth from our hungry eyes and ears.

This is all by way of suggesting that I think it may be the wrong question to ask where Whitman's disappearance (as uncanny slave) would leave *us,* and that we should instead look away from Whitman our canonical genius and toward Whitman in the text and in his times, the 1850s, before there was a canonical Whitman. In gazing at Whitman the other way—in striving ever and always for his canonical attentions—we are in fact looking at him as we would look at Emerson. Or we are seeing Whitman as Emerson has trained us to see the speaker-orator and public, self-reliant man. Allen Grossman, too, is somehow seeing Whitman this way—as Emerson sees—when he worries over the uncanniness of the nearly lost or just plain lost Whitmanian voice and vision of the catalogues.

How does Emerson see? The answer, helped along by Newfield, might be that he doesn't. Or rather, he sees beyond, he sees not feelingly, but transparently, beyond to the *greater* inclusivity, the greater stakes in a different world of clarity.

But politically, Whitman's vision (and sometimes his other senses as well) may be staging in the catalogues a mode of virtual representation in which, by means of *his* virtual absence (that loss of presence about which Allen Grossman is worried), specificity and particularity (those working men in their costumes) are not lost. In Emerson, on the other hand, specificity is always lost, or often lost. These processes may be visible in Emerson's poem "The Rhodora," which opens with the pointed observation of the single flower—"In May, when seawinds pierced our solitudes, / I found the fresh Rhodora in the woods"—but slips by the end into a generalized diffidence that leaves the flower an all but entirely obscured catalyst and the poet-speaker, at the very least, sharing the spotlight:

Why thou wert there, O rival of the rose!
I never thought to ask, I never knew:
But, in my simple ignorance, suppose
The self-same Power that brought me there brought you.
                              (Lines 13–16)

In fact, the point in Emerson may well be this loss of specificity, in favor of the transcendent, the universal. As Newfield writes, "Emerson imagines not those contemporaries who are extraordinary for their independence, originality, or freedom, but those who submit like children to the highest authority."[26] But Emerson—unlike the

Whitman of the catalogues—himself always supervises these actions; he is present to us in the mediated apprehension of the rhodora (and "The Rhodora"), and his interrogation largely fills out the substance of the poem after the opening lines.

One finds a similar version of the catalogic virtuality of Whitman's speaker even in those places—such as the opening lines of "Song of Myself"—in which something like an authoritarian power play seems to be at least one of the text's multiple operations. For when the speaker asserts "And what I assume you shall assume," the autocratic tendencies that grow out of his heightened awareness and insight are coupled with what is rarely found in the Emersonian version: an acknowledgment of the reader as a distinct entity, invited to *participate* in a dynamic that is at once highly structured and shared (or, as the first poem in 1855 [eventually "Song of Myself"] ends: "I stop somewhere waiting for you").[27] It depends, as it so often does, on an embedded ambiguity: Shall we read "shall" ("you shall assume") as future tense or as an imperative? This space of negotiation, this dynamic of interchange, however, functions just as the logic of parataxis might require, since the representational dynamics of the Whitmanian line at the very least impede—and may do a great deal more—the movement toward some universalized or totalized claims, toward the claims of the virtual, except the virtuality of Whitman's speaker himself. And that is a virtuality that, I am arguing, Emerson first and last rejects (and one Whitman rejects sometimes, too, of course).

Other passages in the Whitman corpus reflect not so directly a refusal of the virtual and its hierarchies and filtrations, as a sometimes uneasy and sometimes empowering oscillation. For example, the description of the poet from the 1855 Preface—"The others are as good as he, only he sees it and they do not"—registers at once a strict egalitarianism and something else less easily demarcated, though it is interesting to ponder how the second clause's qualification shifts the grounds of the relation in a decidedly Emersonian direction, especially if we recall the importance of vision in Emerson's conception of the poet for whom he says he *looks* in vain: "We have yet had no genius in America, *with tyrannous eye*, which knew the value of our incomparable materials" ("The Poet," *LAE* 465). Is *this* what Emerson was teaching Whitman? Is this why he was "simmering"?

Similar questions might be asked of a passage that occurs later in "The Eighteenth Presidency!": "I am not afraid to say that among them ["the great masses of the mechanics"] I seek to initiate my name, Walt Whitman, and that I shall in future have much to say to them. I perceive that the best thoughts they have wait unspoken, impatient to be put in shape" (*LAW* 1323). Once again: speaking for or speaking with? And where shall our interpretive emphasis be placed in the first lines—upon the initiation of the singular name or upon the collective "among," which echoes a similar such declaration in "Song of Myself": "I troop forth replenished with supreme power, one of an average unending procession" (1855, *LG* 43)? Once again, the disappearance of the speaker, a virtual Whitman, present only as one of the mob or perhaps absent as one of the mob and so enacting again the uncanniness to which Allen Grossman has alerted us.

I want to suggest—for there is little space in the present context to do more—that the origins of these complications may be found in the Jacksonian revision of the nation's representative and political ground rules: the movement toward party participation, toward an acknowledgment of the ordinary citizen's stake and role in the nation's governance. This is a dynamic partially glimpsed in Jackson's 1832 veto of the National Bank's charter, where he turns his attention toward his fellow citizens with "republican language . . . [that] was readily embraced and embellished by nascent radical movements," rather than simply, traditionally addressing his veto message only to the people's elected representatives in the Congress. (Moreover, Jackson believed the 1832 election to be the people's referendum on the same issue: Jackson and No Bank vs. Clay and the Bank.)[28] As Harry L. Watson has argued, while "direct popular democracy . . . was never a reality in Jacksonian America, . . . 'Jacksonian democracy' did liberate ordinary white men from many of the deferential constraints of eighteenth-century political culture, and it gave their feelings and opinions a new respect in the public sphere."[29] It is perhaps then not inappropriate to recall here Emerson's journal entry, written at the prospect of a second Jackson administration: "Yet seemeth it to me that we shall all feel dirty if Jackson is reëlected" (*JMN* IV: 57).

It may be equally fitting to conclude by remembering William Charvat's characterization of Emerson's "American Scholar" address as "essentially a plea to his own class to recapture cultural power,"[30] a plea, that is, to found and project visionary, representative men, to take hold, perhaps, of the virtual and sometimes unguided masses of the Whitmanian catalogue. The peroration of that address captures rather neatly the dynamic and the tensions I have been discussing:

> Patience,—patience;—with the shades of all the good and great for company; and for solace, the perspective of your own infinite life; and for work, the study and the communication of principles, the making those instincts prevalent, the conversion of the world. Is it not the chief disgrace in the world, not to be an unit;—not to be reckoned one character;—not to yield that peculiar fruit which each man was created to bear, but to be reckoned in the gross, in the hundred, or the thousand, of the party, the section, to which we belong; and our opinion predicted geographically, as the north, or the south? Not so, brothers and friends,—please God, ours shall not be so. We will walk on our own feet; we will work with our own hands; we will speak our own minds. (*LAE* 70–71)

These concluding lines register the dilemma of democratic exclusivity (the exclusivity of democratic virtuality?), professing an aversion to any sense of either collectivity or collective accountability ("Is it not the chief disgrace in the world . . . to be reckoned in the gross, in the hundred, or the thousand"), only to invoke (indeed, produce), virtually simultaneously, such a distinct, and elite, community ("Not so, brothers and friends . . . *ours* shall not be so. *We* will walk . . . "). And is there any doubt who will be at the head of this new grouping, who has, in fact, called it into a certain—dare I say, catalogic—being?

Opening out a space of contention between Emerson and Whitman at the figure of poetry, then, begins to expose for us the manifold political and representative contingencies that their writings reflect, refract, and produce. Let me conclude by attempting to clarify the space of this essay's intervention, with a caveat and then a summary. I have been attempting to place Emerson's and Whitman's writings in relation to the political discourses they reflect and help to shape, and I have begun to sketch out a territory of contestation between the two of them at a site that we might call participatory democracy. In Whitman, I believe we are looking at something like Reading as participatory democracy. Or, Reading as if participatory democracy. And, as Michael Warner and others have made clear, *vice versa*.[31] I would not want, however, to discount the "as if" in that last formulation, for it figures at a range of levels: the "as if" of a play of compromise insistently on the verge of registering as mere ploy; the "as if" of the Jacksonian gesture toward a people's power within the machinery of the party;[32] and finally, the "as if" of the Constitution's preamble, around which these disputes are first set in motion, and the crux of which Thomas Gustafson has described this way: "They, the few, invoke 'We, the People,' the alpha of democratic radicalism, to inaugurate a Constitution that explodes in deed the center of power it installs in theory."[33]

Part of the challenge here may be to find a space in our interpretations of Emerson for these autocratic or authoritarian positions, for Emerson the deliverer of a unitary truth as much as Emerson the antinomian and the proponent of self-reliance. And as for Whitman, we have still to uncover the full complexities, and the historical referents, for the poet as Common Man whose initial project nevertheless reads like a variation of Publius's plans for what he tellingly calls Union: "Through me many voices."

But returning to the 1856 edition of *Leaves of Grass*, we might come to see that Whitman's use of Emerson's letter as endorsement for a book filled with additional poems that, as Justin Kaplan notes, "Emerson could not possibly have seen" (207), may actually serve as a microcosm of the different conceptions of literary property and social propriety—not to say poetry—that the two men bring to their newly begun relation in 1856. Indeed it does sometimes seem as if the whole of the relations I have been attempting to sketch out return again to those two cognates, property and propriety, terms that the work of William Charvat calls to our attention as suitable and then necessary features in our historical reconstructions of the literary nineteenth century. What is the proper subject matter of poetry and what the proper use of a private letter? How does a former newspaper editor and editorialist, accustomed to writing always in the first-person plural, read, or deploy in print, the singular, first-person pronoun of Emerson's congratulatory letter? Who, to Whitman's eye, greets, when Emerson greets him at the beginning of his great career? And which career anyway?

Notes

Photographs of the 1856 edition of Whitman's *Leaves of Grass* are published courtesy of the Rare Book and Manuscript Library, University of Pennsylvania.

References to works frequently cited appear within the text in parenthesis along with page numbers. The abbreviations for these works appear below.

JMN *The Journals and Miscellaneous Notebooks of Ralph Waldo Emerson,* ed. William Gilman et al., 16 vols. (Cambridge: Belknap Press of Harvard University Press, 1960–82).
LAE Ralph Waldo Emerson, *Essays & Lectures,* ed. Joel Porte (New York: The Library of America, 1983).
LAW Walt Whitman, *Poetry and Prose* (New York: The Library of America, 1982).
LG Walt Whitman, *Leaves of Grass,* eds. Sculley Bradley and Harold W. Blodgett (New York: Norton, 1973).

1. F. O. Matthiessen, *American Renaissance: Art and Expression in the Age of Emerson and Whitman* (1941; repr. New York: Oxford University Press, 1968), xii.
2. I follow Michael Lopez and Lawrence Buell, among many others, in furthering these critical reappraisals of Emerson and his place in American literary history; see Lopez, "De-Transcendentalizing Emerson," *ESQ: A Journal of the American Renaissance* 34 (1988): 77–139, and *Emerson and Power: Creative Antagonism in the Nineteenth Century* (De Kalb: Northern Illinois University Press, 1995); and Buell, "The Emerson Industry in the 1980's: A Survey of Trends and Achievements," *ESQ: A Journal of the American Renaissance* 30 (1984): 123–29.
3. William Charvat, *The Profession of Authorship in America, 1800–1870,* ed. Matthew J. Bruccoli (Columbus: Ohio State University Press, 1968), 46–47.
4. George Monteiro also notes that Emerson never calls Whitman's writing "poetry"; see Monteiro, "Fire and Smoke: Emerson's Letter to Whitman," *Modern Language Studies* 15 (Spring 1985): 4. I'm indebted to his essay, though I came to it after having formulated the argument upon which this essay is based. Page references refer to the 1856 edition of *Leaves of Grass* and are included parenthetically in the text.
5. Matthiessen, *American Renaissance,* 650.
6. David S. Reynolds, *Walt Whitman's America* (New York: Knopf, 1995), 341–42. Emphasis added.
7. Quoted in Jerome Loving, *Emerson, Whitman, and the American Muse* (Chapel Hill: University of North Carolina Press, 1982), 195, n. 5.
8. Cowley offered the theory in his introduction to the Penguin reprint of the first edition of *Leaves of Grass,* first published in 1959 (New York: Penguin, 1986). He utilized a somewhat less specific version of the same model in his significantly entitled "Walt Whitman: The Miracle": "There was a miracle in Whitman's life; we can find no other word for it. In his thirty-seventh

year, the local politician and printer and failed editor suddenly became a world poet. No long apprenticeship; no process of growth that we can trace . . .; not even much early promise: the poet materializes like a shape from the depths" (*The New Republic* [March 18, 1946]: 385). Henry Binns's fabrication in 1905 of a mysterious romance for Whitman with a woman in New Orleans to explain the genesis of *Leaves* may well be the prototype of this common strand in Whitman studies (*A Life of Walt Whitman* [New York: Dutton, 1905], 50–52).

9. Cf. Reynolds: "The first edition . . . had brought together all aspects of cultural experience into an organic whole, and its wholeness was matched by Emerson's response, which moved beyond details straight to the health-affirming, fortifying effects Whitman had tried to achieve" (*Walt Whitman's America*, 342).

10. On the reverse of the title page, as "Walter Whitman," and in the first poem that would become "Song of Myself" section 20, as "Walt Whitman."

11. On *Parnassus*, see Monteiro, "Fire and Smoke," 7.

12. Justin Kaplan, *Walt Whitman: A Life* (New York: Simon and Schuster, 1980), 205–6.

13. We should not, however, miss the excremental connotations implicit in Whitman's name for this "appendix" that may mark, to say the least, a particularly noisome example of the complexity of his relation both to Emerson and to Derridean supplementarity more broadly; I'm indebted to Michael T. Gilmore for pointing out this connotation of the title. See also Kenneth Price's discussion of Whitman's relation to Emerson in his *Whitman and Tradition: The Poet in His Century* (New Haven: Yale University Press, 1990), chap. 2.

14. My thanks to David R. Johnson for this point.

15. As Price shows (*Whitman and Tradition*, 40–44), Whitman's long reply to Emerson—printed immediately after Emerson's letter in the 1856 edition (see fig. 2)—makes some of these complexities particularly clear.

16. Charvat, *Profession of Authorship*, 104, 105.

17. This has a wide range of consequences, I think, not least in complicating Matthiessen's insistence that each of his Big Five shared a common "devotion to the possibilities of democracy" (ix).

18. This image of the orator capturing his audience's attention with a sceptre transmutes in another of Emerson's journal entries into an image even more remarkable: "Let [the orator] come to them in solemnity & strength & when he speaks he will chain attention with an interesting figure & an interested face" (*JMN* I: 8). Derived from a famous Renaissance emblem of "eloquence" with which Emerson was surely familiar—that of the orator chaining his audience's attention through the ears—the image seems also to suggest both the great chain of being and the chains associated with slavery.

19. Allen Grossman, "The Poetics of Union in Whitman and Lincoln:

An Inquiry toward the Relationship of Art and Policy," in Walter Benn Michaels and Donald E. Pease, eds., *The American Renaissance Reconsidered* (Baltimore: The Johns Hopkins University Press, 1985), 185.

20. "[John Quincy] Adams had, of course, early abandoned the sinking ship of Federalism . . . , but in every other way he aptly illustrates the main literary, professional, theological, and ideological features of this subgroup within the New England dominant class" (Kevin Van Anglen, *The New England Milton: Literary Reception and Cultural Authority in the Early Republic* [University Park: Pennsylvania State University Press, 1993], 59, n. 23).

21. Christopher Newfield, *The Emerson Effect: Individualism and Submission in America* (Chicago: University of Chicago Press, 1996), 13, 38.

22. Newfield, *The Emerson Effect*, 45–46.

23. Van Anglen, *The New England Milton*, 119. Emphasis added.

24. Grossman, "The Poetics of Union," 188, 193, 195.

25. Grossman, "The Poetics of Union," 195.

26. Newfield, *The Emerson Effect*, 23.

27. Michael Moon makes a related point in *Disseminating Whitman: Revision and Corporeality in "Leaves of Grass"* (Cambridge: Harvard University Press, 1991), 83.

28. Harry L. Watson discusses the full context of the Bank crisis in chapter 5 ("Killing the Monster") of his *Liberty and Power: The Politics of Jacksonian America* (New York: Hill and Wang, 1990), esp. 143–50. The quotation appears on 148.

29. Watson, *Liberty and Power*, 13. Cf. Sean Wilentz: "Jackson's war on the Second Bank of the United States was a turning-point in the building of his party's constituency and identity: his veto message brilliantly rearticulated the old republican discourse into a ringing defense of small producers against the alleged schemes of merchant capitalist financiers and foreign investors to subvert the Constitution and equal rights" ("Society, Politics, and the Market Revolution, 1815–1848," in Eric Foner, ed., *The New American History* [Philadelphia: Temple University Press, 1990], 65).

30. Charvat, *Profession of Authorship*, 65.

31. Besides Michael Warner's *The Letters of the Republic: Publication and the Public Sphere in Eighteenth-Century America* (Cambridge: Harvard University Press, 1990), I have in mind Jay Fliegelman's *Declaring Independence: Jefferson, Natural Language, and the Culture of Performance* (Stanford: Stanford University Press, 1993), especially his arguments about eloquence and "Jefferson's Pauses," 1–28.

32. "Jackson's democratic wish sought more active, participatory forms of political representation. . . . Jackson himself helped bury 'King Caucus,' which had nominated presidential candidates behind closed congressional doors; it was replaced by party conventions (crowded with delegates 'fresh from the people'). . . . However, the Jacksonian Democrats faced a problem.

Their party constituency ... was an unstable amalgam of contending regional factions. Their message about national government was essentially negative. What were they going to mobilize participation for? The answer was participation itself. The Democrats celebrated the mechanisms of participation, the political party.... The contending factions of a heterogeneous nation were united through their participation in the party processes" (James Morone, *The Democratic Wish: Popular Participation and the Limits of American Government* [New York: Basic Books, 1980], 184–85).

33. Thomas Gustafson, *Representative Words: Politics, Language, and the American Language, 1776–1865* (Cambridge: Cambridge University Press, 1992), 286.

The Transatlantic Book Trade and Anglo-American Literary Culture in the Nineteenth Century
Michael Winship

In the past several decades an increasing number of scholars of American literary and cultural history have come to recognize the important pioneering work and legacy of William Charvat. Renewed interest in Charvat's work has to an extent coincided with the emergence of a new scholarly field, the history of the book, clearly signaled by the emergence of an energetic and active new organization, the Society for the History of Authorship, Reading, & Publishing (SHARP). Of particular interest to scholars of American culture, though, are the earlier founding of the Program for the History of the Book in American Culture at the American Antiquarian Society and that program's sponsorship of a project for a collaborative, multivolume *History of the Book in America* to be published by Cambridge University Press. This American project is just one of a series of national histories of the book. French scholars led the way with their four-volume *Histoire de l'édition française* (1982–86), prepared under the direction of Henri-Jean Martin and Roger Chartier, which has in turn inspired a projected six- or seven-volume *History of the Book in Britain*, also to be published by the Cambridge University Press. A number of other similar projects are already planned or contemplated, including histories of the book in Germany, Italy, the

Netherlands, and Spain, as well as in Scotland, Ireland, Wales, Canada, Australia, and New Zealand.

There is a certain irony that the history of the book, which from its beginnings has been an international and interdisciplinary field, should have focused so much effort on national projects. Books—those international agents of intellectual and cultural exchange—are no respecters of national borders, though this fact can only be accommodated in national histories of the book in limited and awkward ways. But if national histories of the book tend to overlook or ignore the international trade, they only reflect long-standing disciplinary divisions within literary and cultural history along national lines, divisions that tend to emphasize, for example, American exceptionalism. Here, I believe, an international history of the book has much to teach by demonstrating the great extent to which books and texts have been shared across borders and oceans. Unless this fact is recognized, American literary historians run the risk of conceiving of print culture too narrowly, without recognizing its full transatlantic dimension.

It is not difficult to establish that during the nineteenth century the United States was fully and actively involved in the international, and especially the transatlantic, trade in books. Customs records—as abstracted in the American serial set and British parliamentary papers—document the nature and extent of that involvement.[1] A series of graphs based on that evidence (see Appendix) gives an overview of American and British imports and exports of books (measured in dollars and hundredweights) from 1828 to 1868. One feature is immediately obvious: the tremendous, even exponential, growth in international trade over the period, especially exports from Britain and imports into the United States. Between 1828 and 1868, American book imports grew by a factor of more than nine, exports by a factor of almost seven and one-half. The growth in both seems especially marked around mid century, though low figures in 1838 no doubt reflect curtailed economic activity caused by the severe financial panic in the United States in the late 1830s. British book exports grew even more rapidly over the same period, increasing by a factor of nearly fifteen, and were almost equally divided between exports to foreign countries and those to British colonies and possessions. In contrast, book imports into Britain little more than tripled between 1828 and 1868 and consisted almost entirely of imports from foreign countries.[2]

A second series of graphs (also in the Appendix) breaks down American and British book imports and exports in three years (1828, 1848, 1868) for selected countries or regions.[3] Clearly, Great Britain was the chief source for books imported into the United States, though Germany and France were also significant, if less important. American books were exported to Britain, Canada, several South American countries, and, curiously, China. For Great Britain, France predominated as the source for imported books in 1828, but in later years other foreign countries, including the United States, became relatively more important. Though British exports were fairly evenly spread in 1828, in later years the United States and, especially by 1868, Australia predominated in the export trade, though clearly throughout the period the chief foreign market for British books outside its colonies and possessions was the United States.[4]

One important feature of an examination of the international trade in books is the availability of such extended series of statistics that provide a long overview of the trade in books. If similar records for the domestic book trade were available for these years, historians of the book could determine the relative importance of the international trade in books in relation to the domestic trade. Nevertheless, it is important to remember the reason that one set of statistics survives and the other does not: customs statistics are a direct result of governmental regulation of international trade, a form of control that many Americans feel would be an inappropriate abridgment of our first-amendment rights if applied to the domestic book trade.[5] In contrast, government regulation of the foreign trade in books through the collection of tariffs, a duty on foreign books as merchandise, has been widely accepted not only as a source of revenue but as a means of protecting the domestic manufacture and trade in books.

Tariff rates on books in both the United States and Great Britain indicate that the second of these functions was the more important during the nineteenth century. In the United States between 1824 and 1846 duties on imported books were charged according to a complicated schedule depending upon the language in which they were printed, the number of years since original publication, and binding. In 1846 the Walker tariff simplified the duty on books, which was set at a flat rate of 10 percent *ad valorem*, and 20 percent on any book "in the course of printing and republication in the United States." These rates were lowered in 1857 to 8 and 15 percent respectively, then raised in 1861 to a flat 15 percent, in 1862 to 20 percent, and in 1864 to 25 percent.⁶ At mid nineteenth century, the British government charged a duty on imported books at a basic rate of five guineas per hundredweight, reduced by half (two and one-half guineas per hundredweight) for books printed in a "living" foreign language or printed in English in a British colony or possession, and further reduced to one guinea per hundredweight for all books printed prior to 1801.⁷ In both countries the use of tariffs to restrict the international trade in books must have been made acceptable, in part, by the support it provided the domestic book trade.

Governments can regulate the foreign trade in books in a second way, copyright. As opposed to *tariffs,* which charge a duty on physical books as merchandise, *copyright* establishes ownership in the texts contained within books and thus determines which books can be legally imported, exported, or produced. In theory tariffs and copyright are independent of each other, though (just like the books and texts that they concern) they have often become entangled.

Compared to the history of tariffs, the history of international copyright in the United States and Great Britain during the nineteenth century is complex and confusing. Before attempting a brief summary, let me point to the useful distinction between *de jure* and *de facto* copyright, between copyright as established by law and copyright as actually practiced by publishers and booksellers.⁸ It is tempting to suppose that once one has mastered the legal details of copyright complete understanding of practice will follow, but this is rarely the case: copyright law will only partly explain the workings of authorship and the literary marketplace in the nineteenth-century United States. For example, although American publishers were under no legal obligation to recognize copyright in any text written by a foreign author during the nineteenth century, modern scholars often fail to recognize that the economic realities of publishing at the time fostered the establishment of a set of conventions known as "trade courtesy" that established a publisher's right to a text, in essence a *de facto* copyright.⁹

In the United States, from the first copyright act of 1790 until the passage of the Chace Act in 1891, legal copyright protection was granted only to citizens and permanent residents; the works of foreigners were provided no legal protection.¹⁰ In Great Britain international copyright was first addressed by Parliament in the Copyright Amendment Act of 1842, which protected the rights of British copyright holders within Britain and its possessions but made no provisions to protect the rights of British authors abroad nor to protect the rights of foreign authors in Britain. Case law provided, however, that works by foreign authors (including Americans) could be copyrighted in Britain if they were first published there. But in August 1854 the House of Lords ruled that copyright protection also required that an author be resident in Britain at the time of publication. Throughout the period the rights of British authors in their works were given only limited legal protection abroad, though an 1844 act empowered the Crown to enter into agreements with foreign states for the exchange of copyright privileges. Over the following decades Britain negotiated several such agreements with European countries, until in 1886 Britain joined the Berne Convention. This Convention, originally comprising fourteen European countries, established a Copyright Union that provided protection throughout the Union for any work that had been properly copyrighted in the proprietor's own country. The United States did not join the Berne Convention until 1989, nearly a century after the Chace Act of 1891 first allowed British or other foreign authors to establish copyright in their works in the United States.[11]

Many, both Britons and Americans, believed that the situation was unfair and expressed their unhappiness in an almost endless stream of speeches, articles, and petitions on the subject of international copyright.[12] British authors thought that they were being denied due profits from the sale of their works in the large American market; American authors believed that they were disadvantaged by having to compete in the market with British works that could be produced more cheaply since there was no legal requirement for American publishers to pay royalties to foreigners. My understanding is that the actual situation was a great deal more complicated: many American works were pirated in England, and trade courtesy meant that many American publishers sent money across the Atlantic to establish or confirm their claim in British works. Although Britain and the United States did not finally settle the legal problems of international copyright until the end of the century, the heated discussions of the issue and the accommodation represented by trade courtesy both attest to the long-standing and continued importance of the transatlantic trade in texts as well as books.

Looking at the international book trade in terms of tariffs and copyright agreements leads to the consideration of guineas per hundredweight or dates of publication and deposit but fails to give any sense of just what books and texts were traded across the Atlantic and just how the business was managed. Accordingly, I would like now to shift focus from the "macro" to the "micro" level and to examine several examples of the transatlantic trade between London and the Boston literary publishers and booksellers Ticknor and Fields at mid century.[13]

In order to participate successfully in the transatlantic trade in books and texts, a firm needed to be linked to three separate communication networks, designed for the transfer of information, merchandise, and credit. The information network enabled the partners of Ticknor and Fields in Boston to learn what books were available in London. They relied primarily on advertisements, notices, and reviews in periodicals—especially trade journals such as Sampson Low's *Publishers' Circular*—as well as on publishers' and booksellers' catalogs. Public sources of information did not fulfill all the firm's needs, however, for the conventions of trade courtesy required that the partners have early knowledge of gossip, especially of forthcoming London publications. To this end, both partners made several trips to England to establish personal acquaintance with London publishers and authors. More important, the firm had an agent in London to keep them abreast of new and interesting publications.

A letter of April 7, 1856, to Nicolas Trübner indicates what was expected:

> Touching the works we wish you to buy for us for reprinting, we meant to have explained to you, when you were here, and thought we did, the class of publications which we naturally choose. You see how impossible it is for us to name authors as you suggest, for new ones are springing up every day. Books like Rogers' 'Table Talk', Mrs. Gaskell's 'Life of Jane Eyre', Tennyson's 'Poems', &c. &c. are what we want. First rate things you know as well as we do. A new poet, for instance, we should be shy of, but another shot from Alexander Smith, for instance, would suit us exactly. Will it not be a good plan for you to enquire of publishers occasionally what is *talked* of as coming out?[14]

The nineteenth-century networks for the transfer of merchandise and credit used by Ticknor and Fields were also well established and relatively stable. For most of the century packet lines (the Cunard line was the most famous) connected Liverpool to Boston and New York with regular, twice-a-month service, first sail then steam. The packets carried the mails—thus supporting the information network—and all but the very largest shipments of books that Ticknor and Fields ordered from London. The credit network provided Ticknor and Fields with the means to pay for its London purchases and involved the firm with large international bankers. Typically the firm purchased a bill of exchange with cash from the Boston bankers Brown Brothers and deposited it with Baring Brothers, bankers in London. Ticknor and Fields could then pay the London trade for purchases with promissory notes drawn on Baring Brothers.

By mid century Ticknor and Fields was well situated within these three communication networks and very much involved in the import book trade. The firm regularly imported some works in bulk for wholesale distribution and also imported small quantities of other London publications for retail sale. Books were not the only imports, however, for once the connections were made the firm began to import all sorts of other products related to the book trade. These included type, ink, paper, binding cloth, leather, stationery, and, on occasion, stereotype or electrotype casts of relief engravings done by British artists—at one point the firm inquired if there were a promising young British engraver that they could lure to Boston and set up in business.

To return to books. Which books did Ticknor and Fields import from England? The range was considerable. For wholesale distribution the firm regularly imported British bibles and testaments, as well as illustrated children's books, including the so-called "indestructible" books printed on cloth for the very young. Another specialty was elegantly illustrated gift editions for the Christmas trade—including British editions of the firm's own American authors Henry Wadsworth Longfellow and Oliver Wendell Holmes. Smaller quantities of British books and magazines were regularly received for retail sale at the firm's Old Corner Bookstore. Finally, the firm sent special orders for single books to London for its retail customers, who included many of the intellectual elite of Boston and Cambridge.

Let me describe a single transaction to give some sense of the range of the firm's activities as an importer of books. On March 12, 1858, Ticknor and Fields received a shipment of books from the firm's London agents, Trübner and Company, via the Cunard steamship *Niagara*, which had just arrived from Liverpool. The contents of "Case #206" were various. It contained small shipments of new books ordered directly from two London publishers, Richard Bentley and

H. G. Bohn, which had been ordered on January 27 and February 9 respectively and which had a total value of £14.13.0. From Bentley the firm received eleven copies of volume 8 of a new edition of Horace Walpole's works; from Bohn a selection of sixty-six volumes from his famous "library" series. A third group of new books, eleven titles valued at £4.10.5, had been gathered together by the London agent and included three dozen copies of *Our Favorite Picture Books* (presumably for children). Several newly published books detailing the siege at Lucknow, which had been lifted only the preceding autumn, provided current intelligence of imperial politics. Boston customers could also keep up with the latest London serials, for Trübner also sent a collection of recent issues of magazines and newspapers, valued at £5.1.6, including eight copies of Dickens's *Household Words*, five each of *Chambers Journal* and *The Illustrated News*, and twelve copies of the most recent monthly part of Thackeray's *The Virginians*, then being serialized in London. The shipment also contained special orders for individual patrons: twenty-one titles in all, valued at £7.1.2 1/2, including medical books, sheet music, and back issues and bound volumes of magazines. Finally, the agent had included with the shipment fourteen parcels that had been delivered in London for transfer to Boston. This was a service that Ticknor and Fields regularly performed for its customers, and included with this shipment were parcels for Ralph Waldo Emerson, Mrs. Eliza Follen, and the American Board of Commissioners for Foreign Missions.

The total cost of the books in this shipment came to just over £31. The packing case cost another 7s. 6 1/2d.; freight came to £1.12.5 (paid to Baring Brothers in Liverpool); a further 3 shillings was charged for postage. Trübner and Company also charged a commission of 7.5 percent on the value of the books that it had gathered (a total of £1.5.10) and included a report with the shipment to keep the Boston firm up-to-date on its book orders and to provide the latest news of the London trade. For example, Trübner reports that the London firm Kent and Company was not able to supply a portrait of Tennyson that Ticknor and Fields wished to use as the frontispiece for a collected edition of that poet's works as no copies were in stock.[15]

Just as important as the importation of merchandise—books, serials, and other items—was the transatlantic trade in texts. As I have suggested, the conventions of trade courtesy allowed American firms to acquire the right—if not a *de jure* copyright at least a trade-sanctioned *de facto* right—to English publications. These conventions required that the firm be the first American firm to announce its intention to publish a work. Furthermore, a claim in a work was considered stronger if the American firm had made a direct payment to the London publisher or author. Since British copyright law required first publication in the United Kingdom, American publishers usually strove for simultaneous or nearly simultaneous publication in order to discourage competition. This frequently resulted in a payment to the British publisher or author for early sheets, proofs, or even a second copy of the manuscript, sent from London. Thus the trade in texts, as well as books, also called into service the three communication networks: information, merchandise, and credit.

The trade in texts—as opposed to their piracy—was much more important and regular than many modern scholars recognize. Ticknor and Fields, for example, made a payment of $150 to Alfred Tennyson when they published a two-volume edition of his *Poems* in 1842 and, having established their "rights" to his work, remained the sole American publisher of this very popular British poet for many decades. On the other hand, the Boston firm was never able to add the poetry of Elizabeth Barrett Browning to its list, which already included the works of her husband, because trade courtesy gave a New York firm prior claim. In 1856, Ticknor and Fields went so far as to offer that firm $200 in hope that it would give up its claim to *Aurora Leigh*.[16]

From time to time, when the firm acted as the sole "authorized" American distributor of a British edition, it could be said to be involved in the importation of both books and texts in a single transaction. These imported editions (which included works by Mary Russell Mitford, Richard Hengist Horne, and Mayne Reid, among others) were shipped in sheets or bound, but usually had a specially printed title page with the Ticknor and Fields imprint. A typical example of this type of transaction involving the collected works of Charles Dickens, a vocal supporter of international copyright and critic of American publishers for their so-called piracies, is illustrative.

On March 9, 1858, Ticknor and Fields wrote to the London publisher Chapman and Hall to inquire what price and size of order would guarantee exclusive rights to the American market for an authorized edition of Dickens's collected works that the London firm had announced for serial publication. Terms were quickly agreed to, and on June 15 the first shipment containing five hundred copies each in sheets of *Pickwick, Nickleby,* and *Chuzzlewit* left London. Chapman and Hall charged two shillings per volume, a total of £300; the cost of packing cases, bills of lading, dock charges, entering, clearing, insurance, and so on, was another £12.9.5, though the Boston firm received a "drawback" (refund of the paper duty) of £20.10.10. The total cost of the shipment thus came to £291.18.7 ($1297.46), which was posted to Chapman and Hall's account on October 24, 1858. When the sheets arrived in Boston their cost came to 86.5 cents per copy. Another 30 cents was charged for binding, but the total cost per copy ($1.165) was less than half the retail price of $2.50. Because Ticknor and Fields was the sole American distributor, the firm was able to increase further the profit on the work by reducing the trade discount to only 20 percent, or 25 percent on orders of twenty-five copies or more.[17]

The first lot of sheets was shipped by freight directly from London and not, as was normal, via the Liverpool packets. It was not received in Boston for three months, and this delay held up publication of subsequent volumes in the set that arrived in Boston before the first were in hand. Furthermore, freight costs on the shipment (£12.9.5) were heavy, and further charges came due upon arrival in Boston.[18] When the firm finally began to distribute the series at the end of October, a fourth volume—*The Old Curiosity Shop*—was included, though it had not been issued in London until well after the original three titles.

Before I get lost in the multitudinous details of the transatlantic book trade, let me stop. My goal has been to demonstrate how and especially in what quantities both books and texts crossed the Atlantic during the nineteenth century. Particular arrangements and costs varied from place to place, time to time, transaction to transaction, but a glimpse of the importing activities by Ticknor and Fields shows that during the nineteenth century the transatlantic trade in both books and texts was an active and thriving business.

William Charvat was just one of many scholars to recognize the importance of Ticknor and Fields as a firm that published the works that helped define nineteenth-century American literary culture, whether we understand that culture traditionally as an American literary renaissance or more expansively as we are now inclined to do. But I believe that the history of the book should encourage us to understand that accomplishment from a broader, international perspective. Just as the firm was part of an international, especially transatlantic, trade in books, Ticknor and Fields should be recognized as fostering an international, Anglo-American literary culture. I would insist that we must recognize not only that they published works by Bryant, Dana, Emerson, Hawthorne, Holmes, Longfellow, Lowell, Stowe, Thoreau, and Whittier, but also that they published these works together with—for the same market and for the same audience—those by Browning, De Quincey, Dickens, Kingsley, Mitford, Reade, Scott, Tennyson, and Thackeray.

Appendix: Foreign Trade in Books in Britain and the United States, 1828–1868

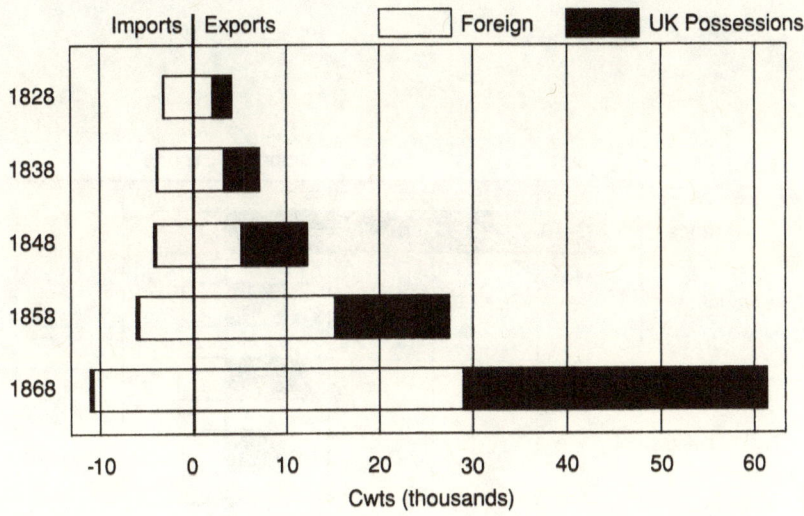

Britain, 1828–1868

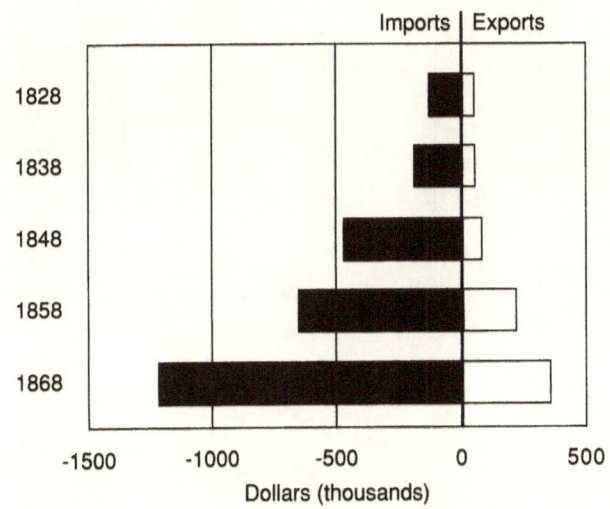

United States, 1828–1868

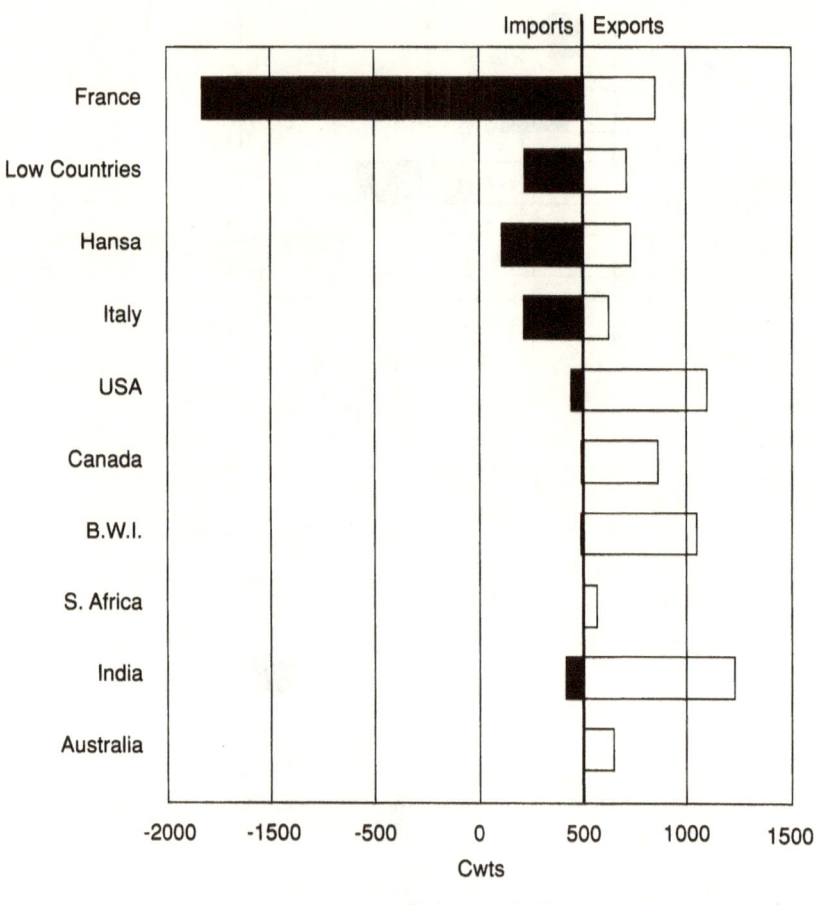

Britain, 1828

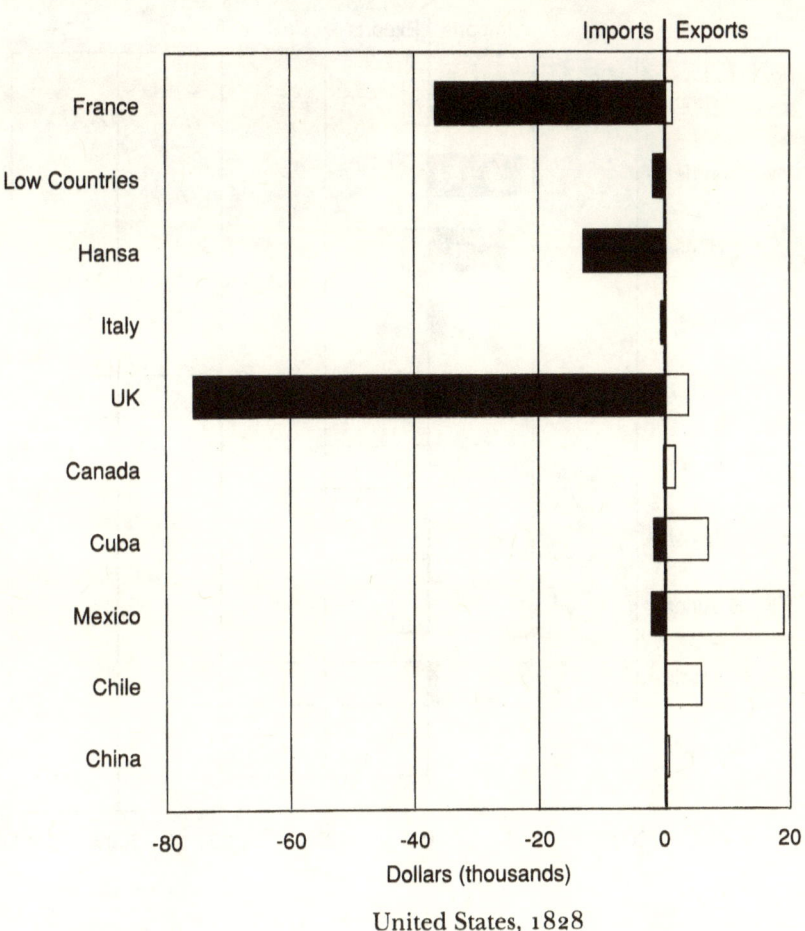

United States, 1828

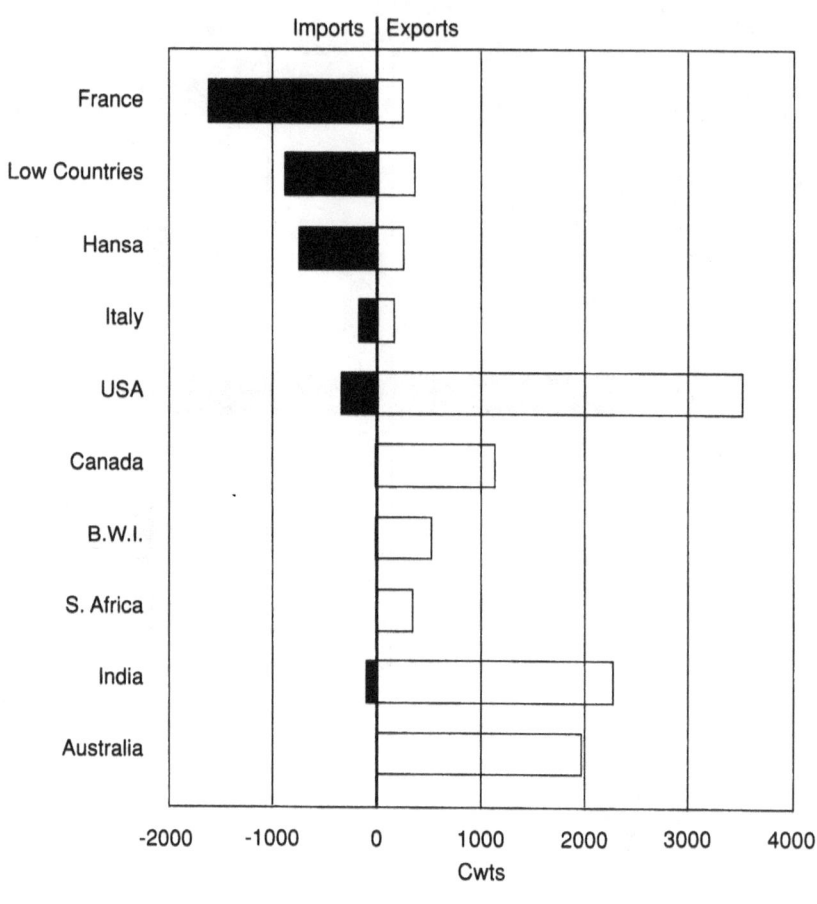

Britain, 1848

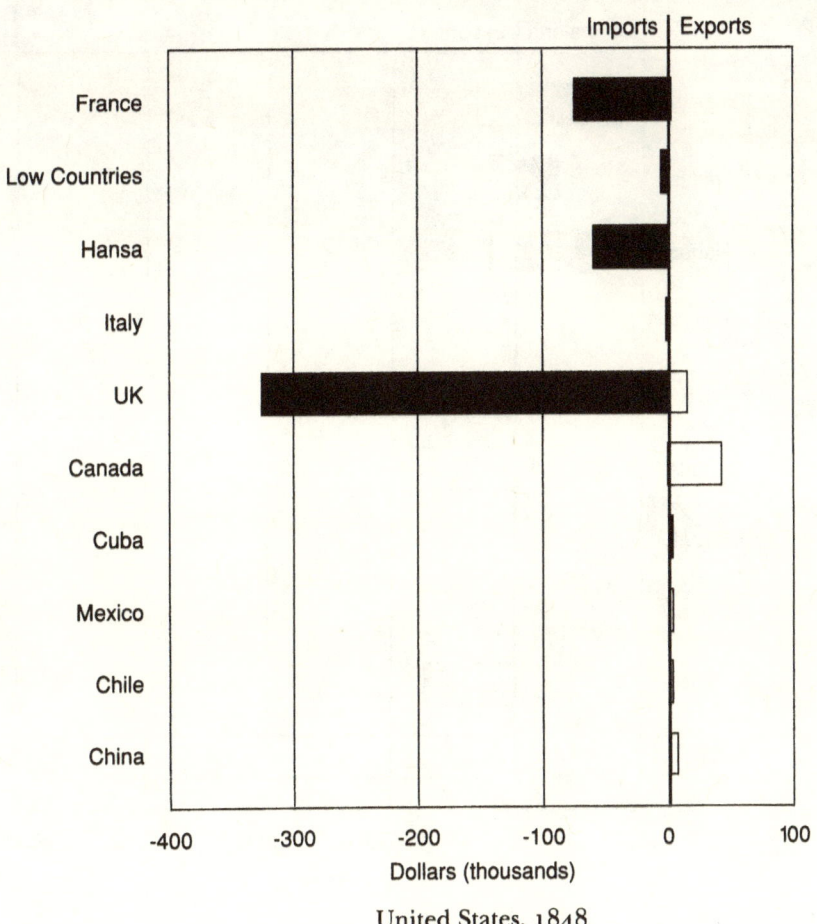

United States, 1848

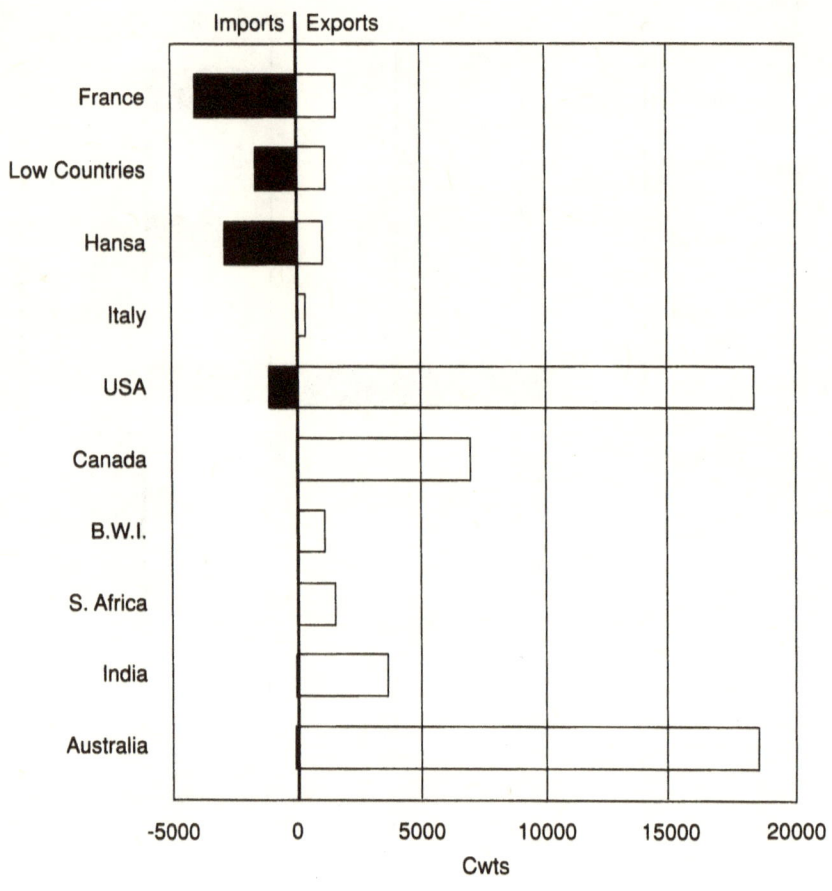

Britain, 1868

THE TRANSATLANTIC BOOK TRADE 117

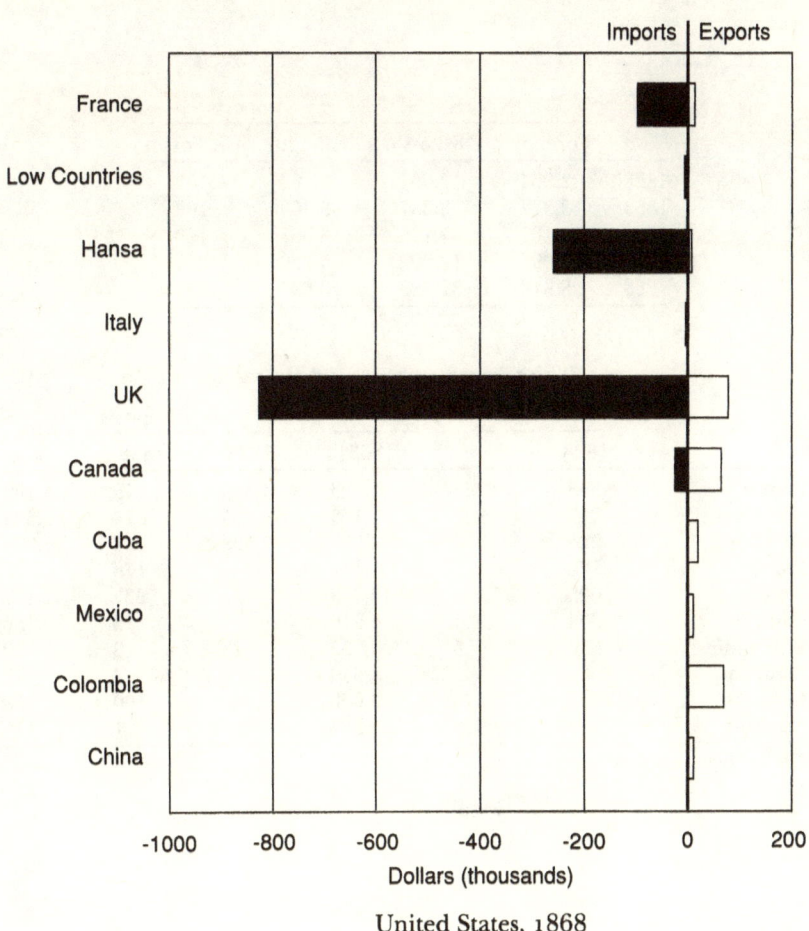

United States, 1868

	Exports		Imports	
	Foreign	UK Poss'n	Foreign	UK Poss'n
1828	2,054	2,064	3,163	107
1838	3,227	3,837	3,760	107
1848	5,161	7,125	3,961	165
1858	15,093	12,292	5,720	251
1868	28,919	32,489	10,695	281

With selected countries and regions

	Exports			Imports		
	1828	1848	1868	1828	1848	1868
France	348	243	1,623	1,849	1,615	4,102
Low Countries	219	352	1,133	285	874	1,593
Germany	228	258	1,056	388	737	2,900
Italy	125	165	352	286	178	77
USA	605	3,518	18,379	53	337	1,157
Canada	364	1,131	6,919	3	18	56
B.W. Indies	550	525	1,055	13	18	10
S. Africa	67	348	1,540	1	2	12
India	738	2,275	3,660	80	100	68
Australia	148	1,968	18,583	1	1	115

Note: All figures in cwts.

Figures for Britain

	Exports	Imports
1828	46,937	133,677
1838	50,913	193,575
1848	75,193	472,872
1858	209,774	654,080
1868	349,933	1,220,426

With selected countries and regions

	Exports			Imports		
	1828	1848	1868	1828	1848	1868
France	1,018	833	11,734	36,727	75,652	95,955
Low Countries	0	490	550	1,676	7,484	4,700
Germany	170	730	9,762	12,810	60,853	259,058
Italy	0	135	300	307	800	2,040
UK	3,866	14,660	77,524	75,807	326,602	826,117
Canada	1,635	41,861	64,556	250	1,016	24,800
Cuba	6,929	1,256	19,951	1,776	90	1,209
Mexico	18,993	2,178	9,772	1,981	0	22
Chile	5,738	1,883	1,642	0	0	140
Colombia	1,490	618	70,477	211	0	142
China	459	5,348	9,446	85	15	573

Note: All figures in dollars

Figures for the United States

Notes

1. United States Congress, *House Document* 137, 20th Cong., 2nd sess., 1828 (serial set 187), 4–5, 84–85, 140–41, 226–27; *Senate Document* 306, 25th Cong., 3rd sess., 1838 (serial set 342), 6–7, 104–7, 194–95, 246–47; *House Executive Document* 42, 30th Cong., 2nd sess., 1848 (serial set 541), 40–41, 84–85, 188–89; *Senate Executive Document* 15, 35th Cong., 2nd sess., 1858 (serial set 989), 12–13, 120–21, 248–49, 312–13, 385, 484–85; *House Executive Document* 87, 40th Cong., 3rd sess., 1868 (serial set 1384), 30–31, 140–41, 289, 384–85, 504–5; Great Britain, *Parliamentary Papers*, 1868/69 (99), Vol. LVI, 365–70.

2. The 1828 figures for Britain are roughly equivalent to the largest recorded for any year during the entire eighteenth century, as recorded in Giles Barber, "Books from the Old World and for the New: The British International Trade in Books in the Eighteenth Century," *Studies in Voltaire and the Eighteenth Century* 151 (1976): 185–224.

3. The reader should take care to note that the scale changes from graph to graph and that liberties were taken in grouping together statistics for countries or regions that were undergoing political change during this period. Omitted from these graphs are re-exports and indirect trade. While these are not particularly relevant to my argument here, they do remind us just how much Britain and the United States dominated Atlantic shipping during the nineteenth century. Re-exports are books imported into Britain or the United States for immediate re-export to another country. In 1868, for example, Britain re-exported 133 hundredweights to Turkey, 103 to South America, and 73 to the United States. Figures for indirect trade account for such books in a different way, recording the origin of the books—for example, books from the Netherlands arriving in the United States via English ports. Indirect trade could be considerable: in 1868 the United States imported only $2,040 worth of books directly from Italy, but another $16,011 of Italian books indirectly through non-Italian ports.

4. Before leaving customs statistics, let me note that they suggest another trend of the nineteenth-century book trade, the change in the value of books. In 1828 the average value of a hundredweight of British books exported to foreign countries was £23.3, to British possessions £25.8; by 1868 these had fallen to £12.7 and £9.8 respectively. Although these figures are incompletely recorded and difficult to interpret, I have no doubt that the

reduction in value by approximately one-half resulted from the introduction of new materials and technologies to book production during the industrial era.

5. The British government did, however, exercise some control over the internal book trade through its so-called "taxes on knowledge," and the record of government receipts from the duty on paper—not repealed until 1861—is another source of useful statistics for British book production in the first half of the nineteenth century. For an interesting statistical study of the British book trade that draws on these and other sources, see Simon Eliot, *Some Patterns and Trends in British Publishing, 1899–1919* (London: Bibliographical Society, 1994).

6. United States, *Statutes at Large*, vol. 5, 557–58; vol. 9, 47–48; vol. 11, 192; vol. 12, 187, 551; and vol. 13, 213. See also United States Congress, *Senate Document 72*, 62nd Cong., 1st sess., 1911, 3v. (serial set 6086–88), "Tariff Proceedings, 1839–57"; Donald Marquand Dozer, "The Tariff on Books," *Mississippi Valley Historical Review* 36 (1949/50): 73–75.

7. The basic rate of five guineas would have increased the cost of imported books by more than a third, while the total revenue produced from 1841 to 1850 from this duty was £87,363. In comparison the internal excise tax on paper paid was an important source of government revenue: in the single year 1850 it was £852,996—almost ten times as great as the import duty for the decade. Great Britain, *Parliamentary Papers*, 1850 (85), Vol. LII, 341, and 1852 (1466), Vol. LII, 34–35.

8. I believe that this distinction was first made by Graham Pollard; see his "The English Market for Books," *Publishing History* 4 (1978): 27–29.

9. For a fuller discussion see my *American Literary Publishing in the Mid-Nineteenth Century: The Business of Ticknor and Fields* (Cambridge: Cambridge University Press, 1995), 135–39.

10. Thorvald Solberg, *Copyright in Congress, 1789–1904* (Washington: GPO, 1905), is a useful guide to copyright legislation in the nineteenth-century United States.

11. Simon Nowell-Smith, *International Copyright Law and the Publisher in the Reign of Queen Victoria* (Oxford: Clarendon Press, 1968), provides an excellent summary of British copyright law and its implications. Even the 1891 Chace Act was not strictly reciprocal, for it contained the infamous protectionist "manufacturing clause" requiring that a book be printed from type set in the United States for American copyright protection.

12. James J. Barnes, *Authors, Publishers and Politicians* (London: Routledge and Kegan Paul, 1974), gives a full account of the debates and struggles over international copyright.

13. During the 1850s Ticknor and Fields emerged as one of the preeminent—if not the preeminent—literary publishers, especially of poetry, in the United States. The firm's list included works by many of the most

important New England literary figures, as well as major Victorian British writers. For a full account see my *American Literary Publishing*, which is based on the surviving business archives of the firm now in the collections of the Harvard College Library. The discovery and preservation of these archives was largely due to the efforts of William Charvat.

14. Ticknor and Fields, Letter book, foreign (1855–59), 115–16 [shelfmark: MS Am 2030.2 (61)]; quoted by permission of the Houghton Library, Harvard University, and the Houghton Mifflin Company.

15. Ticknor and Fields, Letter book, foreign (1855–59), 340, 347–48; Foreign order book (1858–61), 8–11; and Purchase book (1857–58), 369, 387.

16. Warren S. Tryon and William Charvat, eds., *The Cost Books of Ticknor and Fields and Their Predecessors, 1832–1858* (New York: Bibliographical Society of America, 1949), 52–53, 337; Ticknor and Fields, Letter book, foreign (1855–59), 14, 15–16, Letter book, domestic (1856–57), 255.

17. Ticknor and Fields, Letter book, foreign (1855–59), 357; Foreign order book (1858–61), 33; and Purchase book (1857–58), 511.

18. Ticknor and Fields, Letter book, foreign (1855–59), 452.

American Civil War Poetry and the Meaning of Literary Commodification: Whitman, Melville, and Others
Lawrence Buell

Civil War discourse has a commodity value that is very high and still rising. In the 1990s, its stock has never been higher, owing in good measure to Ken Burns's eleven-part PBS special, said to have been watched by some forty million Americans. One of Burns's expert witnesses, Shelby Foote, has affirmed that the series made him a millionaire. He had sold thirty thousand copies of his war trilogy in the previous fifteen years; but "during the six months after the broadcast, . . . more than 100,000."[1] A recent advertisement for the History Book Club (get three books free, buy one, no further obligation) lists almost as many Civil War-related titles as for the American Revolution and the two world wars combined; and the tear-off inviting you to check which of the types of history interest you most lists "Civil War" as the first option. But even before the Burns series, "no topic from U.S. history had excited as much curiosity from Americans and foreigners [alike]" as had the Civil War.[2]

But do these generalizations fit the case of Civil War poetry? Clearly they apply far better to genres like popular history, film, mass-market novels of the *Gone with the Wind* variety, narrative biographies of Lincoln and various famous generals, and memoirs (like Grant's and Sherman's). It might therefore seem nothing less than perverse to focus on poetry as an illustration of literary commodification. For "Poetry," as William Charvat (the pioneer scholar in the field of American literary economics) long ago declared, "is poor professional stock. . . . Readers will not pay for it in proportion to the work, thought, imagination, tinkering, and time-consuming revision that go into it."³ Julia Ward Howe, author of the most famous and most-reprinted of all Civil War poems, seems to have been paid at most $5 for "The Battle Hymn of the Republic" by the *Atlantic Monthly* (some report $4).⁴ So far as I know, the only clear instance of a volume of Civil War poetry becoming a major money maker is Stephen Vincent Benét's *John Brown's Body* (1928), which topped the best-seller list in 1929, was Doubleday's biggest income producer between the mid 1920s and the mid 1930s, and enjoyed at least twenty reprintings (fueled in part by an immense number of school-text adoptions) in the quarter-century after its publication.⁵ This case bears out every item in the recipe Charvat laid down in another memorable obiter dictum for the kind of poem with the greatest possible chance of popular success:

> It is not conspicuously or radically experimental in form; it does not challenge the reader on grounds where he does not wish to be met; it is not intellectually daring or adventurous; it is not pervadingly cynical or pessimistic. [Stylistically it's to be] clear and lucid; its rhythms and rhyme patterns are unmistakable; its imagery and symbolism are exposed rather than hidden, functional rather than ends in themselves. Its subject matter, not its method or its devices, is its reason for existing. It need not be moralistic in purpose, but it must not be immoral or amoral."⁶

Altogether, *John Brown's Body* certainly tests but just as certainly does not disconfirm the general rule that there simply hasn't been the same market for Civil War poetry as for other, more inherently popular genres—and it's hard to imagine at this late date in the video revolution that we're likely to see a repetition of Benét's success.

The otherwise marginal value of Civil War poetry as saleable commodity isn't, however, from my present standpoint a disqualification but positively an advantage, since one of my two main purposes will be to apply pressure to the notion of "commodity" itself from opposite directions: on the one hand, to make it more elastic, by prying it loose from the image of cash value per se; on the other hand, to make it less pejorative by prying it loose from the image of sheer entrepreneurial self-interest.

The cases that interest me most are (predictably) Walt Whitman and Herman Melville, who wrote the two best collections of Civil War lyrics. Of the two, I shall emphasize Whitman especially, since my other main purpose will be to revisit his late-life pronouncement about the formation of *Leaves of Grass* (in "A Backward Glance O'er Travel'd Roads") that "although I had made a start before, only from the occurrence of the Secession War, and what it show'd me as by flashes of lightning, with emotional depths it sounded and arous'd . . . —that only from the strong flare and provocation of that war's sights and scenes the final reasons-for-being of an autochthonic and passionate song definitely came forth."[7] At first glance, this is a nonsensical pronouncement, since after all the first three editions of *Leaves* (which contain the majority of Whitman's best poetry) appeared before the Civil War ever broke out. Yet after years of skepticism I've come to believe that his assertion makes perfect sense. For one thing, Whitman seems for some time to have considered the third (1860) edition of *Leaves of Grass* a finished experiment, in clear distinction from his book of Civil War poems, *Drum-Taps* (1865–66).[8] Under pressure of the war experience, however, he not only began tinkering with the texts of many of his previous poems[9] but also, starting in 1871, re-absorbed *Drum-Taps* back into *Leaves of Grass* and reconstructed the volume so as to make the war both central and pervasive, the pivotal event in the intertwined lives of both the nation and the persona.[10] What emboldened him to do this was not simply the interplay of personal growth and the tide of epochal historical events; it was also the opportunities and exigencies of the literary marketplace.

In order to flesh this out, it is helpful to situate Whitman in relation to fellow poets whose work was influenced by the trauma of the war. Herman Melville is of course the most famous case. *His* collection of war poems, *Battle-Pieces* (1866; still strangely neglected), marked a new stage in *his* career—a departure, indeed, far more dramatic than Whitman's in the sense that from this time on until the end of his life Melville abandoned fiction for poetry, save for the posthumously published *Billy Budd*.

Yet *Drum-Taps* and *Battle-Pieces* were only two of at least a score of single-authored volumes of poetry largely or entirely about the Civil

War published either during the war or just a year or two afterward. To these can be added another score or two of book and pamphlet compendia of war poems by various hands, ranging from lyrics for musical performance to charity projects to benefit war widows and orphans to coffee table books illustrated by fine woodcuts.[11] Quite a range of market niches, clearly. Nor does this begin to give a sense of how widely war poems were scattered through contemporary magazines like *Harper's Weekly* or documentary compendia like Frank Moore's nine-volume *Rebellion Record* (1862–65; a major source for Melville).

The single-authored volumes included, at the high end, a number of well-known literati published by major houses. Whittier authored two, as did Henry Howard Brownell (dubbed by Oliver Wendell Holmes, Sr., "Our Battle-Laureate").[12] Each cannibalized liberally from his earlier volume the second time around. James Russell Lowell, George Boker, and Thomas Buchanan Read each produced one: Lowell's being his second series of satiric *Biglow Papers;* Boker's including a much-reprinted encomium to the *Cumberland* (the Union ship sunk by the Confederate ironclad *Merrimack* before *it* was disabled by the *Monitor*); and Read's containing the much-*more*-reprinted ballad of "Sheridan's Ride." Both of Whittier's books, Brownell's second, Lowell's, and Boker's were published by Ticknor and Fields; Read's by Lippincott. On the low end were such obscure gems as *The Talisman of Battle*, by disabled veteran A. O. Ganyard (out of the Rochester [New York] *Democrat* office); *Lenore; Story of the Southern Revolution, and Other Poems*, by someone identified simply as L'Eclair (New Orleans: Bouvain and Lewis); and Methodist missionary M. B. Bird's *The Victorious*, a fervidly bibliocentric chronicle of the history of abolitionism falsely subtitled "A Small Poem on the Assassination of President Lincoln," issued out of Kingston, Jamaica. These last three were local publications, of limited distribution, by persons moved much more by the force of events than by literary aspiration as such.

Arranging this mélange on a continuum of entrepreneurialism based on publisher prestige, elegance of physical product, and book promotion, *Drum-Taps* looks about middle of the pack. The second and more important of the two versions, the one with the so-called *Sequel* including "When Lilacs Last," Whitman arranged to have printed independently (in a format quite drab and unremarkable), then contracted for distribution with a reputable New York publisher

(Bunce and Huntington) such that the book gained a modest public relations boost, even though the firm's name did not appear on the title page. In the event, *Drum-Taps* did manage to garner a goodly number of reviews in major magazines and newspapers, the majority more positive than not.[13]

Battle-Pieces, by contrast, was a quality production: as attractively printed and bound as any of the single-author volumes, with clean, distinct typeface and more generous margins, by a leading house (Harper's) that promoted it vigorously. Harper's ran six poems in its monthly magazine (with one of the best, on Sherman's march to the sea, displayed in an unusual large-type two-page spread format); distributed a quarter of the volumes as review copies;[14] and touted the book in a *Harper's Magazine* review. The fact that *Battle-Pieces* sold only 525 copies in ten years (somewhat less than twice the number of review copies) cannot be blamed on the publisher.[15]

Yet in fact *none* of these various Civil War poetry volumes were spectacularly successful. The biggest sellers were Whittier's two books. *In War Time and Other Poems* included, among other items, the already famous "Barbara Frietchie," in which a heroic Maryland nonagenarian confutes Stonewall Jackson, leader of the invading Confederate army: "'Shoot if you must this old gray head, / But spare your country's flag,' she said." *National Lyrics* cannibalized heavily from the earlier volume but added such new pieces as "Laus Deo," which celebrated the Emancipation Proclamation. Between 1863 and 1867 the print runs for the two collections were 7,100+ and 9,200+ respectively, as against 1,260 for *Battle-Pieces* and probably 500 for *Drum-Taps*. Contrast this, however, with Whittier's idyll *Snow-Bound*, which sold 32,000 copies in its *first year* of publication (1866–67), not to mention the 41,000 of Tennyson's *Enoch Arden* sold in *its* first year (1864–65), when the war was at its height. (Not for nothing has Tennyson been called America's favorite nineteenth-century poet.) Meanwhile, domestic sales of Lowell's *Biglow Papers*, second series, for the entire decade of the 1860s were well below 4,000; Brownell's Ticknor and Fields collection never quite sold out its run of 1,500; nor did Boker's *its* first run of 2,000.[16] All this didn't mean that readers preferred escapist books to war books, however. On the contrary, Harper's biggest seller for 1865 was Major George Ward Nichols's gripping eyewitness *Story of the Great March* of General Sherman through Georgia and South Carolina, which enjoyed at least thirty printings in that year alone.[17]

At this point, though, we need to ask what counts as commodity value, anyhow. Clearly not just the kind of statistics I've been rehearsing. The case of *Drum-Taps* is instructive here. By no coincidence, it was the appearance of *Drum-Taps*, its incorporation within the fourth edition of *Leaves of Grass* the next year (1867), together with a practically concurrent (1868) bowdlerized English edition of Whitman's poems and a more assertive, favorable critical promotion of his work both at home and abroad, which set the stage for Whitman's acceptance by a wider reading public, first in Britain and then in the United States. From 1867 on, Whitman was able to place 60 percent of his new poems in newspapers and magazines before their book publication, as against zero in the 1850s.[18]

This success was directly proportional to Whitman's increasing reliance on shorter, more accessible, and somewhat more conventionally stylized verse forms, including a number of explicitly occasional pieces: poems in which sensuality was sublimated by ethical idealism. *Drum-Taps* marked the start of this shift, as Whitman clearly realized when he predicted (wrongly as it turned out) that the volume "may be a success pecuniarily" and contrasted it to *Leaves of Grass* as a work of greater artistic control and engagement with current events (expressing "the pending action of this *Time & Land we swim in*").[19] But though the comparative commercial success of his subsequent work clearly pleased him—and indeed, Whitman was typically blunt to the form of crassness in setting prices on the poems he sent to magazines—money was hardly as important to him now as fame and admiration.

As we follow one key index of Whitman's acceptance—namely appearance of individually reprinted pieces in poetry anthologies—we find that for the first two decades (late 1860s through late 1880s), certain of the war-era poems are the most crucial—and not just the egregious "O Captain! My Captain!" In particular, I want to dwell on the first Whitman poem to get so reprinted: "Come up from the Fields, Father"—about a Midwestern farming family that receives a letter from their soldier son in another person's hand informing them that he's in a military hospital. The letter claims that the son will soon be better, but the mother doesn't buy it—and with good reason, for the speaker adds, "While they stand at home at the door, he is dead already; / The only son is dead." The poem ends with the image of the mother in deep mourning, getting ready to follow the son to the grave.

It was a nice fortuity for this essay, based on a lecture given at a conference in Columbus, Ohio, that "Come up from the Fields, Father" was the only Whitman poem set firmly in the Buckeye state: in early autumn,

> . . . where the trees, deeper green, yellower and redder,
> Cool and sweeten Ohio's villages, with leaves fluttering
>   in the moderate wind;
> Where apples ripe in the orchards hang, and grapes on the
>   trellis'd vines
>
> . . . the sky, so calm, so transparent after the rain,
>   and with wondrous clouds;
> Below, too, all calm, all vital and beautiful—and the farm
>   prospers well.[20]

More to the point at hand, however, is that this poem is both the first Whitman lyric known to have been anthologized in the first decade of Whitmanian anthologizing, and also the most so. It appeared in no less than five collections from England to the United States to (finally) Germany, including *The Household Book of English Poetry* (London), *Public and Parlor Readings: Prose and Poetry for the Use of Reading Clubs for Social Entertainment* (Boston and New York City), and *A Handbook of English Literature Intended for the Use of High Schools* (Boston and New York).[21]

It was especially by means of his wartime lyrics that Whitman entered the ken of some of the major poets of the century (one of the few Whitman poems known to Gerard Manley Hopkins was "Come up from the Fields, Father"—"Pete," Hopkins called it);[22] further, these war lyrics were not only the means by which Whitman infiltrated Anglo-American high culture, but the way by which he entered Anglo-American parlors and schools as well. Indeed, in modern times the latter (if not the former) still holds. Five of the seven Whitman items in Charles M. Coffin's anthology of *The Major English Poets* (Harcourt, 1954; rev. 1969), assigned in three different high schools over a thirty-year period to two generations of the Buell family (first to my wife and me, then to both our daughters), were *Drum-Taps* poems.[23]

Obviously the explanation of Whitman's eventual enshrinement as an American cultural icon is not susceptible to any single-thesis explanation. The suitability of certain Whitman later lyrics for middle-

American schoolrooms hardly suffices in itself to account for it. Numerous other factors also came into play, such as the vocal endorsement of an increasing number of major literati (especially British); the advent of poetic modernism; the displacement of the first, patriotic-affirming American canon by the oppositional paradigm in the nineteen-teens, such that Whitman begins to supersede Longfellow, Thoreau begins to rival Emerson, and the way is prepared for the Melville revival. But clearly important to the timing, if not the eventual result, was Whitman's willingness to participate actively in the remaking of himself as the good gray poet of his friend O'Connor's 1865 tract (which happily coincided with the publication of *Drum-Taps*); and to this end Whitman's war literary representations were crucial.

In the short run, as numerous Whitmanians have observed, the war enabled Whitman to redefine his persona from the brash unwashed omnisexual cosmic-anarchic force to the compassionate, maternal nurturer and patriotic chronicler of historic events. In the longer run, Whitman became increasingly adept at promoting his literary fortunes via making the war his insignia subject, beginning with the double periodical publication of the most ambitious new poem of the 1867 *Leaves*, "The Return of the Heroes," which was Whitman's equivalent of Winslow Homer's famous swords-into-ploughshares painting *The Veteran in a New Field* (1865), which shows the ex-soldier's jacket lying next to the spot where he's wielding his scythe. Whitman then very self-consciously rearranged *Leaves of Grass* as a whole so as to place the war material at the center—the point up to which all in a sense leads, and from which everything is made to fall away into autumn, parting, and death. (He called attention to this in one of the manifestos he attached to the two-volume Centennial edition of *Leaves of Grass* and *Two Rivulets* 1876.) Finally, in late life, after his paralytic stroke in 1873, which Whitman believed had its roots in wartime fatigue in the army hospitals, Whitman consolidated to an even greater degree his sense of identification with disabled war veterans on the one hand and on the other hand with Abraham Lincoln himself, the latter via a public lecture on Lincoln Whitman gave nineteen times between 1879 and 1890, which typically ended with a rousing recital of "O Captain! My Captain!"—a poem Whitman professed to hate but which he fully recognized as a passport to middlebrow respectability.[24] This performance seems to have netted Whitman $100 or more a pop, and on one occasion as much as $600. Near the end of his life, biographer David Reynolds reports, "So identified was [Whitman] with Lincoln that" a major publisher "offered him five hundred dollars to write a sixty-thousand-word book on the president."[25]

Although *Drum-Taps* probably earned Whitman nothing at the time, its carefully cultivated rebound effect yielded him a modest financial return and, far more important from his standpoint (and I think ours as well), helped advance him to the threshold of canonicity. Hence my earlier caveat about wanting to define commodity in more elastic terms than just the cash value of the original produce.

But I also want to put the notion of commodification under pressure from another angle by questioning the usual assumption that it must entail some sort of aesthetic debasement. In "Come up from the Fields, Father," Whitman obviously does exploit images of loss and grief in a mass-marketish Currier-and-Ives depiction of the traditional American farming village household and of mainstream domesticity-discourse, as contrasted for example with the more convoluted, obliquely symbolic high romantic death exaltation of "Lilacs." It's telling that Whitman received at least two effusive fan letters about the former poem from young women in 1880, one of whom had moved her audience of community neighbors to tears by reading the poem at a Decoration Day service in church, the other recalling an in-class recitation of "Father" by her teacher ("a lady of unusually broad education, and also a lover of your writings"): "I do not think any of us moved for a moment after the poem was ended, and then such a spontaneous, unpremeditated burst of applause, rose from girlish & boyish hearts, and surprised our teacher. It was the outburst of admiration from honest hearts, for something we all felt very keenly."[26] It would be a great mistake (I think) to interpret these anecdotes as ipso facto evidence of meretricious pandering to middle-brow conventionalism. For one thing, unlike "O Captain! My Captain!" "Come up from the Fields, Father" was a poem that retained Whitman's characteristic experimental form. Not only does he force his reader to come to him prosodically (by refusing to give up free verse, catalogue rhetoric, or idiosyncratic syntactical fragmentation), Whitman also invests the poem with a most delicate subtlety of conception via the device of the letter from the son in another's hand.

Even if one knows as little of Whitman biography as his two correspondents probably did, reading this poem attentively in its *Leaves of Grass* context, placed between "By the Bivouac's Fitful Flame" and

"Vigil Strange I Kept on the Field One Night," it dawns on one that this isn't just a simple heartstrings piece, but also a meditation both self-reflexive and revelatory upon the poetics of comradeship and the comradeship of poetics: imaging an alter ego of the poet—the nurse-amanuensis—exercising a long-distance impact through an epistolary impersonation that's an image and analogue at the narrative level of the potency of this scene of reception for the reader. Of course what the poem foregrounds, and what his two young admirers and their companions were no doubt responding to especially, is the pathos of the domestic tragedy of the folks on the home front. But this hardly constitutes any debasement or deflection of poetic purpose on Whitman's part. From the start, one of his central objectives had been to recuperate and make luminous the experience of obscure average Americans. To that end his most formidable challenge was how to make his idiosyncratic, heterodox style intelligible to such people, the "young mechanics" and so forth. This poem is one of those moments in the Whitman canon where the "avant-garde" dimensions of Whitman's aesthetics (his metapoetics, his prosodic experimentalism, his maternal/erotic tenderness for beautiful young men) fuse in synergy with the period's conventions of narrative, portraiture, feeling.

In short, a case like this shows that "commodification" may unleash creative energies as well as impose self-censorship. So too with Herman Melville's *Battle-Pieces*. This collection is normally and with some justification treated as symptomatic of Melville's retreat from the literary marketplace,[27] yet in point of fact not only was it subjected (as I've explained) to a considerable media hype, it's also the case that no other book Melville ever published was so dependent upon images from the mass media. The distilled, ironic detachment of the collection, on which Melvillians have often remarked, was not simply a logical outgrowth of the style of narrative rhetoric toward which Melville had developed by the time of his final novel, *The Confidence-Man* (1857), it was also the result of having imbibed most of his images of the war second-hand, through magazine stories and illustrations (from *Harper's Weekly* and *Harper's Monthly*, in particular) and the omnibus documentary compendium *The Rebellion Record*.[28]

A good example of Melville's symbiosis with the emphases of the literary marketplace in *Battle-Pieces* was the poem mentioned earlier to which *Harper's* gave special billing: "The March to the Sea." Students of Civil War poetics sometimes praise Melville at Whitman's expense for undermining rather than catering to cultural platitude.[29] To this there is indeed some basis. "March to the Sea," for instance, is written in a deceptively rollicking, celebratory balladish style until the very last stanza, when, in a sudden twist, Melville yanks away the veil:

> For behind they left a wailing,
>   A terror, and a ban,
> And blazing cinders sailing,
>   And houseless households wan,
> Wide zones of counties paling,
>   And towns where maniacs ran.
>   It was Treason's retribution
>   (Necessity the plea);
>   They will long remember Sherman
>   And his streaming columns free—
>   They will long remember Sherman
>   Marching to the sea.[30]

This *looks* like (and to some extent actually is) the mordant Melville we moderns know and love trying to fool and humiliate the complacent Amasa Delano-ish reader—all the more so when you note that the book version reworks the key mitigating statement as a question by asking: "Was it Treason's retribution— / Necessity the plea?"[31] Yet if we compare Melville's text to Major George Ward Nichols's bestselling account of Sherman's march (of which Melville was surely aware, since excerpts appeared in *Harper's* during the same time *Battle-Pieces* was being excerpted), we shall see some quite comparable mood swings, albeit in different proportions over the long haul: patriotism more firmly containing the sense of disorientation and dismay.[32]

In short, *Harper's* had good reason to believe that the mixture of exuberance and horror in Melville's poem would not in itself be bad for business—although such juxtapositions in the popular discourse were also calculated to trigger idiosyncratic as well as culturally symptomatic resonances in Melville's ironic sense.

Altogether, then: Whitman's and Melville's ventures into Civil War poetry suggest that it's much easier to build a case for why this or that work did or didn't sell well than to establish either that a work with seeming pretensions to seriousness (*however* one defines "seriousness") was generated independently of commodity motives and popular commodity forms, or conversely, that commodity motives and popular commodity forms are deleterious to artistic achievement. Those who argue the contrary are surely naive; and to insist on doing so will simply make themselves unhappy and the world no wiser.

Other Americanists before me have made versions of this same argument: witness for example the critical rehabilitation of so-called sentimental fiction and David Reynolds's documentation in his book *Beneath the American Renaissance* of the impact of various popular forgotten genres from the literary substrate on the work of canonical eminences. But such arguments, on the one hand, tend to rest heavily either upon appeal to some principle of inherent subversiveness or to counter-hegemonic disaffection within the ostensibly conventional, or, on the other hand (as in Reynolds), upon an attempt to reinstate some version of high canonicalist orthodoxy in order to explain how those base metals got transmuted into gold. What still seems to be a no-no is the notion that attunement to popular consciousness itself might produce significant literary work. Therefore late Whitman has to be conceived in terms of senescence or compromise and late Melville as disaffected retreat from the marketplace. My own position isn't that these images are totally wrong, but that literary commodity forms can act as focalizers and energizers as well as containers and constrictors.

This is not, of course, to deny Whitman and Melville agency in their repossession of popular forms. No mid-nineteenth-century poet but Whitman could have written his seventh stanza, for example:

> Ah, now the single figure to me,
> Amid all teeming and wealthy Ohio, with all its cities
>   and farms,
> Sickly white in the face and dull in the head, very
>   faint,
> By the jamb of a door leans.

Nor, on the other hand, need one feel driven to treat the symbiosis of canonical and popular as an unqualified good. On the contrary, the limits of these poems' conceptual horizon become more apparent as we historicize them: how both are, for example, manifestly poems of white angst that mourn the forcible disruption of civil order much more explicitly than they sustain the ideals for which the

Yankees supposedly fought, union and abolitionism. In this they anticipate the postbellum reconciliation longings that produced the relatively speedy reunion of white society at the freedmen's expense. Melville even goes so far as to make a mockery of the word "free."[33] The 1880 memorial service at which Whitman's schoolgirl fan recited his poem would have been one among hundreds of such post-Reconstruction healing rituals. If it is true, as I believe, that we gain more from placing Whitman and Melville on a continuum with Whittier and Stephen Vincent Benét and Ken Burns as well than by putting them on opposite sides of a canonical fence, the gain comes more at the level of understanding than at the level of apotheosis. But far be it from me to quarrel with that, historian as I like to think I am, especially if it is also true—as I strongly suspect—that Whitman and Melville themselves would have preferred it that way.

Notes

1. Robert Brent Topkin, Introduction to Topkin, ed., *Ken Burns's The Civil War: Historians Respond* (New York: Oxford University Press, 1996), xvi.
2. Topkin, *Ken Burns's The Civil War,* xix.
3. William Charvat, "The Popularization of Poetry," in *The Profession of Authorship in America, 1800–1870: The Papers of William Charvat,* ed. Matthew J. Bruccoli (Columbus: Ohio State University Press, 1968), 101.
4. Mary H. Grant, *Private Woman, Public Person: An Account of the Life of Julia Ward Howe from 1819 to 1868* (Brooklyn: Carlson, 1994), says $5 (p. 141—citing other authority); Madeline Stern, "Julia Ward Howe," in Joel Myerson, ed., *Dictionary of Literary Biography: The American Renaissance in New England* (Detroit: Gale, 1974), 114, says $4.
5. Charles A. Fenton, *Stephen Vincent Benét* (New Haven: Yale University Press, 1958), 219.
6. Charvat, "The Popularization of Poetry," 105.
7. "A Backward Glance O'er Travel'd Roads," *Leaves of Grass: Comprehensive Reader's Edition,* ed. Harold W. Blodgett and Scully Bradley (New York: New York University Press, 1965), 569–70. "Without those three or four years and the experiences they gave," Whitman immediately reiterated, "'Leaves of Grass' would not now be existing."
8. See his May 10, 1860, letter to his brother Jeff while the third edition was in press, as well as his January 6, 1865, letter to William O'Connor characterizing *Drum-Taps* as a new departure (Edwin Haviland Miller, ed., *The*

Correspondence of Walt Whitman [New York: New York University Press, 1961], 1: 53, 246–47).

9. See *Walt Whitman's Blue Book: The 1860–61 Leaves of Grass Containing His Manuscript Additions and Revisions*, ed. Arthur Golden (New York: New York Public Library, 1968).

10. Wynn Thomas, *The Lunar Light of Whitman's Poetry* (Cambridge: Harvard University Press, 1987), 252–80, is particularly astute on this subject.

11. F. O. C. Darley, *A Selection of War Lyrics*/With Illustrations on Wood (New York: James G. Gregory, 1864).

12. *Atlantic* 15 (1865): 589.

13. For detailed reconstruction of the circumstances of *Drum-Taps'* publication, see F. DeWolfe Miller's editorial introduction to *Drum-Taps* (Gainesville, Fla.: Scholars' Facsimiles and Reprints, 1959), xxvi–liii. I'm not convinced, however, that the publisher's name did not appear on the title page because the firm "balk[ed]" at Whitman's scandalous reputation (l–li), if only because shortly thereafter Bunce and Huntington published William O'Connor's defense of Whitman, *The Good Gray Poet*. Whitman's chronic micromanagement of the publication of his poems (see Whitman, *Correspondence*, ed. Edwin Haviland Miller [New York: New York University Press, 1961], I: 53) might conceivably have kept him from using Bunce and Huntington as anything but a marketing agent (*Correspondence*, I: 270). For reviews of *Drum-Taps*, see Kenneth M. Price, ed., *Walt Whitman: The Contemporary Reviews* (Cambridge: Cambridge University Press, 1996), 111–32.

14. Eugene Exman, *The House of Harper* (New York: Harper and Row, 1967), 98. Total edition = 1,260; reviewer copies = 300. By comparison, the two printings of *Drum-Taps* were 500 and 1,000 copies, respectively; and it would appear that by the mid-1870s only a few remained (see Joel Myerson, *Walt Whitman: A Descriptive Bibliography* [Pittsburgh: University of Pittsburgh Press, 1993], 148 and cf. Whitman, *Correspondence*, II: 273).

15. Garner, *The Civil War World of Herman Melville* (Lawrence: University Press of Kansas, 1993), 441.

16. These Ticknor and Fields statistics are gleaned from cost book and royalty records in the Houghton Mifflin Papers, Houghton Library, Harvard University.

17. Exman, *House of Harper*, 96; *Harper's New Monthly* 32 (December 1865): 122.

18. David Reynolds, *Walt Whitman's America: A Cultural Biography* (New York: Knopf, 1995), 450.

19. Whitman, *Correspondence*, I: 210, 246–47.

20. *Drum-Taps and Sequel to Drum-Taps* (1865–66; rpt. 1959), 40, 39.

21. Data from Myerson, *Bibliography*. I am also indebted to Ed Folsom, "'Affording the Rising Generation an Adequate Notion': Whitman in Nineteenth-Century Textbooks, Handbooks, and Anthologies," in Joel My-

erson, ed., *Studies in the American Renaissance 1991* (Charlottesville: University Press of Virginia, 1991), 351ff., which remarks discerningly about this poem's nineteenth-century popularity in the context of arguing that Whitman's work circulated a good deal more widely in late Victorian Anglo-America than Whitman himself led others to believe or, perhaps, really did himself believe.

22. Gerard Manley Hopkins to Robert Bridges, quoted in Gay Wilson Allen and Ed Folsom, ed., *Walt Whitman and the World* (Iowa City: University of Iowa Press, 1995), 33.

23. I.e. (in the revised edition): "Give me the Splendid Silent Sun," "Cavalry Crossing a Ford," "By the Bivouac's Fitful Flame," "As Toilsome I Wander'd Virginia's Woods," and "When Lilacs Last." The other two were "When the Full-Grown Poet Came" and "Good-bye My Fancy!"

24. Reynolds, *Walt Whitman's America*, 531. Folsom remarks in "Whitman in Nineteenth-Century Books" that "it was during the 1880s that 'O Captain!' became firmly entrenched as the 'great' Whitman poem" (355). Folsom bases this statement on the poem's print circulation—of which Whitman would certainly have been well aware.

25. Reynolds, *Walt Whitman's America*, 575.

26. Quoted in Folsom, "Whitman in Nineteenth-Century Books," 352.

27. See for example the aftermath status accorded this phase of Melville's career by Sheila Post-Lauria, *Correspondent Colorings: Melville in the Marketplace* (Amherst: University of Massachusetts Press, 1996), 229–30.

28. On Melville's printed sources, see especially Hennig Cohen's annotated edition of *Battle-Pieces* (New York: Thomas Yoseloff, 1963). For an understanding of Melville's dependence on magazine illustrations, I am especially indebted to Paul M. Wright's ms. paper "Herman Melville's *Battle-Pieces and Aspects of the War* and the Representation of the Civil War in the Illustrated Press." I am most grateful to Dr. Wright for sharing with me his work in progress.

29. E.g., Timothy Sweet, *Traces of War* (Baltimore: Johns Hopkins University Press, 1990).

30. *Harper's Monthly Magazine* 32 (February 1866): 367.

31. Melville, *Battle-Pieces, and Aspects of the War* (New York: Harper's, 1866), 132.

32. Here, for example, are some of Nichols's observations for November 13, 1864, on the destruction of Atlanta: "As for the soldiers, they do not stop to ask questions. Sherman says, 'Come,' and that is the entire vocabulary to them. A most cheerful feature of the situation is the fact that the men are healthful and jolly as men can be; hoping for the best, willing to dare the worst." But then (on the next page), he turns to survey the city itself. "Atlanta is entirely deserted by human beings, excepting a few soldiers here and there. The houses are vacant; there is no trade or traffic of any kind;

the streets are empty. Beautiful roses bloom in the gardens of fine houses, but a terrible stillness and solitude cover all, depressing the hearts even of those who are glad to destroy it. In the peaceful homes at the North there can be no conception how these people have suffered for their crimes" (*The Story of the Great March,* 22nd ed. [New York: Harper, 1865], 37, 38). Melville's poem might be seen as rising to the challenge of Nichols's final sentence.

33. See especially *re* Melville, Nina Silber, *The Romance of Reunion: Northerners and the South, 1865–1900* (Chapel Hill and London: University of North Carolina Press, 1993), who emphasizes that postbellum northerners "transformed their anger against the southern aristocracy into feelings of pity and respect" (6).

Negotiating an Audience for American Exceptionalism: *Redburn* and *Roughing It*

Julian Markels

In his formulation of the reciprocal influences involved in the writer-reader-book trade triangle, Charvat acknowledged from the outset that the scholar's most difficult challenge is to find reliable evidence of the reader's influence. He was himself a sophisticated reader and more than once suggested in conversation that this challenge is further complicated by internal evidence that the male writer is often self-consciously courting a reader response that he is uncertain of in advance, and in that process frustrating rather than facilitating his incipient rhetorical purpose.

Something like that occurred in the apprentice novels of Melville and Twain, who often looked over their rhetorical shoulders at confusedly imagined audiences while on their way to producing eventually the two novels that today lay greatest claim to evoking the collective reader response of an entire nation. *Moby-Dick* and *Huckleberry Finn* are everybody's choice as novels that speak for us all in articulating a national character and culture. *Moby-Dick*'s two protagonists acting out our Calvinist and Enlightenment traditions in a formal structure that is all but unique have been construed by the learned as constitutively American. *Huckleberry Finn*'s protagonist and narrative viewpoint, its vernacular style, its picaresque ethnography of the

Mississippi Valley, and its thematizing of racial slavery in Huck's conflict between "a sound heart and a deformed conscience," also have converged until recently to make readers of all kinds, and readers in many countries, apprehend this novel as uniquely American.

Both novels are also formal and thematic breakthroughs, and my argument here is, first, that the daring they required also entailed a transcendence of self-consciousness about reader response and a new if still anxious self-reliance; and second, that this daring enabled them, at least in part, to create rather than court their audiences in producing the rhetorical and epistemological responses that define the American exceptionalism(s) they have come to embody.

Nobody has explained the American-ness of *Huckleberry Finn* better than Henry Nash Smith in his analysis of Mark Twain's rhetorical development in staging a conflict between what Smith calls "two ways of looking at the world," the "genteel" and the "vernacular" in language and taste, religion and ethics, and even finally philosophy. Although this conflict originated in Southwest humor, Smith denies that it is a geographical conflict:

> The conflict was rather between the conventional assumptions he [Twain] shared with most of his countrymen and an impulse to reject those assumptions, also widely shared, that found expression in humor.
>
> If geography has any meaning in this connection, it lies in the fact that spokesmen for the conventional American culture attempted to maintain a connection with Europe.[1]

Here Smith is indirectly hypothesizing Twain's readers' response, and, as if to illustrate the difficulty Charvat foresaw in doing that, we can question whether humor was always assured of a homogeneous national audience. A distinction can be made, for example, between Mark Twain's two principal targets of vernacular irreverence, the religious culture of American Calvinism and the religion, history, and literature of Europe. I would hypothesize that the genteel Calvinism at which he poked so much fun was not geographically differentiated for his American audience. But European culture often was, and it can also be argued that Smith's genteel spokesmen who affirmed a connection with Europe didn't always share a universal American impulse to reject genteel assumptions through humor.

That possibility must certainly have been worrying Mark Twain in his reaction to his audience's reaction to his 1877 speech at the Whittier birthday dinner. There he felt guilty afterward for his mockery of Emerson, Longfellow, and Holmes—spokesmen who affirmed a connection with Europe—through the rhetorical device that had first made him famous for his jumping-frog story and that was to lead him eventually to *Huckleberry Finn*. This was the frame narrative in which a genteel Easterner elicits from a Western rustic a vernacular narrative that mocks the Easterner's religious, literary, and ethical culture. A California miner tells Mark Twain that he is the fourth writer to visit the miner's cabin in twenty-four hours—after Emerson, Holmes, and Longfellow, who had all been drinking and looked pretty seedy. Holmes, whose double chins hung down to his stomach, had inspected the cabin disapprovingly and urged the miner to "Build thee more stately mansions,/O my soul," and then the miner continues with similar parodies of Longfellow and Emerson. Finally Mark Twain assures him that these visitors must have been imposters, and the miner replies, "Ah—imposters, were they? Are *you?*," turning the screw one more time on the genteel narrator.

Although that punch line links Mark Twain sympathetically with the writers he had just parodied, both he and his sponsor Howells were hugely embarrassed by the speech. Howells called it a "bewildering blunder," and Twain wrote an abject letter of apology to Emerson, Longfellow, and Holmes. But neither the principals' reactions at the dinner nor the next day's newspaper reports suggest anything like the public scandal that, according to Smith, Twain and Howells had "simply invented."[2] Lacking a sure instinct for either the dining or newspaper audiences, they regretted Twain's use of the rhetorical strategy whose later permutations were to give *Huckleberry Finn* so much of its exceptionalism—in Emmeline Grangerford's poetry, for example, or Huck's and Jim's argument whether King Solomon was wise, or the King's parodies of Shakespeare and genteel religion. Thus despite Smith's initial claim that Mark Twain shared with his countrymen both a commitment to conventional assumptions and an impulse to reject those assumptions, one of his conclusions from the Whittier birthday episode is that "the confusion of tastes and attitudes in nineteenth-century American culture made it impossible for Mark Twain to arrive at a workable idea of his vocation"[3]—a conclusion that coalesces Twain's idea of his vocation with a far from confident idea of his audience.

Smith goes on to demonstrate that between the Whittier dinner and the composition of *Huckleberry Finn,* Twain moved closer to a workable idea of his vocation by turning for his subject matter to the river world of his boyhood in "Old Times on the Mississippi" and *Adventures of Tom Sawyer.* This immersion in memory no doubt helped him overcome his rhetorical self-consciousness, and here I want to focus on an earlier apprentice novel based on Twain's transcontinental journey and mining adventures—*Roughing It*—in which that self-consciousness is still unmistakable. *Roughing It* came five years before the Whittier dinner; it is sprinkled with stagings of the vernacular-genteel conflict, and among these are some highly self-conscious passages confusedly addressed to disparate audiences. The rhetorical confusion of these passages, moreover, parallels Melville's confused self-consciousness in passages where he can't settle on his audience in another apprentice novel based on a journey in the opposite direction—*Redburn.*

Redburn anticipates *Moby-Dick* at roughly the same rhetorical distance at which *Roughing It* anticipates *Huckleberry Finn,* and at that distance we can see Melville trying out some of Twain's trademark rhetoric and Twain trying out some of Melville's. In the first example below, you might almost think you were in a Twain frame narrative, and in the second you could almost be reading a Melville vignette from *Israel Potter* or "The Encantadas."

> But I felt very little like doing as I was bid, for I had some scruples about drinking spirits; and to tell the plain truth, for I am not ashamed of it, I was a member of a society in the village where my mother lived, called the Juvenile Total Abstinence Association, of which my friend, Tom Legare, was president, secretary, and treasurer, and kept the funds in a little purse that his cousin knit for him.[4]

> The mere handful of miners still remaining, had seen the town spring up, spread, and flourish in its pride; and they had seen it sicken and die, and pass away like a dream. With it their hopes had died, and their zest of life.... They had accepted banishment, forgotten the world and been forgotten of the world. They were far from telegraphs and railroads, and they stood, as it were, in a living grave, dead to the events that stirred the globe's great populations, dead to the common interests of men, isolated and outcast from brotherhood with their kind. One of my associates in this locality, for two or three months, was a man who had had a university education; but now for eighteen years he had decayed there by inches, a

bearded, rough-clad, clay-stained miner, and *at times among his sighings and soliloquizings he unconsciously interjected vaguely remembered Latin and Greek sentences — dead and musty tongues, meet vehicles for the thoughts of one* whose dreams were all of the past, whose life was a failure, a tired man, burdened with the present, and indifferent to the future; a man without ties, hopes, interests, waiting for rest and the end.[5]

But the first is in fact from *Redburn* and the second from *Roughing It.* In these early works the two writers all but crossed paths, and the different paths they finally took can perhaps tell us not only about personal differences but about rhetorical and generational "reader-response conditions" for the American exceptionalisms later embodied by *Moby-Dick* and *Huckleberry Finn.*

Both novels begin as initiation stories and then, around halfway through, become picaresque miscellanies in which the narrative persona keeps shifting character to suit the material at hand. He is sometimes the still young initiate describing local color in the streets of Liverpool or Virginia City, sometimes a much older hand moralizing about sailors or Goshoot Indians, sometimes a Byronic *poseur,* and sometimes a stand-up comedian. His material is partly autobiographical reminiscence, partly cribbed from guidebooks or scrapbooks, and partly fictional invention.

Mark Twain referred to his plot as a "narrative plank" into which he had plugged anything he thought he could fit, and that included throughout the novel episodes of vernacular/genteel confrontation. Two of these have often been anthologized: chapter 32, under the title "Lost in the Snow," and chapter 43, "Jim Blaine and His Grandfather's Ram." The Jim Blaine story is built on the pattern of the jumping-frog and Whittier's birthday stories: the tenderfoot "Mark Twain" is duped by a drunken miner's shaggy dog story whose endless digressions involve a running burlesque of genteel religion. And "Lost in the Snow" records Twain's and his friends' pious renunciations of alcohol and tobacco when they think they are about to die in a blizzard:

> Ollendorf got his voice again and forgave me for the things I had said and done. Then he got out his bottle of whiskey and said that whether he lived or died he would never touch another drop. He said he had given up all hope of life, and although ill prepared, was ready to submit humbly to his fate; that he wished he could be spared a little longer, not for any selfish reason, but to make a thorough

reform in his character, by devoting himself to helping the poor, nursing the sick, and pleading with the people to guard themselves against the intoxications of intemperance, make his life a beneficent example to the young, and lay it down at last with the precious reflection that it had not been lived in vain.[6]

Now that is a foretaste of the King's speeches at the camp meeting and the Wilks farm in *Huckleberry Finn*—speeches that Huck describes as "All tears and flapdoodle"—and in *Roughing It*'s many episodes mocking genteel religion Mark Twain takes his audience confidently for granted. But it's a whole different story with the Western landscape that inevitably claims attention in this novel.[7] Then as now, any narrative of Western travel is duty-bound to ooh and aah about the landscape, and Mark Twain is perfectly aware that landscape description gives him another opportunity to mock genteel assumptions, as when he says at the end of chapter 17 that "it was a comfort in those succeeding days to sit up and contemplate the majestic panorama of mountains and valleys spread out below us and eat ham and hard boiled eggs while our spiritual natures reveled alternately in rainbows, thunderstorms, and peerless sunsets. Nothing helps scenery like ham and eggs."[8] But *Roughing It*'s several succeeding landscape descriptions revert to picturesque ideality, as if totally oblivious to the ham-and-eggs philosophy. The following passage comes 150 pages after the ham-and-eggs passage and cozies up to an audience that Twain must have identified with European literature and such of its epigones as Emerson, Longfellow, and Holmes:

> From Virginia's airy situation one could look over a vast, far-reaching panorama of mountain ranges and deserts; and whether the day was bright or overcast, whether the sun was rising or setting, or flaming in the zenith, or whether night and the moon held sway, the spectacle was always impressive and beautiful. Over your head Mount Davidson lifted its gray dome, and before and below you a rugged cañon clove the battlemented hills, making a sombre gateway through which a soft-tinted desert was glimpsed, with the silver thread of a river winding through it, bordered with trees which many miles of distance diminished to a delicate fringe.[9]

Where *Roughing It* is rhetorically assured and consistent in its deflation of establishment religion, it is self-conscious and inconsistent in its address to establishment literature. Where the rhetorical strategies that constitute its reprobate miners clearly anticipate *Huckleberry Finn*, nothing in its narrator's landscape confusion remotely anticipates Huck's descriptions of the fog or of dawn on the river or of the Phelps farm.

Those descriptions of Huck's reflect a global vernacular sensibility rather than a local narrative strategy. They reflect a new experience of nature and society, and Twain understandably needed time, risk, and struggle to find his way into that affirmative sensibility long after mastering Southwest humor's boilerplate device for deflating the genteel. The revolutionary jump to Huck's point of view, when it did occur, required Twain to give up on the audience he was trying to appease in the landscape of *Roughing It* and in his apology for the Whittier speech—or rather, perhaps, to take his chance on that audience by enlarging on his reprobate miners in the persona and language he invented for Huck.[10]

Melville in *Redburn* is struggling to appease an apparently different imagined audience. Where Twain's rhetorical hesitancy typically occurs in his narrator's landscape descriptions, Melville's occurs in his narrator's moral and political reflections on the degeneracy of sailors or the indifference of capitalists or the protection of immigrants. The initiation story in the first half of *Redburn* casts the narrator in the satirical role of genteel tenderfoot parallel to that of "Mark Twain" in the first half of *Roughing It*, and Melville's sailors then play the potentially vernacular role of the miners whose culture initiates "Mark Twain." But Redburn when initiated does not become one of "the boys," as "Mark Twain" does, and thus put Melville in rhetorical position to enlarge the language and viewpoint of these sailors into those of a vernacular Ishmael. Instead Redburn holds himself apart as already an Ishmael, keeps reminding his reader of his elite origins and downward mobility, and then wonders whether the sailors whose life he now shares may be too morally depraved to be redeemable.

That's where Melville's rhetoric typically waffles. Chapter 29 is entitled "Redburn Deferentially Discourses Concerning the Prospects of Sailors," and it is a nice question to whom his deference is directed. He says that vulnerable sailors in port are preyed upon by landlords, bar-keepers, and "denizens of notorious Corinthian haunts in the vicinity of the docks, which in depravity are not to be matched by any thing this side of the pit that is bottomless." But then he also says that the sailors love it, that the very fact of their being sailors "argues a certain recklessness and sensualism of character, ignorance, and depravity." He goes on to mock the hypocritical philanthropists who subscribe to sailors' charities but avoid sailors in the flesh, and then asks whether the sailors' condition can be ameliorated by anything less than "ameliorating the moral organization of all civilization."[11] But then he also doubts that, and in the chapter's penultimate paragraph he says that no matter how well intentioned an educational program might be, "the thought of lifting them [sailors] up seems almost as hopeless as growing the grape in Nova Zembla" (140). Then he reverses his field again and concludes the chapter with the following paragraph, which Huck Finn would surely describe as a pious goody-goody Amen:

> But we must not altogether despair for the sailor; nor need those who toil for his good be at bottom disheartened. For Time must prove his friend in the end; and though sometimes he would almost seem as a neglected step-son of heaven, permitted to run on and riot out his days with no hand to restrain him, while others are watched over and tenderly cared for; yet we feel and we know that God is the true Father of all; and that none of his children are without the pale of his care. (140)

There is no way to construe that paragraph as ironic when taken in context, and in many similar passages in *Redburn* Melville spreads himself rhetorically all over the place. In chapter 47, for example, Redburn discourses on the victimization of emigrants in the same way he did earlier on the condition of sailors, and with the same confused courting of incommensurate audiences. He tells how the immigration agents deceive their clients, how the ship captains cheat them, how the cabin passengers disdain them. Then he concludes with the following passage, where the first paragraph denounces the exploiters and the second retracts the first:

> Lucky would it be for the pretensions of some parvenus, whose souls are deposited at their banker's, and whose bodies but serve to carry about purses, knit of poor men's heart-strings, if thus easily they could precisely define, ashore, the difference between them and the rest of humanity.
>
> But I, Redburn, am a poor fellow, who have hardly even known what it is to have five silver dollars in my pocket at one time; so, no doubt, this circumstance has something to do with my slight and harmless indignation at these things. (242)

In Melville's rhetorical waffling two preoccupations of his later writing struggle for expression: in the example of the sailors a preoccupation with what he was later to call a "depravity according to nature," and in the example of the immigrants a preoccupation with equality and social justice. The lead sailor Jackson in *Redburn* has long been recognized as a prototype for Claggart in *Billy Budd*, and the immigrants in *Redburn* anticipate such exploited groups as the scriveners of "Bartleby" and the textile-mill women of "The Tartarus of Maids." *Moby-Dick* is of course the climactic expression of both preoccupations, in Ahab's obsession with cosmic demonism and in Ishmael's pervasive egalitarian commentary. And just as Mark Twain finally had to risk alienating the audience for his polite landscapes if he was to get to *Huckleberry Finn*, Melville had to risk alienating the audience for his pious social reflections if he was to get to *Moby-Dick* and beyond.

It turns out, then, that on one side of their waffling both writers were courting the same establishment audience despite their different subjects. It's on the other side of their waffling, and beneath their mutual courting of this audience, that Twain moves toward the specific vernacular exceptionalism of *Huckleberry Finn* while Melville is cut off from making that move. Even when ignoring his imagined genteel audience, Melville could not follow through on *Redburn*'s vernacular first step in satirically exposing his hero to the sailors' culture because he had no way to give that culture a positive vernacular charge. Having made his sailors entirely a subject for condescending reflection, he was rhetorically impelled to reverse direction and, so to speak, to initiate these sailors to Redburn's culture on their way to becoming Ishmael and Ahab. And in that reversal he had to reauthorize Redburn's sensibility instead of mocking it.[12]

An explanation of the two writers' different trajectories may begin with generational and geographical considerations. Melville's imagined readers were surely more Eurocentric than Twain's and thus more self-consciously American. His generation kept issuing manifestos of American exceptionalism, Melville's conspicuously among them, and Redburn's eastward voyage into the European past introduces him to a miscellaneous population of sailors, starving people, leisure classes, and immigrants who when taken together are collective evidence for America's mission to the world. Twain's generation had by now had time to ripen America's internal disunities and to replicate the earlier generation's America-Europe engagement in

North-South or East-West engagements that precluded much talk about America's singular mission.

But these generational and geographical considerations also entail deeper epistemological considerations. In order to affirm America's mission in his Atlantic culture, Melville had to expand in Ahab and Ishmael Redburn's essentialist, universalized, and humanistic narrative of cosmic evil and social equality. This is the narrative that he said in his essay on Hawthorne would produce American exceptionalism, and it is the epistemological opposite of Twain's social constructivist, historicized narrative of Huck's and Jim's struggle for freedom and equality in their particular circumstances.

Twain's narrative, with its epistemology, won a large audience where Melville's didn't win any, and it can be questioned whether *Moby-Dick* has ever rivaled *Huckleberry Finn* in being perceived as the paradigm for a national literature. Early in our century a bargeman on the Thames told the Labor Party theorist Harold Laski that *Moby-Dick* is "the greatest piece of literature ever produced by man,"[13] which is as universal as you can get in a universe without women. At roughly the same time William Dean Howells called Mark Twain the Lincoln of our literature, and later Hemingway said that all modern American literature comes from *Huckleberry Finn*—all of which, ironically enough, is as nationally particularized as Melville hoped our literature would turn out to be.

Yet *Huckleberry Finn* ends in impasse, and I think its ending is latent in the two-cultures paradigm of Southwest humor where Mark Twain began. That paradigm's implied audience needs a winner for the humor to succeed, and it creates terrific rhetorical pressure against accommodation between the two cultures.[14] Even so, Twain is impelled by the history he still shares with the audience he has newly created to keep *Huckleberry Finn*'s vernacular victory qualified and incomplete. Thus the rhetorical battle initiated by Southwest humor ends for him in an intra-American standoff that then invites external intervention by what Henry Nash Smith called the "God-figure"—Colonel Sherburn or the man that corrupted Hadleyburg or the mysterious stranger—who invokes a plague on both houses and damns the whole human race. I think this rhetorical and cultural problematic rather than his family or financial misfortunes is the source of Twain's later nihilism. And that nihilism as narrativized in his late stories, in which nineteenth-century Hadleyburg and sixteenth-century Eseldorf are interchangeable, is no longer socially constructed and historically contingent but universalized, essentialized, and, so to speak, humanistic. The rhetorical problematic of *Huckleberry Finn* led Mark Twain eventually back into Melville's epistemological world, where this chief icon of American exceptionalism was finally moved to write that "it was wonderful to find America, but it would have been more wonderful to lose it."

Notes

1. Henry Nash Smith, *Mark Twain, The Development of a Writer* (Cambridge: Harvard University Press, 1962), 3-4.
2. Smith, *Mark Twain*, 98.
3. Smith, *Mark Twain*, 110.
4. Herman Melville, *Redburn. His First Voyage*, ed. Harrison Hayford, Hershel Parker, and G. Thomas Tanselle (Evanston, Ill.: Northwestern University Press, 1969), 42.
5. Mark Twain, *Roughing It*, ed. Harriet Elinor Smith and Edgar M. Branch (Berkeley and Los Angeles: University of California Press, 1993), 412-13; my emphasis.
6. Twain, *Roughing It*, 214-15.
7. The following analysis extends in another direction that of Leo Marx in "The Pilot and the Passenger: Landscape Conventions and the Style of Huckleberry Finn," in *The Pilot and the Passenger: Essays on Literature, Technology, and Culture in the United States* (New York: Oxford University Press, 1988), 18-36.
8. Twain, *Roughing It*, 120-21.
9. Twain, *Roughing It*, 284.
10. James Phelan has shown me how this is an oversimplification. Part of what's revolutionary in the jump to Huck's point of view is that he is endowed not only with the vernacular irreverence of Twain's reprobate miners but also with a vernacular innocence comparable to the genteel innocence of Twain's victimized frame narrators. Huck's innocence produces a dramatic irony that distances us from him but also engages us on his behalf in a manner that would be impossible with Simon Wheeler or Jim Blaine or the miner of the Whittier birthday speech. I would argue even so that the novel's pervasive irreverence toward establishment culture, manifested not only by Huck's adventures but by the King's and the Duke's as well, entails substantial risks with the audience Twain had courted in the landscapes of

Roughing It. Those risks are also reflected indirectly in the shifting grounds of a now hundred-year-long argument whether to teach *Huckleberry Finn* in public schools or allow it general circulation in public libraries.

11. Melville, *Redburn*, 138 (subsequent citations are in the text).

12. In *White-Jacket*, written almost simultaneously with *Redburn* and published immediately following, Melville's lead sailor is Jack Chase, who could not be more different from Jackson in *Redburn*. Jack Chase is a reader of Byron, Scott, and Camoens, he is all "honor and integrity" (17), and his all-round nobility leads White Jacket to speculate that "Jack must have been a by-blow of some British Admiral of the Blue" (14). Forty years later Melville described Billy Budd as "a foundling, a presumable by-blow, and, evidently, no ignoble one. Noble descent was as evident in him as in a blood horse" (16). Instead of finding in these exceptional sailors some hope for sailors in general, or some seeds of an alternative culture, Melville associates them genetically with the genteel Establishment. Quotations from Herman Melville, *White-Jacket; or, The World in a Man-of-War*, ed. Harrison Hayford, Herschel Parker, and G. Thomas Tanselle (Evanston, Ill.: Northwestern University Press, 1970).

13. Hershel Parker, "Historical Note. VIII," in Herman Melville, *Moby-Dick*, ed. Harrison Hayford, Hershel Parker, and G. Thomas Tanselle (Evanston, Ill.: Northwestern University Press, 1988), 752.

14. The great exception is "The Big Bear of Arkansas," whose vernacular hero's Falstaffian rhetoric not only disarms his genteel skeptics (whom he begins by mocking for their understanding of the word "game"), but then converts those skeptics to his final perception of union with the bear. True, the frame narrator of this story performs the conventional function: he remains oblivious to Jim Doggett's table-turning answers to his condescending questions, and at the end he holds himself aloof from the mystical experience of union shared by the others. But this time the frame narrator's Malvolian aloofness only serves to highlight the reconciliation Doggett has accomplished with those others.

Writing with an Ethical Purpose: The Case of Elizabeth Stuart Phelps
Susan S. Williams

In 1892, Elizabeth Stuart Phelps confessed to a friend that she suffered severe stage fright whenever she spoke in public. "I have had to abandon all public reading," she wrote. "I am . . . by no means strong enough to undergo the strain and loss of vitality involved in the stage fright insomnia, and general demoralization of a work to which I am not physically adapted."[1] Phelps's stage fright, I want to suggest, is intimately connected to her profession of authorship. On the surface of it, her fear of public speaking seems unwarranted and unnecessarily modest. After all, when she made this comment, Phelps was a well-established figure in the American literary scene who had achieved popular as well as critical success. She had written a number of best-selling novels, including the phenomenally successful *The Gates Ajar* (1868), and was regularly serialized in the pages of the *Atlantic* and *McClure's*. She also enjoyed a critical reputation as one of the best living American writers. In William Charvat's terms, she had succeeded both as "a literary artist" and as a "professional writer." This dual success, however, created its own tensions; she could not, as Charvat puts it, "solve the problems of one function without reference to the other."[2]

These functions were particularly interrelated for Phelps, because she viewed herself as a moral realist. This realism, she believed, would allow her to find professional success while also writing with certain literary standards. In her memoirs, *Chapters from a Life* (1896), she hinted at these standards when she defined moral realism as an effort both "to tell the truth about the world [she] live[d] in" and to write "with an ethical purpose."[3] Truth-telling, for her, necessarily included an attention to the moral dimension of life.

If morality and realism went hand in hand for Phelps, however, her position as a moral realist created a conflict between seeing and doing, between recording the truth and working to effect social change. It is this particular conflict, I think, that manifests itself in her stage fright. On one hand, she understood the importance of public speaking, especially on behalf of temperance and women's rights. But she also knew that such public speaking would leave her physically exhausted and unable to write. "My intellect may go with [these platform women]," she admitted in her memoirs, "and my heart may throb for them, but my time and vitality have always been distinctly the property of my ideals of literary art" (*CL* 253). As we saw in the passage with which I began, she also worried about the "general demoralization of a work to which [she was] not physically adapted." I am struck here by the word "demoralization": to speak in public leaves her not only exhausted but also demoralized, so discouraged that she can no longer capture the morals that are an implicit part of her literary art. "I was made to live curled up in a shell somewhere (an oyster shell perhaps!) on the seashore," she wrote to her friend John Greenleaf Whittier.[4] Her analogy is instructive; she wants to claim immunity from public events in order to stay in her protective shell and create beautiful "pearls" of art.

Phelps's stage fright seems at first to fit the paradigm of literary domesticity that Mary Kelley describes in *Private Woman, Public Stage*, in which writers assume a public voice by remaining essentially private, often hiding behind a veil of anonymity.[5] Phelps did in fact use a pen name: christened Mary Gray, she wrote under her mother's name, Elizabeth Stuart Phelps. Her mother, who was also a writer, had died when Phelps was only twelve. But Phelps's use of this name was more of a memorial to her mother than a true mask, a way for the daughter to create a legacy to the woman she believed had died from the strain of being both a mother and a writer. Similarly, Phelps's decision not to be a "platform woman" stemmed as much from personal choice as it did from societal constraints. She saw her authorship as enabling her to define her "time and vitality" as "the property of [her] ideals of literary art" rather than of social action. Since writing itself made her "often ill with the strain" (*CL* 267), it allowed her to just say no to other forms of labor.[6]

Two aspects of Phelps's authorship, then, are marked by her stage fright. The first is her sense of herself as a moral realist who can serve an ethical purpose while also telling the truth. As such, she can work for social good from her study just as well as from the speaker's platform. This justification of her privacy, in turn, leads to a second aspect of her authorship: her particular valorization of literary labor as both socially and personally productive. In this view, writing paradoxically becomes at once a form of self-sacrifice in which one trades physical "vitality" for ethical morality and a form of self-protection that enables one to channel one's energies into "the ideals of literary art." For Phelps, these literary ideals were wholly compatible with moral realism.

In the rest of this essay, I want to sketch more fully the ways in which moral realism defined Phelps as an author. I will focus in particular on her 1894 temperance novel, *A Singular Life*. This novel tells the story of Emanuel Bayard, a Christ-like hero who is murdered while doing missionary work in Angel Alley, the bowery district of a New England fishing town. Bayard actively fights for social change in a way that Phelps herself could not, enabling her to "mount the platform" vicariously if not in fact. For this reason, he provides a helpful lens through which to view Phelps's ambivalence about her decision to pursue literary rather than ministerial labor. Bayard, I will argue, becomes a figure for the author, one who shares Phelps's stage fright but resolves it in a different way. Having looked at this connection between Phelps and Bayard, I will end my essay by briefly discussing Phelps's relation to two writers who influenced her definition of moral realism: William Dean Howells and Harriet Beecher Stowe. Her connection to these writers provides a crucial bridge between the traditions of women's writing and the traditions associated with realism: a bridge that makes her work a particularly important case for understanding the profession of authorship in the later nineteenth century.

In *A Singular Life*, Phelps's moral realism is manifested most directly in her narrative stance as a "biographer" who leaves no detail unsaid. "I see no reason why one should hesitate to give a man full credit for personal beauty because one chances to be his biographer," the narrator says when she first describes Bayard.[7] She continues such direct address when she describes Bayard's attempts to follow the social gospel. When he struggles to find a job, she reminds us that her factual narrative, unlike fiction, "omits nothing of the grim details" (*SL* 78). To this end, Bayard is not allowed to suffer from "an interesting delirium or deadly fever," as he would have in a "respectable fiction"; instead he has "one of those serious nervous collapses which seem ignominy to a young man" (*SL* 83–84). Even as the narrator is attracted to Bayard's personal beauty, she avoids overly romanticizing him. Her rather heavy-handed reassurances, however, remind us of the constructed nature of such truth: it does not come easily but rather occasions profound narrative anxieties.

A Singular Life contains more subtle gestures toward realism as well. For instance, Bayard's thoughts are often portrayed in photographic terms. As he courts Helen, he pictures the lowly house in which they would live, and "his fancy, with terrible distinctness, took forbidden photographs by flashlight" (*SL* 287). One thinks here of the photographs of tenements in Jacob Riis's *How the Other Half Lives* (1890) more than of the romanticized pictures usually associated with Phelps. Riis rarely asked permission to take his photographs and admitted that "the spectacle of strange men invading a house in the mid-night hours armed with [flash] pistols was hardly reassuring." Riis justified such practices by arguing that they enabled him to capture the "unventilated and fever-breeding" tenements as they were. Bayard's aversion to living in a "lowly house" betrays his genteel roots, but it also leads him, like Riis, to confront the possibilities of living like "the other half."[8]

As she wrote *A Singular Life*, Phelps herself had certain photographs in her head: she based the town of Windover largely on her own experiences as a summer resident of Gloucester, Massachusetts. She first became interested in the temperance movement after seeing a man murdered during a brawl in a Gloucester rum shop. Phelps took it upon herself to deliver the news to the man's wife, and it was "the short sunset hour which [she] spent in that devastated home" that "did for [her] what all the temperance conventions and crusades of America . . . had failed to do" (*CL* 206). In *A Singular Life*, she recreated this intimate scene of pathos for her readers, thereby encouraging them too to join the temperance movement. For some readers, however, her thinly veiled allusions to Gloucester hit too close to home. One resident, Munroe Stevens, was so irate that he felt compelled to write a response. In a pamphlet entitled *The "A Singular Life" Reviewed and Gloucester Vindicated* (1897), Stevens condemned Phelps for writing a story that "is libellous to all the New England fishermen, and more especially to the good people of Gloucester." This libel was particularly galling to Stevens because Phelps spent her summers in Gloucester, "seeking rest, recreation and peace among the hospitable people she defames." Worse still, she presented this "work of scandal" under the guise of her religion: "It is boldly and unblushingly published abroad that the book is a good, honest Christian work."[9] Even as Stevens insisted that *A Singular Life* was factually inaccurate, however, he also took pains to show the ways in which Phelps's particular descriptions corresponded to real places in Gloucester. As a reader, he assumed that the novel would have a realistic agenda, and he criticized it on those grounds.

Within *A Singular Life*, Phelps's own realistic agenda is figured in Bayard's personal conflict between social action and private contemplation. He gives his life to the temperance cause, insisting on ministering to the thieves, prostitutes, and alcoholics in Angel Alley even when he knows that his life is in danger. Yet he is an uneasy and at times unwilling reformer. After working in Angel Alley all day, he returns to his boarding-house room with a palpable sense of relief. Similarly, he visits his childhood home with fetishistic delight. He revels in its Persian rugs, its mahogany hat-tree, and the "luxurious mattresses" in his well-heated room (*SL* 353). The bed, flanked by a portrait of his mother, offers maternal comfort, while the old pipes, fishing rod, and silk menus in the room attest to the kinds of leisure activities that he had enjoyed as a youth. Bayard's Christian mission has led him to renounce such activities along with his other material comforts, but this renunciation is not easy. Even as Bayard is committed to self-sacrifice, he also longs to be "curled into the shell of his solitude contentedly" (*SL* 10). The fact that self-sacrifice does not always come easily makes him a more realistic character. It also creates a certain connection between him and Phelps's own life: as we have seen, she too desired to "live curled up in a shell somewhere ... on the seashore."

Bayard's love of material comforts makes his character realistic in another sense as well: he understands that working on behalf of the underclass does not necessarily erase the material needs of middle-class reformers. Bayard longs for a room filled with books, art works, pipes, and fishing rods: the products of the leisure class that has trained him for the ministry. Much of the plot of *A Singular Life* is taken up with Bayard's attempts to earn enough money to provide a suitable home for the woman he wants to marry, Helen Carruth. Helen is the daughter of one of his seminary professors and is used to material comforts, and Bayard marries her only after he has inherited some property from his uncle. He initially rejects the idea of marriage on the grounds that it is incompatible with his work; he cannot imagine fulfilling his social role as middle-class husband while also laboring among the poor in Angel Alley. Yet he also cannot imagine marrying anyone other than a middle-class, conventional heroine.

Bayard realizes that to earn a good living as a minister he will have to succumb to the increasing professionalization of the clergy. As the narrator comments, "It is at once the saddest and healthiest thing about the work of a man of God that it is subject to market laws, to fashion, to prejudice, to envy, and to poor judgment, like other work" (*SL* 79).[10] From Bayard's perspective, this subjection is often more sad than healthy, and at various points in the novel he and his readers cringe as he compares job offers with his seminary classmates; undergoes a job interview in a stuffy, wealthy church; and is snubbed by other clergymen for attempting to do God's work from outside the bounds of institutionalized religion. At the same time, Bayard shares his classmates' concern with material wealth and comforts, and for that reason his status as martyr is all the more conflicted.

The fact that Bayard has to try to overcome his class-consciousness in order to be a social reformer also helps make him a realistic practitioner of Christian socialism, leading one contemporary reviewer to praise the novel's "timeliness . . . in the present days of Brotherhood Churches and men of Dr. Herron's stamp."[11] In the 1890s George Davis Herron's influential sermon, "The Message of Jesus to Men of Wealth," had denounced the false virtues and competitive individualism of the wealthy and promoted the importance of a socially responsible, applied Christianity. Bayard rejects the competitive individualism he sees in main-line churches, working instead to reform the oppressed. In doing so, he joined a line of other fictional ministers who left the church to work among the underclass, including those depicted in Mrs. Humphrey Ward's *Robert Elsmere* (1888) and William T. Stead's *If Christ Came to Chicago* (1894).[12]

Contemporary reviewers of *A Singular Life* saw Phelps's writing as more "artistic" than these "popular books," especially ones "that have no other quality than . . . an assault on the feelings."[13] Phelps probably would have been happy with this comment, especially since she believed that if a writer sacrifices "truth or beauty to didactics, he is, in so far, no artist" (*CL* 265). Bayard represented for her a figure of truth and beauty who could recognize the problems of the underclass while still retaining his aesthetic sensibilities and physical beauty. In *The Story of Avis* (1877), a book written earlier in Phelps's career, she had seen these qualities as being inherently opposed. Avis, who is a gifted painter, has "to be a little color blind to misery for beauty's sake."[14] Once she loses this color blindness in her efforts to be a good wife and mother, she also must renounce her art. Bayard comes closer to combining beauty and truth than Avis had been able to do, but he finally cannot be both a middle-class husband for Helen and a minister to the poor. Death seems to be the only way for him to escape the conflict these dual roles pose. In this sense, he faces a dilemma similar to that of Perley Kelso in another of Phelps's early novels, *The Silent Partner* (1871). Perley wants to improve the lives of the workers in the factory that her father owns, attaching herself in particular to a woman named Sip Garth. They develop a strong partnership, both renouncing marriage in order to work for their cause of reform. But in the end, an insoluble division separates them: "I was only *among* [the workers]," Perley says, while "Sip is *of* them; she understands them and they understand her; so I left her to her work, and I keep to my own."[15] So too can Bayard at best be among the destitute alcoholics in Angel Alley, not of them; his death saves him from becoming fully assimilated into their underclass world.

It is fitting, in this context, that one of Bayard's most prized possessions is a copy of Guido Reni's painting of Saint Michael the Archangel (fig. 1).[16] At various points in the novel Phelps creates a parallel between Bayard and Michael: Bayard adopts a "grand Saint Michael look" that is "half of scorn and half of pity" (*SL* 185). When Bayard himself looks at the painting in his study, he encounters this same look: Michael stares at him "with that absence of curiosity which belongs to remote superiority" (*SL* 175). Michael too is in the world but not quite of it, his "foot on the dragon" and "his head . . . in the skies" (*SL* 397). Furthermore, the painting does its work within the safe confines of the study, representing worldly concerns while also remaining distant from them. Like Bayard, and like Phelps, it works its ethical purpose by maintaining some detachment from the real world.

As *A Singular Life* was going to press, Phelps wanted to title it either "Emanuel Bayard" or "Bayard." She eventually chose a more general

Figure 1. Guido Reni, *Saint Michael the Archangel* (1635), from a copy of the Tauchnitz edition of the *Marble Faun*, in the author's collection.

title, but her working title suggests the intense identification she had with the character whom she would later call her "dearest hero" (*CL* 273). "The book is twice as long as any I have written, and my soul is in it," she wrote to Henry Oscar Houghton, indicating her personal investment in it.[17] This identification stems, I think, largely from Bayard's embodiment of the conflict between social action and private contemplation—the desire to curl into a "shell of solitude"—that she faced in her own life. Yet Bayard also bears striking similarities to Phelps's father, Austin, a minister and professor at Andover Seminary who suffered extreme insomnia and nervousness because of vocational anxieties. As a professor of homiletics, Austin Phelps argued that pulpit oratory was a strong agent of personal and social change. He also felt guilty that his time writing sermons and books took him away from more overt social action. "My conscience condemned what my intellect craved," he wrote in his memoirs, "and my intellectual aspirations crushed my conscientious convictions. Repose in my work was impossible."[18] Only in death, his daughter concluded, did he end these personal struggles, when "he who starved for rest" at last found "the repose of The Still Hour."[19] Phelps herself, in the meantime, had no such moment of repose; she seems to have inherited some of his ambivalence about the twin callings of the life of the mind and a life of public service.

In one sense we can read Emanuel Bayard's struggles in terms of Phelps's attempts to confront the death of her father. (She wrote *A Singular Life* just three years after editing Austin's memoirs.) Like Austin Phelps, Bayard is a minister who struggles to reconcile his pleasure at leading an intellectual life in his study with his desire directly to effect social change. And like Austin, he finds repose in the "still hour" of death; in his final moments he "fell into a sleep so gentle that [his wife's] heart leaped with hope" (*SL* 419). By rewriting her father in *A Singular Life*, Phelps specifically locates this hope in the possibility of a life in which "intellectual aspirations" and "conscientious convictions" can coexist.

If Bayard helped Phelps cope with the death of her father, we can also see him as reflecting some of the specific anxieties that marked Phelps's profession of authorship. Like Bayard, to take one example, Phelps valued the time that she spent writing in her own private study. Ironically, she was so associated with the calm of her study that one biographical account of her includes an engraving of her at work in it (fig. 2). "All the day the sun shines in as cheerfully as it can," we are told, "struggling through those little windows and those little panes. There are subdued green curtains at these windows; and about the room are books, pictures, a few easy chairs, tables, and many of the nothings which make a study pleasant."[20] Just as the sun can only partially penetrate this private space, so too can readers of this account only get a carefully constructed glimpse of a woman who

Figure 2. Elizabeth Stuart Phelps's study, Andover, Mass., from R. H. Stoddard et al., *Poets' Homes* (Boston, 1879). Courtesy, Peabody Essex Museum, Salem, Mass.

herself rarely appeared in public: a privacy that she justified by an appeal to the higher "ideals" of her art.

Yet also like Bayard, Phelps had to practice that art within the context of an increasingly professionalized marketplace. She spoke contemptuously of the "transcendent sphere" occupied by those who claimed that they "[did] not write for money" (*CL* 79), and she made sure that she herself was well paid for her labor: she negotiated a payment of $5,000, for example, for serialization and book rights to *A Singular Life*.[21] Phelps's concern with the market value of her fiction was in part practical. Single until age forty-four, she supported herself through her writing. She married Herbert Ward in 1888 (six years before publishing *A Singular Life*), but she continued to assume financial responsibilities, specifically for the marriage while her husband (himself a writer and minister) spent time yachting and pursuing other leisure activities.[22]

During the 1890s, however, it became increasingly difficult for Phelps to maintain her market value in the face of competition with mass-produced fiction. Although *A Singular Life* sold relatively well—

54,000 copies within four years—it paled in comparison to "bestsellers" like *Ben Hur*, which at the height of its popularity sold 4,500 copies monthly.[23] At the same time, Phelps's editors were becoming less generous than they had previously been. As Susan Coultrap-McQuin has shown, Phelps was vexed when some editors began to reject her work and insist that she submit a completed manuscript before she received a contract. Having made her first successes writing for "gentleman publishers" like James T. Fields, she found herself becoming impatient with the market laws enforced by a new, professional class of editors and publishers, who possessed expert managerial as well as literary skills.[24] She was particularly irritated when her own father-in-law, who was also her editor, requested that she reduce her fee. "I cannot remember that a *reduction* of my price has ever been offered me," she wrote him. "I cannot, of course, afford to write for your columns upon the terms proposed."[25]

Even as Phelps negotiated this growing commercialization of letters, she also worked to develop a theory of moral realism that identified literature, like her father's oratory, as a practice that could combine high intellectual standards with the promotion of social change. Her interest in realism was part of her parental legacy; as a writer, her mother had focused on everyday life—a practice that her father endorsed. Indeed, Austin Phelps reported that

> it was one indication of the growth of [his wife's] mind during the closing years of her life, that she attached less value than she had previously done, to *fiction* as a medium of conveying truth. In her maturest efforts, she drew but little upon the resources of her own invention. Real life became more exclusively her chosen source of materials. Upon principle and by preference, she made real characters the object of her study, and facts the subject of her pen. For this purpose, she kept a distinct diary whenever she went on a journey; and scarcely would she suffer a brief excursion from her home to pass, without some contribution to her stores.[26]

Such a passage gives further support to Joan Hedrick's recent discussion of nineteenth-century "parlor literature" as a precursor to women's writing generally and realism in particular. The personal diaries and letters that women routinely wrote helped them develop detailed skills of observation, which in turn led them to claim authority as observers of everyday life. As Henry James put it in *The Nation* in 1865, "We believe ... that the greatest successes in this line [of realism] are reserved for that branch of the school which contains the most female writers; for if women are unable to draw, they notoriously can at all events paint, and this is what realism requires."[27] James's assumption here seems to be that drawing requires more originality and invention (coded masculine) than does the imitation or copying associated with painting (coded feminine), a view that is similar to that expressed by Austin Phelps.

As the younger Phelps worked to define her sense of realism, she was less invested than her father in the distinction between dangerous "invented" fiction and actual facts. Instead, she focused her attention on the way in which literary fiction could be motivated by an ethical purpose. As we have seen, truth-telling, for her, necessarily included an attention to the moral dimension of life. For this reason, she saw little difference between the goals of "the realist," "the romanticist," and "the idealist." If there was a distinction among these "contending schools," she claimed, it was "not so much one of artistic theory as of the personal equation," the artist's "personal impression as to what life is" (*CL* 259–60). In this sense, too, Phelps's literary practice was linked to a strong sense of individualism: subjective "personal impressions" were at once a key to "the real" and a justification for self-reliance and authorial control. "'Your work is what you are,'" Phelps wrote in her memoirs, echoing a comment made by Hall Caine at a meeting of the Century Club (*CL* 260). Inherent in this comment is the potentially disabling assumption that no writer can rise above his or her own experiences. But Phelps endorsed it ("Just here, I venture to suggest, lies the only important, uncontested field in a too familiar war," she added) in order to suggest that literary labor promotes—and defines—a strong sense of individuality.

Phelps ultimately identified work as her primary life-force and, even more, as the source of the immortality of the soul. In "A Plea for Immortality" (1880), she captured this idea in a quote attributed to Victor Hugo: "I perceive that the soul shall live forever because I know what I have done."[28] And doing for her was intimately related to writing. As a writer, she claimed individual authorial rights that led her to demand fair compensation for her writing and to reject other kinds of work. These rights, in turn, were grounded in her conception of eternal life. Drawing on social-Darwinian conceptions of the survival of the fittest, Phelps eventually developed a belief in a "law of spiritual selection" in which the "strength of individuality" is "proportional to the strife for eternal existence." This struggle, moreover, "is no light matter, like ladies' calisthenics"; instead, "the athletics of the soul are virile."[29] Phelps's notion of eternal life, then, justified her practice of a mode of individualism that was usually associated with the "virile" activities of men. In this way, Phelps used biblical precepts to convert spiritualism from "women's work" into a model of strong "masculine" individualism. And within this model she found a particular model for her own authorship: a model that justified literary labor as part of the valid—and "virile"—work that will eventually win the struggle for immortality.

Armed with this well-developed sense of individualism, Phelps was able to pitch her practice of moral realism against the realistic project associated with William Dean Howells, whom she called the "chief exponent" of realism in America. In her memoirs, she explicitly challenged a passage in *Literary Friends and Acquaintance* in which Howells claimed that the work of writers such as Hawthorne, Emerson, and Stowe was "marred by the intense ethicism that pervaded . . . the New England mind. . . . They still helplessly pointed the moral in all they did. . . . New England yet lacks her novelist, because it was her instinct and her conscience to be true to an ideal of life rather than to life itself" (*CL* 260–61). Phelps disagreed, arguing that "moral character is to human life what air is to the natural world; —it is elemental" (*CL* 261). If moral character is part of "the truth," furthermore, and being "an accurate truth-teller" is necessary to being a "literary artist," then there is no conflict between defending literary value and having moral influence.

Even as Phelps was willing to challenge Howells's definition of realism, she also realized that his comment in *Literary Friends and Acquaintance* was only "one of the latest phrases of the school of art" associated with realism (*CL* 260). For this reason, it would be misleading to take this comment as the definitive word on Howells's critical stance. Later in his career, Howells himself endorsed some of the tenets of Christian socialism, and his novel *Annie Kilburn* (1888) anticipates *A Singular Life* in its depiction of the minister Julius Peck. What interests me is the fact that Phelps chose to (mis)read Howells in this way, setting her own emphasis on writing with an ethical purpose against his criticism of an "intense ethicism." She distinguished herself from Howells not in order to denigrate her own art but rather to make a claim for its importance within theories of realism. Unlike a reviewer in the *Dial*, who claimed that Phelps was "an idealist of the old school, the school of Ouida on the one hand and Ruskin on the other; an idealist of the kind that is sternly opposed to the realist with an impassable bar between," Phelps saw herself as a writer who could practice realism without sacrificing the "idealism" of a certain ethical stance.[30] In this respect, her position complicates the assumption—voiced most recently by Michael Davitt Bell—that American women writers at the turn of the century "were more concerned with achieving distinction as 'serious' artists than with securing wide moral influence."[31] "Serious" art and moral influence were not antithetical concepts in Phelps's view, and she was willing to take on a writer like Howells precisely because he seemed to her to suggest that they were.

Phelps's disagreements with Howells are also revealed in their correspondence during the ten years when he was editor of the *Atlantic*. In 1874, for example, she sent him some poems that were, as she told him, "in punishment for the bad opinion you expressed of some verses" she had sent earlier. "If you do not like these," she continued," I shall write you an epic, and so on till you treat me better."[32] She was even more annoyed with him in 1881 when he asked her to cut her serialized novel *Friends: A Duet* in order to make room for a piece by Henry James. "The very fact that there is so much of Mr. James makes it more important to me that my story should have its fair artistic effect. You will know, from your own experience, how vital these matters are to an author."[33] That same year, Howells published *Dr. Breen's Practice,* an account of a woman doctor who ends up forgoing her career in order to get married. When this novel appeared, Phelps already had in press *Doctor Zay,* a competing account of a woman doctor who manages to combine marriage and career. Acknowledging the similarity of the books, Phelps wrote to Howells with her blunt assessment of Dr. Breen. "I don't feel that Dr. Breen is a fair example of professional women," she wrote; "indeed I know she is not for I know the class thoroughly from long personal observation under unusual opportunities." Yet Phelps felt that this was "all the better for *my* doctor, who will contrast as gloriously in that respect, as Alas! she will suffer in comparison with your work in others."[34] Phelps neither trashes Howells's novel nor assumes a false modesty; she seems to see herself as a peer who, in this case, has a certain narrative authority based on experiential knowledge. Phelps's complaint with Howells here is not so much about ethics as it is about the powers of observation. She ends her letter by quoting Herbert Spencer's praise for novels that "diverge from those 'plots' which rarely occur in actual life." In this case, Phelps claims to know more about such actuality than Howells does.

Although many of Phelps's disagreements with Howells sprang from substantive disagreements about the nature of her art, they were also motivated by her loyalty to other writers whom she saw as writing with an ethical purpose. The list of writers whom Howells identified as marred by "the New England mind" included not only Phelps but also a number of her friends, including Stowe, Oliver Wendell Holmes, and John Greenleaf Whittier; and Phelps was eager to defend these allies. She was especially adamant in her defense of Stowe, whom she considered "the foremost woman of America" (*CL* 138).[35] Even as Phelps identified herself as a realist, she also allied herself with Stowe's tradition of social writing. In Phelps's 1881 novel *Friends: A Duet*, the character Reliance Strong had prophesied that someone would "do for these poor slaves [to drink] what Harriet Stowe did for the black [slaves]."[36] *A Singular Life* was Phelps's attempt to fulfill this prophecy. Once it was published, it was even identified as such; one newspaper claimed that "the book may be related to the moral welfare of to-day as Uncle Tom's Cabin was to the slave issue."[37] In this light, we can also see *A Singular Life* as Phelps's attempt to extend the sentimental tradition established by Stowe into a realist novel.

In reaching to these literary precedents, Phelps was also looking for a model of how to be a social reformer without having to be in the public spotlight, how to work for the social good while also making her living as a professional writer. As we saw at the beginning of this essay, that dilemma had everything to do with Phelps's stage fright, which was a sign both of her fear of exposing herself to the public and of her commitment to writing as a "literary art" that required all of her productive energies. This commitment, in turn, suggests three conclusions about how we might think about her authorship, as well as that of other nineteenth-century women writers.

First, Phelps's case suggests that writing was valuable to her because it produced certain individual rights: in this case, the right to save one's energy for intellectual labor; to mediate "the truth" through oneself; and to haggle with editors and publishers about the conditions of production. If "your work is what you are," as Phelps argued, then you are your work; authority to write comes from your knowledge of yourself. Although Phelps did not write in a vacuum, she did value solitude, working in a study away from her house; refusing to read reviews of her own work; and not sharing manuscripts of her work with anyone until they were completely finished. To this extent, Phelps embodies a Romantic ideal of authorship that privileges the solitary artist who has certain rights over her work. Yet she also saw her solitude, ultimately, as a form of social action; although she endured stage fright on the public platform, her solitary writing gave her a means through which to be connected to the world.

The maxim that "your work is what you are" also suggests a certain parallel between life and art: a parallel that, in Phelps's case, makes it particularly inviting to see the character Bayard as a figure of the author. In this sense, the displacement of author into character becomes a mode of self-revelation. Phelps herself admitted that not all writing was self-revelation, especially when it involved hack writing commissioned by a particular publisher: a kind of writing that Phelps found herself doing more of at the end of her career. ("This is not literature," Phelps wrote to Jordan about *The Whole Family*.)[38] But by creating such a strong alliance between authorship and selfhood, Phelps presents a strong case for biographical readings of her work, challenging us to consider the critical implications of reading an author into her text.

A second issue that Phelps's case raises is the importance of class in thinking about notions of authorship. Neither Phelps nor her characters, I have suggested, can escape their own white middle-class consciousness; they can be among the working class but never of them. As Amy Schrager Lang has pointed out in a recent reading of *The Silent Partner,* Phelps's moral realism is always informed by her middle-class values: a fact that effectively alienates her writing from the underclass she wants it to serve. This underclass is also often presented in racialized terms, being described as darker or "dirtier" than the white reformers. Characters in Phelps's novels reach out to this underclass by giving them French prints or taking them shopping or inviting them to afternoon soirees in which they read Dickens and listen to Beethoven. We need to give more attention to the ways in which such class formations undergirded women's writing in the nineteenth century, thinking not only about the ways in which authors struggled to become part of a newly formed professional class, but also about how that class affected the production and reception of their works.

If authorship defined the self for Phelps, my final point is that her authorship was also influenced by her publishers and by other writers and editors, such as Howells and Stowe. Rethinking Phelps in relation to these various influences leads us to ask fundamental questions about literary history and the classifications that we employ to structure that history. Given that Phelps was once in a circle of writers that included Stowe and Howells, why did she lose the battle for literary recognition? Her decision to retreat to her study, rather than to work as a literary editor as Howells did, ultimately may have made her less able to make her ideas have critical currency. Phelps's own ideals—and a moralism stemming from an earlier form of evangelism—may have made her lose literary credibility.

It was difficult to place Phelps into the realist canon as it came to be formed in the early twentieth century. Even critics and publishers who respected her moral purpose did so on the grounds that it remained understated. In 1905, for instance, the editor of *Harper's* admitted to her that in general he was against "any moral preachment as a main *motif*, in fiction," but that he would continue to accept her work as long as she continued to write "a sympathetic human story of such spiritual value that the reader forgot the moral, it was so beautifully veiled."[39] After Phelps's death, any such moralism—veiled or otherwise—became increasingly distasteful to modernist critics. By 1930, Vernon Parrington identified her importance as one of New England's first industrial novelists, but then condemned her as "an emotional woman who lived in a world of sentiment rather than reality."[40]

Studying Phelps's authorship, however, makes it difficult to categorize her—or the realism that she practiced—in any such simple terms. Sentiment and reality were for Phelps inextricably bound together; her role as observer and social critic led her to see sentiment as an elemental part of everyday life. In this sense, we can see realism not simply as a reaction against the excesses of the sentimental and domestic novel, but in some ways as a logical continuation of it. Here I agree with Sharon Harris, who has argued that "while women's literature of the period was also insistent upon the maintenance of a high moral plane, their own position as creator was one of disclaiming superiority except in the realm of observation. It is small wonder, then, that their romanticism or sentimentalism was so often a literature of place and so often ventured into the realms of realism.... All of which signifies the necessity of rethinking the rise of American realism."[41]

Ultimately, then, Elizabeth Stuart Phelps's profession of authorship asks us to consider her contribution to the development of realism even as it recognizes that she was a conflicted practitioner of it: a writer who never fully resolved the tensions between Stowe's sentimental tradition and a new social progressivism and aesthetic of realism. She also never fully resolved the conflicts between being a "professional writer" and a "literary artist." Indeed, one could say that she did not want to resolve these conflicts, since being a professional writer meant earning the money and respect that enabled her to practice her art on her own terms. Nancy Glazener has recently claimed that "the construction of realism" was also "the construction of sentimental and sensational authorship as unprofessional."[42] This particular construction was most strongly voiced by "high" realists such as William Dean Howells and Henry James. But the very fact that Phelps was willing to challenge their constructions, all the while still negotiating fair contracts for her own writing, suggests that such constructions did not silence her but, in many ways, authorized her to define realism in her own terms. And as I hope I have shown, an understanding of Phelps's particular construction of realism can in turn lead us to a deeper understanding of the terms of her work, of realism as a genre, and of the profession of authorship in America.

Notes

1. Elizabeth Stuart Phelps to Gould, October 28, 1892. Quoted in Susan Coultrap-McQuin, "Elizabeth Stuart Phelps: The Cultural Context of a Nineteenth-Century Professional Writer" (Ph.D. dissertation, University of Iowa, 1979), 109.

2. William Charvat, *The Profession of Authorship in America, 1800–1870: The Papers of William Charvat*, ed. Matthew J. Bruccoli (Columbus: Ohio State University Press, 1968; rpt. New York: Columbia University Press, 1992), 3.

3. Elizabeth Stuart Phelps, *Chapters from a Life* (Cambridge: Riverside, 1896), 259, 257. Future references to this work will be cited in the text with the abbreviation "*CL.*"

4. Elizabeth Stuart Phelps to John Greenleaf Whittier, April 5, 1878, Houghton Library, Harvard University, Cambridge, Mass., bMS Am 1844 (325). Published by permission of the Houghton Library, Harvard University.

5. Mary Kelley, *Private Woman, Public Stage: Literary Domesticity in Nineteenth-Century America* (New York: Oxford University Press, 1984).

6. Coultrap-McQuin gives a more extended discussion of Phelps as an invalid in "Elizabeth Stuart Phelps," 103–13.

7. Elizabeth Stuart Phelps, *A Singular Life* (Boston: Riverside, 1894), 11. All subsequent quotations from this text will be to this edition and will be cited in the text with the abbreviation "*SL*."

8. On Riis and his relation to realism, see David E. Shi, *Facing Facts: Realism in American Thought and Culture, 1850–1920* (New York: Oxford University Press, 1995), 190–92.

9. Munroe Stevens, *The "A Singular Life" Reviewed and Gloucester Vindicated* (privately printed, 1897).

10. As I will discuss later in this essay, Phelps's father Austin, a professor of homiletics at Andover Seminary, bears striking similarities to Emanuel Bayard. Specifically, he worried, like Bayard, about the professionalization of the clergy and the interest of young ministers in "careers" and upward mobility rather than preaching the word of God. "A preacher had better work in the dark . . . than to vault into an aerial ministry in which only the upper classes shall know or care anything about him," he wrote in 1881 (quoted in Russel Hirst, "The Sermon as Public Discourse: Austin Phelps and the Conservative Homiletic Tradition in Nineteenth-Century America," in Gregory Clark and S. Michael Halloran, eds., *Oratorical Culture in Nineteenth-Century America* [Carbondale: Southern Illinois University Press, 1993], 101).

11. Edith Baker Brown, "A Novel of Emotion," *The Bookman* 3 (May 1896): 262.

12. On Herron and the social gospel, see Susan Curtis, *A Consuming Faith: The Social Gospel and Modern American Culture* (Baltimore: Johns Hopkins University Press, 1991), 195–206.

13. Brown, "A Novel of Emotion," 262.

14. Elizabeth Stuart Phelps, *The Story of Avis*, ed. Carol Farley Kessler (New Brunswick: Rutgers University Press, 1985), 159.

15. Elizabeth Stuart Phelps, *The Silent Partner* (Old Westbury, N.Y.: The Feminist Press, 1983), 293. Also see Amy Schrager Lang, "The Syntax of Class in Elizabeth Stuart Phelps's *The Silent Partner*," in Wai Chee Dimock and Michael T. Gilmore, eds., *Rethinking Class: Literary Studies and Social Formations* (New York: Columbia University Press, 1994), 284. It is notable that Perley, like Bayard, sees marriage as being incompatible with her social work.

16. Although Phelps alludes to a painting of St. Michael with the dragon, the only painting of St. Michael by Guido Reni that I have been able to locate pictures him conquering the devil (*Saint Michael the Archangel*, now

located at the Santa Maria della Concerzione, Rome). Phelps may have had the wrong painter in mind, or she may have conflated the devil with the form of the dragon.

17. Elizabeth Stuart Phelps [Ward] to Henry Oscar Houghton, August 12, 1894, Houghton Papers, Houghton Library, bMS Am 1648. Publication is by permission of the Houghton Library, Harvard University.

18. Quoted in Elizabeth Stuart Phelps, *Austin Phelps, A Memoir* (New York: Charles Scribner's, 1891), 40. For a general discussion of Austin Phelps's oratory, see Hirst, 78–109.

19. *Austin Phelps: A Memoir,* 183.

20. R. H. Stoddard et al., *Poets' Homes: Pen and Pencil Sketches of American Poets and Their Homes,* 2 vols. (Boston: D. Lothrop, 1879), II: 98.

21. Coultrap-McQuin, "Elizabeth Stuart Phelps," 203; see also letter from Elizabeth Stuart Phelps Ward to Henry Oscar Houghton, May 4, 1894, Houghton Papers, Houghton Library, bMS Am 1648 (903).

22. Susan Coultrap-McQuin gives an account of this problematic marriage in *Doing Literary Business: American Women Writers in the Nineteenth Century* (Chapel Hill: University of North Carolina Press, 1990), 177–78.

23. James D. Hart, *The Popular Book: A History of America's Literary Taste* (New York: Oxford University Press, 1950), 163, 170.

24. On this shift in Phelps's relation to her publishers, see Coultrap-McQuin, *Doing Literary Business,* 168–92. On the rise of publishing as a managerial profession, see Christopher Wilson, *The Labor of Words: Literary Professionalism in the Progressive Era* (Athens: University of Georgia Press, 1985), 40–62.

25. Elizabeth Stuart Phelps Ward to William Hayes Ward, August 5, 1893, Elizabeth Stuart Phelps Ward Papers (MSS 229), Peabody Essex Museum, Salem, Mass.

26. H. Trusta [Elizabeth Stuart Phelps], *The Last Leaf from Sunny Side,* with a Memorial of the Author, by Austin Phelps (Boston: Phillips, Sampson, and Company, 1853), 86.

27. *The Nation* 1 (September 14, 1865): 345. For a discussion of "parlor literature" and its influence on women's writing, see Joan D. Hedrick, *Harriet Beecher Stowe: A Life* (New York: Oxford University Press, 1994), 76–88.

28. Elizabeth Stuart Phelps, "A Plea for Immortality," *Atlantic Monthly* 45 (February 1880): 279.

29. Elizabeth Stuart Phelps, *The Struggle for Immortality* (Boston: Houghton Mifflin, 1889), 148, 141, 146.

30. Review of *Chapters from a Life, Dial* 22 (January 16, 1897): 58.

31. Michael Davitt Bell, *The Problem of American Realism: Studies in the Cultural History of a Literary Idea* (Chicago: University of Chicago Press, 1993), 172. For a related view, see Elizabeth Ammons, *Conflicting Stories: American*

Women Writers at the Turn into the Twentieth Century (New York: Oxford University Press, 1992), who argues that late nineteenth-century women were united by their "avowed ambition . . . to be artists" (4).

32. Elizabeth Stuart Phelps to William Dean Howells, September 24, 1874, Houghton Library, Harvard University, Cambridge, Mass., bMS Am 1784 (515). Publication is by permission of the Houghton Library, Harvard University.

33. Elizabeth Stuart Phelps to William Dean Howells, February 9, 1881, Houghton Library, bMS Am 1784 (515). Published by permission of the Houghton Library, Harvard Library. In 1906, Phelps would have a similar reaction to James's contribution to *The Whole Family*, a composite novel by twelve authors that was the brainchild of Howells and Elizabeth Jordan. This novel was first published in serial form in *Harper's Bazar*, which Jordan edited, and Phelps was commissioned to write a chapter immediately after James's. She found James's contribution "long and heavy" and took her own character in an entirely different direction. She was paid $750 for her efforts while James earned $400: Phelps's vision for the novel clearly had a higher market value. See Alfred Bendixen, Introduction to *The Whole Family, A Novel by Twelve Authors* (New York: Ungar Publishing, 1987), xxxii, xix. Howells, James, and Phelps contributed to one other collaborative book as well. *In After Days: Thoughts on the Future Life* (New York: Harper and Brothers, 1910) included essays on the afterlife by these three writers as well as by John Bigelow, Thomas Wentworth Higginson, Henry M. Alden, William Hanna Thompson, Guglielmo Ferrero, and Julia Ward Howe.

34. Elizabeth Stuart Phelps to William Dean Howells, November 2, 1887, Houghton Library, bMS Am 1784 (515). Published by permission of the Houghton Library, Harvard University. For a brief discussion of these two novels, along with Sarah Orne Jewett's *A Country Doctor*, see Nancy Glazener, *Reading for Realism: The History of a U.S. Literary Institution, 1850–1910* (Durham: Duke University Press, 1997), 135–40.

35. One of the most humbling moments of her life, she later reported, was having Oliver Wendell Holmes read one of her poems to Stowe on the occasion of Stowe's seventieth birthday (*CL* 138).

36. Quoted in Carol Farley Kessler, *Elizabeth Stuart Phelps* (Boston: Twayne, 1982), 96. Kessler also points out that Phelps wrote in a letter to Richard Watson Gilder that her novella *Jack the Fisherman* owed more than half of its success "to its great moral story; as with 'Uncle Tom' on the larger plan."

37. Quotation from *The Union Signal* in Stevens, *Gloucester Vindicated*, 7.

38. Quoted in Kessler, *Elizabeth Stuart Phelps*, 117.

39. Letter from H[enry] M[ills] Alden to Elizabeth Stuart Phelps Ward, September 22, 1905, Miscellaneous Manuscripts "A," American Antiquarian

Society, Worcester, Mass., Box 1, Folder 3. Ironically, the next letter in this collection from Alden to Ward, dated May 29, 1906, rejects a story she had sent him.

40. Vernon Parrington, *Main Currents in American Thought*, 3 vols. (New York: Harcourt Brace, 1930), III: 61.

41. Sharon M. Harris, *Rebecca Harding Davis and American Realism* (Philadelphia: University of Pennsylvania Press, 1991), 18.

42. Glazener, *Reading for Realism*, 13.

Periodicals Back (Advertisers) to Front (Editors): Whose National Values Market Best?

Martha Banta

Scholars who depend upon the material evidence provided by print texts are increasingly concerned over the consequences as libraries and archives rush to save space by converting the book from its tactile "thingness" into an "essence" that hovers inside computer data banks. Placing that particular crisis aside (if crisis it is), I begin by referring to another kind of annihilation of evidence, one that occurred decades ago: the serious defacement visited upon serial runs of popular magazines once they began to turn up in library collections in sadly reduced form, their covers and advertising pages ripped away by various hands.

One reason for the disappearance of periodical covers is easy to determine; works by popular artists such as Thomas Nast, Charles Dana Gibson, Maxfield Parrish, J. C. Leyendecker, and Norman Rockwell have been pilfered for personal pleasure or as saleable commodities. The motives for such venal vandalism of cover illustrations are, regrettably, understandable, but the eradication of advertising sections would seem to have been caused by simple idiocy or by the more complex idiocy caused by bottom-line concerns. It costs more to bind bulk; eliminating "unnecessary" advertisements saves libraries money.

After all, is not the only material that counts front-of-the-book editorial matter? Is it not up there that a magazine's vision is made solely, wholly manifest?

This essay suggests that "the whole story" is not told until we "read" all the evidence that is spread before us from the front to the back of the book. It is necessary to understand, however, that the examples offered here—taken from issues of *Life* that appeared between 1883 and 1918—form a special case, a particular set of circumstances whereby various interests came into intriguing (often conflicting) juxtaposition, but the case is one that still has applicability to any number of periodicals once advertisements became an integral part of their material entity.

Call up the references made by Steven Fink's essay to the various phases by which an author moves from being unpaid and unread to an author who has become part of a paying corporate enterprise. In doing this, we can see that the front of the book is, for *Life*, the fourth phase in action: the place where authors and editors are at work for a magazine publisher. The back of the book represents the third phase: it is the space wherein authors receive public notice by means of publishers' advertisements. The following examples from *Life* remind us also that, while effective advertising implies that authors will be read and will receive royalty checks, periodicals and publishing houses are alike in their need to advertise themselves.

What took place within the covers of *Life* largely resulted from the convergence of two basic factors: the degree to which advertising revenue had become vital to *Life*'s fiscal health by the turn of the last century and *Life*'s self-designated role as a medium for casting a satiric and comical eye upon the flaws and foibles of American society, culture, and politics. This essay focuses upon but one element of the many that make any analysis of *Life* a worthwhile enterprise: the strongly pacifist, anti-imperialist stand taken in the front of the books by its editors, artists, and writers over a thirty-five-year period and the expansionist implications of items put up for sale in the back of the book by advertisers who had quite different views on war, weaponry, and the patriotic call to extend the nation's global reach.

As the corporate entity behind a highly successful ten-cent weekly, the Life Publishing Company gave its readers two magazines: what filled the pages in the front of *Life*, and what was placed on view at the back of the book. Inevitably strange discrepancies appeared over the years as pacifist principles clashed against militant ideologies. As we approach the contradictory ways by which *Life* presented itself both front and back, reflect upon Jay Grossman's essay on the marketing of Whitman's *Leaves of Grass*. It refers to the little "advertisement" Whitman chose to introduce into "Leaves-Droppings," the appendix he placed at the back of the 1856 edition, which includes remarks by an unnamed reviewer regarding the "escaped lunatic" responsible for Whitman's poem. As we shall see, *Life* itself frequently contained both praise and rebuke, claims and counterclaims, within the confines of a single issue. It is this fact that opens up large questions about who was responsible for determining the manner by which *Life* represented itself before the world when taken in its entirety.

First, a look at six front-of-the-book cartoons executed by *Life*'s top-flight cadre of staff artists.

"The Peace of Europe" (December 3, 1885). W. A. Rogers's cartoon neatly lays down *Life*'s editorial view of the lethal situation that has turned the Continent into an armed camp ruthlessly controlled by arrogant aristocrats who place the People at their mercy.

"Next!" (January 26, 1888). Charles Dana Gibson celebrates the manly way by which the United States would quell the war spirit that defines the nature of Europe's corrupt military powers.

"The Old Year's Legacy to the New" (December 31, 1891). W. A. Rogers provides a visual inventory of the sources of social chaos that threaten the "good life" of the nation: on the one hand, problems at home (the Farmer's Alliance, Tammany Hall, Rapid Transit, the Bellamy Solution—socialism, the Silver Question, Labor at War against Capital, the New Rich); on the other hand, problems imported from abroad (Irish Home Rule, the Anarchists, Kaiser Wilhelm, and Armed Peace marked by a mentality of violence that denies the possibility of peaceful solutions).

"A Christmas Satire" (December 22, 1898). F. G. Attwood's cover art continues to project martial blood lust outward upon foreign powers in the year *Life*'s editors were energetically criticizing the war fever sweeping America, stirred by the events of the Spanish-American War and expansionist moves into the Pacific.

"Things of Which We Are Proud" (July 10, 1902). In addition to attacking Trusts, Plutocrats, and corrupt Congressmen, William Walker's cartoon targets the "lynch" mood turned against the Indian, the Filipino, and the Mexican—a mood consistently under attack in *Life*'s editorials.

THE "PEACE OF EUROPE."

NEXT! WHY NOT DISSIPATE THE WAR CLOUD BY A PERSONAL COMBAT, AND LET MR. ALEXANDER, OF PETERSBURG, WORK OFF HIS SUPERFLUOUS ARDOR UPON MR. SULLIVAN, OF BOSTON, FOR INSTANCE.

THE OLD YEAR'S LEGACY TO THE NEW.

"The Gorilla That Walks Like a Man" (December 17, 1914). With the outbreak of war in Europe, cracks began to appear in *Life*'s long-held commitment to pacifism. Charles Dana Gibson's representation of the mythic rape of Belgium testifies to fissures in previous editorial policies that would soon lead to *Life*'s full acceptance of a "Hate the Hun" mentality. Until 1918, however, *Life* used, in addition to the medium of the cartoon, the front of the book to speak through the written word of its abhorrence of war and the imagination of military glory.

"Literature of the War," a book review by Agnes Repplier of September 22, 1898, mocks "the help afforded by the Cuban campaign to the periodical literature of our land."

> How, we wonder, could our magazines have dragged through the long spring and summer months without this splendid stimulus, this never-failing interest and inspiration? The debate which journalism owes the war has been widely and gracefully acknowledged.... But the spirited rivalry of the monthly magazines, their active invasion of the field and the perfection of their equipment, compel us to believe

A CHRISTMAS SATIRE.

THINGS OF WHICH WE ARE PROUD.

THE GORILLA THAT WALKS LIKE A MAN

that most of our literary men, most of our artists, and all of our amateur photographers, have hied them to the war, like the minstrel boy of old, with Kodaks and typewriters slung over their shoulders in place of the obsolete harp. The *Century* for September heads the list, with "Seven Important Articles on the War" printed conspicuously upon its cover; but Scribner presses hard for leadership, playing Mr. Richard Harding Davis as its trump card; the *Review of Reviews* is one long budget of battle; *McClure* and *Munsey* bristle with ships and sailor-boys; and *Harper* and the *Forum* settle down soberly to discuss the situation in a series of political papers.

September 22, 1898, announces a publication in celebration of "The Yankee Navy," purportedly written by Tom Masson, *Life*'s senior humorist in residence.

> Grit, Gumption and Gunnery!—Now Ready. Profusely Illustrated with Original Drawings and by Old Prints of the Period. Price $1.00, bound in cloth, with cover in colors. This work, while being an accurate narrative of the achievements of the American Navy from its inception to the destruction of Cervera's fleet, possesses all the interest and excitement of a story of adventures. The only book on the subject that presents in condensed form the complete history of our Glorious Navy. Other attractive books, illustrated by the best artists, will follow in proper season. LIFE PUBLISHING COMPANY.

A bona-fide advertisement on the face of it, reinforced by the fact of its location outside the magazine's main text, but with Tom Masson's signifying touch (as light-fingered as that of the Artful Dodger), was this not a parody of the real thing?

"The God of Force," a book review of February 15, 1900, allowed no such doubts to weaken its front-of-the-book jabs against the illusory notion of war as high romance.

> It will be remembered that a few years ago a wave of popularity for "bluggy" romances completely wiped out the vogue of sentimentally immoral novels—and most readers welcomed the change, which came as a thunder-storm after a muggy day. The romances were lurid but they cleared the atmosphere. Whether psychologically these stories of war were part of the cause or part of the consequences of a revival of the warlike spirit in England and America, it is difficult to determine. At any rate, within a little while the nations which were reading fighting novels with delight, were engaged in a practical application of the principles of slaughter. And they have been at it ever since—except when busy at Peace Conferences.
>
> In this country, Mr. Crane and Mr. Davis had the courage of their romances, and immediately went to the front to take part in real battles.
>
> In England, Conan Doyle, Kipling and Winston Spencer Churchill have shown an equally prompt desire to get to the scene of real war.
>
> If the men who write the "bluggy" romances show such eagerness to see the actual carnage it is safe to infer that thousands of their readers have been predisposed by these novels to welcome the opportunity of war for adventure. A mind that has fed on warlike images yearns for a glimpse of the reality.
>
> ... Oh, it is a beautiful world that these fighting novelists create for us to live in! Where there is no corner left in it for gentleness, or

charity, or refinement, or art. The god of the world is Force, and they bow down to their leader and follow his flag with enthusiasm.

Life would not let go of its front-of-the-book derision of the public's entrancement by puerile boys' games, fired up by that perennial adolescent in the White House, Theodore Roosevelt. On March 27, 1902, a drama review titled "American Patriotism Dramatized" casts its skeptical eye upon "the new and strenuous light of fighting Imperialism."

> We're getting to be a strenuous Nation, sure enough, and with a large N. We want wars, and if we can't get wars, we want the rumors of wars. If we can't get the rumors of wars, we want plays about wars with heroic or commercial Americans as the heroes. The peaceful and the pastoral can go to the Dickens. We want Yankee Doodle and the Star Spangled Banner, and we want the Yankee and the Spangles emphasized.... Of late we have become very Scrappy Dan, and, therefore, we find great enjoyment in a play like "Soldiers of Fortune" [based on Richard Harding Davis's novel], which has just had its first presentation in New York.
>
> A short time ago there was a class of young men-about-town in New York who were always looking for a fight. The late Recorder Smyth sent one of them to Sing Sing and that particular branch of industry received a set-back. In the West the advance of civilization put rather a damper on the "shooting-up" tendencies of some of its younger inhabitants. But the temperament and youthful hot blood still remained and a lot of it found vent in the Spanish-American war and is still trying to find a fighting chance in the Philippines. All this makes possible "Soldiers of Fortune," which a few years ago, notwithstanding its cleverness of construction and lines, would have been laughed at on Broadway and relegated to the Bowery, where the fighting blood was always on tap.

Twelve years later, on the verge of the onset of the Great War in Europe, an item of May 21, 1914, captioned "There Is No War," derides the home-grown war spirit spreading along the Mexican border.

> Nothing better proves that there is no war than to reflect upon the statements of our military friends during recent years. They have been wheedling us into buying more and more battleships on the ground that that is the best way to prevent war; that the best way to prepare for peace is to prepare for war. If, therefore, our peace

possibilities are to be reckoned by the comparative size of our navy and that of Mexico, it is plain to be seen we are so well prepared for war with Mexico that anything but peace is practically impossible. Accordingly, the news of killings and invadings and mobilizings is not to be credited.

In August of 1914 war erupted across Europe. On September 10 Life Publishing Company placed an advertisement in *Life*'s advertising section—its own satire upon the marketing of war-loving "coffee-table" volumes—that promotes sales of a collection of *Life*'s antiwar cartoons. The advertisement, headed by "War as viewed by *Life*," centers its art work upon the Skeleton of Death and buzzards hovering over a corpse-strewn battlefield. The copy reads, "A handsome art portfolio, printed in colors and black and white, on coated paper. A reproduction in extenso of the famous war pictures, dramatic and satiric, which have appeared in LIFE during the past ten years. A pictorial arraignment of War."

By means of the fake advertisement devised by Tom Masson in 1898 and the directness of this advertisement of 1914, editorial indictments against the war spirit could circle from front to back. However, the time would come, and soon, when the ideological matter contained in *Life*'s own advertisements became increasingly complicitous with the marketing promotions provided by its advertising clients.

Before taking up instances in which the gap between front and back begins to dissolve, look at six sample advertisements in which American book publishers and periodicals herald "The Literature of War" during the gory glory years between the Spanish-American War and the start of the First World War, even as *Life*'s staff of artists and authors continues to insist upon its own antimilitaristic policies.

From the "War Number" of *McClure's Magazine* (May 26, 1898), it would appear that every army general, journalist, and military historian in town was straining to break into the popular publishing scene.

Scribner's and the Review of Reviews Company (December 22, 1898) spread their advertisements across the back of the book in the same issue whose cover features F. G. Attwood's antiwar cartoon "A Christmas Satire" (see p. 178).

In the week prior to *Life*'s censorious editorial declaring that "There Is No War" in Mexico, *Collier's* advertisement of May 14, 1914, banners the news that its own "Land & Sea Forces" have been "Or-

> **10 CENTS.** **WAR NUMBER** **10 CENTS.**
>
> ## McCLURE'S MAGAZINE for JUNE
>
> CONTAINING AMONG OTHER IMPORTANT FEATURES:
>
> GENERAL FITZ-HUGH LEE. Spanish Rule in Cuba.
> Splendidly Illustrated. Many unpublished photographs.
>
> HOW THE WAR BEGAN. By Stephen Bonsal.
> Experiences with the Blockading Fleet. Illustrations from photographs taken on board the "New York."
>
> GENERAL NELSON A. MILES. Military Europe.
> Personal observations and experiences abroad. Fully illustrated.
>
> STORIES OF THE FIGHTING LEADERS. By L. A. Coolidge.
> Character sketches, anecdotes and portraits of notable men in Army and Navy.
>
> IN THE FIELD WITH GOMEZ. By Grover Flint.
> Illustrated from sketches made in Gomez's camp.
>
> AN AMERICAN IN MANILA. By J. E. Stevens.
> With recent unpublished photographs.
>
> SONGS OF THE SHIPS OF STEEL. By James Barnes.
> Spirited poems of the New Navy, of Turret Jack and the Black Gang, of Rapid Fire Guns and Torpedo Boats.
>
> THE COST OF WAR. By George B. Waldron.
>
> WHEN JOHNNY WENT MARCHING OUT. By W. A. White.
> Home scenes. Leaving for the war. A moving, splendid poem in prose. Illustrations by ORSON LOWELL.
>
> THE HOUSEHOLD OF A HUNDRED THOUSAND.
> By Ira Seymour.
> Social Life in the Army.
>
> HYMN IN THE TIME OF WAR AND TUMULT.
> By Henry Newbolt.
> AND OTHER ARTICLES, STORIES AND PICTURES.
>
> NOTE.—"McCLURE'S MAGAZINE" has Representatives, Contributors, Artists and Photographers with Every Branch of the Army and Navy, and at every scene of probable action. The larger aspects and events of the War will be presented in the most authoritative and interesting manner in its pages from personal observation and experience, with interpretation and comment and with authentic and graphic illustrations. The Magazine is represented at Washington, on the Flying Squadrons, on Admiral Sampson's Fleet, at Hong Kong and Manila; at Tampa, Mobile, and in Cuba; and through its London Office the Magazine is able to secure the most apt and important material from foreign sources.
> FOR SALE EVERYWHERE. 10 CENTS A COPY.
>
> **S. S. McCLURE CO., New York.**

dered to Mexico for Action"—its agents prepared to deal with "whatever happens" south of the border.

Everybody's Magazine (December 31, 1914) features "America on Guard!"—a collection of admonitions by ex-president Theodore Roosevelt who cries out for armed preparedness in terms as energetic as those he had voiced in 1897 in his role as Assistant-Secretary to the Navy prior to the start of the Cuban campaign. Next to this advertisement *Life* places Mark Twain's "A 'War Prayer,'" extracted from the *New York Times*. Which voice would be heard here midst the din?

It follows that if it is good business to promote publications about war, the time was right for promoting the business of selling weaponry to the home front; for if words do not kill, guns do.

Under authorization of the United States Government, Smith & Wesson Revolvers (February 5, 1903) make it possible for "Soldier and civilian alike [to] meet dangerous needs with the confidence that no other revolver but a Smith & Wesson gives." Frederic Remington's *The Last Stand* is offered as a buyer's bonus for display in "The Smoking Room or Den," with *Collier's, Munsey,* and *Country Life* prepared to mail out *Hostiles*—"an Indian picture" by Dan Smith, as further proof of Smith & Wesson's claim that, whenever one dips into the history of the West, its products have been ready to meet the nation's "dangerous needs."[1]

Our War in Two Hemispheres.

The Complete History of the Spanish-American Struggle.
ALBERT SHAW, Ph.D., Editor. Special Chapters by more than thirty contributors.
Published by the Review of Reviews Company. Nearly 1,800 pages, and over 500 illustrations. In three magnificent large octavo volumes.

ADDRESS
THE REVIEW OF REVIEWS COMPANY,
13 Astor Place, New York City.

"Roosevelt's Rough Riders."

COL. ROOSEVELT HIMSELF tells the story of his famous regiment in *Scribner's Magazine*. It begins in January (published December 21st) and runs six months. It is accompanied by a wonderful series of illustrations from photographs taken in the field.

Col. Roosevelt is an experienced writer as well as fighter. He was already well known as a depicter of picturesque adventures before he became famous as a soldier.

How the idea started—who the Rough Riders were—anecdotes about various ones—vivid descriptions of their famous fights—the whole story from first to last —a story of real adventure that everyone will want to read. It can be found only in *Scribner's*, which publishes all Col. Roosevelt writes about the war.

FOR SALE EVERYWHERE;
25 CENTS A COPY; $3.00 A YEAR.

CHARLES SCRIBNER'S SONS, 153-157 Fifth Ave., N. Y.

Three Timely Books.

CHARLES SCRIBNER'S SONS, 153-157 Fifth Ave., N. Y.

Inspired by the transport of American troops abroad, Colt's Patent Fire Arms Mfg. Co. (November 7, 1918) provides a one-paragraph history of its own role in the nation's military achievements (to be supplemented, perhaps, by Helen Nicolay's *The Book of American Wars*, listed below the advertisement under "Books Received"). Colt is pleased to announce that "this great experience now seems to have

Collier's Land & Sea Forces Ordered to Mexico for Action

Whatever happens in Mexico, the forces of *The National Weekly* are ready.

Jack London is our War Correspondent with General Wood and General Funston. His first article in the May 16th issue.

Jimmy Hare, our own War Photographer of the Spanish-American, Russo-Japanese, and Balkan conflicts, is with Rear Admiral Badger.

James B. Connolly, Sailor-War Correspondent, writer of sea tales, is also with the fleet.

Henry Reuterdahl, America's foremost naval artist, is aboard the Dreadnought North Dakota.

Arthur Ruhl, authority on Central and South American problems, is at Vera Cruz.

London, Connolly, Reuterdahl, and Hare are working exclusively for the readers of

Collier's
The National Weekly

"The Double-Squeeze at Villa Borghese," a three-part baseball story by Henry Beach Needham, author of "The Jinx," starts in Collier's May 16th.

Julian Street, with Wallace Morgan, the artist, is "Discovering the United States." The first of his articles, "Abroad at Home"—entertaining travel stories of a new type—will appear in the May 23d issue of Collier's. Watch for it.

If you can't get Collier's at your news stand, clip the coupon.

Once in a long time a publishing house is able to offer an opportunity that is really exceptional. P. F. Collier & Son, publishers of the famous Five-Foot Shelf of Books, have acquired the publishing rights of the Lodge History of Nations—former price $120 and up.

A free booklet has been printed *for you* to tell the story of this remarkable work; and now our enormous manufacturing facilities enable us to offer it at a mere fraction of the former price. We want to send you this free booklet. No obligation, merely clip the coupon.

been but preparation to enable us to serve the United States Government during the present world war." It must, however, apologize for the fact that, by aiding military forces, the company will "disappoint many friends who wish to procure some particular model of Colt revolver or automatic pistol for their own use."

In addition to advertisements that promote print publications devoted to extolling military achievements and the sales of weaponry, a third category of advertisements appears back of the book, written

AMERICA— ON GUARD!

THIS is something every American should look squarely in the face. In just what condition are our defenses? Do *you* know? Does *any one* know? Yes, General Wotherspoon knows. When retiring as Chief of Staff the other day he said: "There are only 45,968 soldiers available for the mobile army within the United States; the coast artillery is short 13,018 men; the regular army is lacking in field guns and ammunition."

THEODORE ROOSEVELT

in a splendidly practical, powerful and suggestive article on this very subject points out precisely what we really need to do right now. Every American owes it to himself to read this article in

for

JANUARY

"THE LAST STAND"

AFTER exhaustive tests the United States Government has put Smith & Wesson Revolvers in the hands of its soldiers. Soldier and civilian alike meet dangerous needs with the confidence that no other revolver but a Smith & Wesson gives.

All Smith & Wesson Revolvers have this monogram trade-mark stamped on the frame. None others are genuine.

For Smoking Room or Den we have published a limited number of copies in exact reproduction of Frederic Remington's strong picture, "THE LAST STAND," on heavy plate paper, 14 x 15 inches in size, ready for framing. We will send, prepaid, a copy to any address for ten cents in silver, together with small reproductions of the pictures which have appeared previously. In the March Pearson's, Collier's, Munsey, Country Life and Town and Country we will reproduce "HOSTILES," an Indian picture by Dan Smith.

SMITH & WESSON

42 STOCKBRIDGE STREET   SPRINGFIELD, MASS.

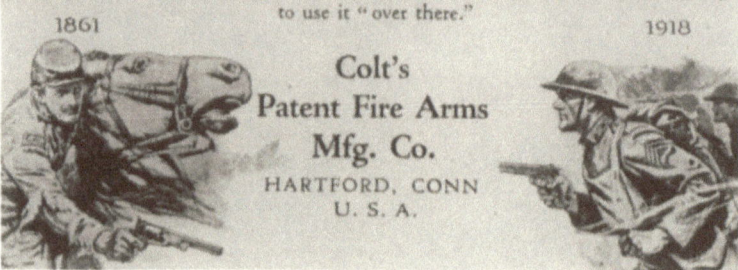

from the slant of all the new "things" there are to sell, now that America's march to war has resulted in the nation's appropriation of new territories.[2]

Advertisements in the January issue of 1899 testify to recently opened up opportunities for travel and commerce. Raymond and

Whitcomb Tours and Tickets touted, "A visit to Hawaii, our new possession, is one of the most delightful possible." A New York agency offered subscriptions to "The Cuba Bulletin"—"indispensable to you because it is alive with topics of vital importance for home-seekers and those . . . contemplating commercial relations with CUBA!" By May 19, 1904, Eastman Kodak felt quite at home around the world.

> In war as in peace the KODAK is at the front. In Cuba and the Philippines, in South Africa, in Venezuela, and now in Korea and Manchuria, the camera most in evidence is the Kodak. The same qualities that make it indispensable to the correspondent make it most desirable for the tourist—simplicity, freedom from dark-room bother, lightness combined with a strength that resists the wear and tear of travel.[3]

Colt Revolvers had the same point to make in May 12, 1914, even before the big war in Europe brought the company back into the active line of military duty.

> Colt Revolvers are unaffected by desert sand or ocean spray. Soldiers and sailors, pioneers and hardy men of action, unhesitatingly intrust their lives to the protection of these arms.

The Heart of Darkness need hold no fears for the new American imperialists venturing into far-flung geographies when equipped with the ever-adaptable American products.[4]

How are we to deal with the discrepancies between back to front of the same periodical? It may help to consider suggestions made by Judith L. Fisher's essay, "Image versus Text in the Illustrated Novels of William Makepeace Thackeray." Fisher works from a narrower base of inquiry than those afforded by the materials drawn from *Life;* she deals solely with discrepancies introduced by Thackeray in the process of his doing double-duty as author and artist for his novels *Vanity Fair* and *Pendennis*. In such a situation (admittedly a rare one), where author and illustrator are one person, readers facing the need to interpret the possible meanings of the prose narrative have their task complicated by the fact that what the author's words say do not necessarily coincide with what the author/artist's pictures show.[5]

Life places an even more arduous demand upon would-be interpreters. First off, there are occasions when gentlemanly objections to foreign wars and expansionism ("America should not impose its policies upon other cultures") expressed on the editorial page are at odds only in degree with the presence of (hardly gentlemanly) cartoons predicated on the same racist arguments ("Why should good Americans, as an advanced race, ever wish to assume the burden of governing unruly savages?") that other anti-imperialists wove into their discourse, whether visual or verbal. Second, on other occasions *Life* might group cartoons that offered sympathetic visual representations of people of color in the same issue in which it cast editorial accusations against Filipinos, Jews, and other non-Ivy League types (for keep in mind that the founding editors of *Life* shared Harvard and Yale in their collective consciousness). Third, to reiterate the fact that is of particular concern to this essay, the magazine's sincere support of antimilitarism rendered in the front of the book is troublingly offset by the products and publications with which it filled its advertising sections.

Judith Fisher's observations are helpful in warning us to take great care when we are faced with visual texts that reside within the same space as print texts, as when Thackeray's single imagination expressed divergent views through his use of both pen sketch and printed text. Fisher remarks, "Readers must determine for themselves how to interweave the visual and the verbal," particularly in cases when illustrations appear "independent of the text and create their own iconography from the details of daily life."[6] Be alert, she suggests, to those "illustrations that seem to be simple reifications of the text but which become symbolic as the reader/viewer moves between text and drawing."

If interpretative snags occur when Thackeray as artist introduces signifying forms at odds with the text offered by Thackeray the author, consider the heightened implications of the conditions created by the contested territory that stretches from the front to the back sections of *Life*. How much more complicated the situation offered by this periodical. Individual issues provide a singular arena up front that mingle the visual and the verbal (differing expressive modes ostensibly channeled through a single editorial mind), while at the back the dual marketing techniques of promotional image and print copy are capable of seeming to subvert all that has come before. What results is nicely summed up by Fisher's comment that "such consistent representation and recurring patterns of juxtaposition between images and between images and words are visual dialogues"—

dialogues "which develop into voices echoing that of the narrator, not really outside the text but not totally embedded within it."

Sharpened awareness of the presence of contentious dialogue certainly aids us when we are in the presence of *Life*'s writers and cartoonists, who push in one direction while still other wordsmiths and illustrators tug at a slant to the periodical's proclaimed ideological stance.

Consider another source of static emanating from the texts provided by *Life:* texts whose meanings hover over the periodical's pages with clashing responses to war and peace that are "not really outside," or "totally embedded within," its covers; texts whose meanings appear to conflict with the marketing of the violence and glory of war in the back of the book because—up front—*Life* is attempting to stand by the credo it laid out in its inaugural issue of January 1883, wherein the periodical was dedicated to the celebration of fun, joy, and the tranquil pursuit of the good life.

Now a shift to a seemingly different set of questions: those posed by yet another of the dual roles *Life* inadvertently found itself enacting: first, what happens when the editors satirize the advertising game as practiced by others; second, what transpires when the editors are enthusiastic participants in self-promotion.[7]

"The Advertising of the Future" (February 16, 1887) merrily casts aspersions against the discomforts of contemporary railroad travel by linking it to the flourishing mortuary business.

"As Advertised" (August 30, 1917) is a compendium of the cliché tags that marketmeisters attach to any and all products, including of course *Life*'s own marketable commodity (see p. 193).

The complicating, complicitous twists and turns by which *Life* tried to clear space between the pleasure it took in satirizing risible advertising ventures and its own absorption in the marketing culture are nicely demonstrated by a sampling of *Life*'s editorial comments set beside examples of *Life*'s own advertisements.

Life's editorial page of December 26, 1901, takes dead aim at the slick techniques used by publishers to sell their novels.

> There is a great deal of money in our national pocket; that's one reason; but another is that novels are being sold like soap, whiskey, cigars, or patent medicine. The publishers advertise them profusely, in the newspapers, in street-cars, on bill-boards, anywhere the public

THE ADVERTISING OF THE FUTURE.

In no spirit of levity LIFE predicts that unless some new method of heating our cars is speedily obtained the railroad advertising of the future, to be honest, will have to read very much as follows:

TO TRAVELERS.

TRY THE
CEMETERY SATCHEL.

One of the greatest conveniences of modern travel. Adds materially to comfort of travelers. In the over-heated cars, holding as it does all the articles of the toilet, together with

OUR POPULAR SHROUD,

which experts state to be the best RECHERCHÉ DUSTER ever manufactured.

THE
Travelers' Novelty Co.,
HOBOKEN.

Trade-Mark.

SECURE BERTHS AT ONCE for the Ice Carnival. Upper Berth, similar in construction to our trade-mark, $4.00. Lower Berth, with ice-box attached, $7.00.

THE SUREDEATH LINE, Limited.
41172 Broadway.

The Holocaust Rapid Transit Company's

Cars are heated by the Celebrated
BURNHARD HEATER.

No difficulty about fires. Fire Insurance Policy and Free Incineration Coupon given away with every first-class ticket on our line.

CLERGYMEN

Of all denominations constantly in attendance. No victim of the Holocaust Rapid Transit Company has ever been known to complain of our service. Low rates to all parts of this world and the next. No return tickets issued.

TICKETS FOR OUR ROUTE AT ALL RESPECTABLE UNDERTAKERS.

NOTICE.

TO GENTLEMEN CONTEMPLATING SUICIDE.

The cars of the Central Railroad of Hohokus are heated by the most approved of modern apparatus, and we feel that we can conscientiously recommend any person who may be tired of life to travel on our road. The chances of escape are **NOT ONE IN TEN THOUSAND**, to say nothing of the crime of which our system relieves our patrons.

E. TERNITY,
General Passenger Agent.

Why Wait?	Full details may be obtained on application	All other means of communication are cold and colorless in comparison.
It is welcome every day in the year.		Now is the *best* time
Don't put it off—do it *now*, while you are thinking about it.		**NOTHING LIKE IT**
No Time For Hesitation	It's a subject well worth considering	It Seems Folly Not to
It's Free Act!	Here's the Opportunity	BEGIN Young Men
Good for Everybody	Are You the Man?	NOW Wanted
START TRAINING WITH US	How Much is It Worth to You?	IT'S YOUR MOVE
The best way to keep good acts in memory is to refresh them.		"Don't make excuses. MAKE GOOD."
"Do it now." Begin tonight		Is Not a Fad
You Will Be Interested		But a Necessity.
ask to be shown **Get Next!**		One Trial Convinces
It is a habit to be encouraged		Get the Original and Genuine
soothing to the senses, satisfying and comforting		The Kind That Will Do You Good
It's easier than you think		No Matter Why Hesitate?
—agrees with everybody.		Where You Live
		Why don't *you* get in line
Keep up with the times!		In a class by itself
"No one thing will give so much pleasure, to so many people, for so long a time, at so little cost."		You can do it Learn to Do It.
GET THE HABIT		*Don't infer, Try it.*
Relished by all. Why Don't *you* try it?		NOW IS THE TIME TO BEGIN
Nothing else compares with it—nothing else is like it.		IF YOU THINK WE'RE TOO ENTHUSIASTIC—see for yourself.
Heard Lots About It	SURELY YOU CAN NOT HESITATE TO AT LEAST INVESTIGATE	
This is a good time **And Here It Is.**	Try This way Next Time:	IN USE ALL OVER THE WORLD!
You'll wonder why you have waited so long.	*Any Man Can Become Expert*	
Once Tried Always Used Act Quickly	It will pay you to inspect this	Don't delay investigating
INSPECTION REQUESTED	SATISFACTION ASSURED	DON'T MISS IT
"THE ONLY WAY" "There's a Reason"	IT'S Don't	THERE is a difference
WAKE UP! NOW IS THE TIME	GREAT Back Out	
ARE YOU ONE OF THE REGULARS? IF NOT, WHY NOT?	It is a present as well as a pressing need	Start
Don't think this over. Be brave, and do it now.	there is no better time than today	Early
IT HAS	There is nothing simpler	**HAVE YOU HEARD ABOUT THIS**
NO	Can you imagine a more delightful way to spend the evenings	LEARN FROM THOSE WHO KNOW HOW
EQUAL	Worth considering **There's Always One Best**	There is no real substitute judge it for yourself

AS ADVERTISED.

eye dwells. The particular fact that they find it most important to bring out is that the books they are selling [do] well. "Our four great stories have all passed the hundred-thousand point," cries one respectable house. "Three binderies, running night and day on our three leading novels, barely keep us supplied," cries another. Another house advertises two books (by the same author) which have sold three hundred and fifty thousand copies apiece. This is the Golden Age of something—one hesitates to call it "letters," yet it is something pleasing and respectable, if not great.... Probably we still spend more for what we drink than for what we read. Good luck, then, to the publishers in their effort to get their full share of the people's spare money. It is better for the country that some of them should get rich, and that successful authors should win modest fortunes, than that the distillers and the brewers should be too abundantly blessed, and bid up the price of race-horses and steam-yachts.

As the clever switch of the tail at the editorial's conclusion suggests, *Life*'s editors were themselves not adverse to filching techniques from the world of commodity salesmanship. During the second week of the infant periodical's existence, the editors helped spank it into lusty life by celebrating *Life* throughout its pages, front and back. They gave center stage to a collection of friendly phrases reprinted under the heading "What Is Said of Us": "bright, attractive countenance," "sensible comment, clever verses, and still cleverer pictures," "fun, persiflage and sarcastic illustrations of passing events," "bright and crisp," "fun and philosophy," "unusual brilliancy and cleverness." This set of commendations culled from *The New York Sun, The New York World, A Woman of Judgment, The Graphic,* and *Mail and Express* was reinforced by the advertisement at the back of the book that heralded "LIFE—a new illustrated weekly. Humorous, Satirical, Refined. Issued Every Thursday. An Able Corps of Contributors."

In 1883 *Life* energetically addressed both potential subscribers and potential advertisers, the two audiences it desperately needed to cultivate during the early months of its struggle to survive. Even after financial welfare was assured, this advertising blurb from September 12, 1889, indicates how adroitly *Life* continued to display itself as a marketable "product" that raised the spirits of sellers and buyers alike by means of joy, escape, fun, the worry-free life.

> Discovered at Last! The elixir of LIFE. One dose every Thursday will positively cure melancholy, moroseness, indigestion, glumness, dullness of trade, blues. Are you glum! Then take LIFE every week. If your business is dull, then advertise in LIFE.

Life's true and enduring product was life, portrayed in its merriest, cleverest, most frolicsome moods. This fact has more than a little to do with the many instances in which the editors expressed how much they deplored all that might threaten life. The periodical's need to define itself (and to market itself) as an antidote to disorder, destruction, and anxiety comes further into focus with two advertisements (one placed by Harper and Brothers, the other by *Life*) that appeared during the first dark days of the Great War.

In the issue of December 31, 1914, Harper's had this to say about its edition of the collected writings of Mark Twain in an advertisement located at the back of the book.

> Be Happy! Now, more than ever, Mark Twain proves a blessing to you! Banish all depression and let in the sunshine of Mark Twain's radiant humor. Revel in the hearty and robust fun of the great storyteller. He is the antidote par excellence for the blues and all species of grouch, melancholy, general debility of the intellect. You may still obtain the Author's National Edition of MARK TWAIN at Special Half Price. "Tomorrow" may be too late!

If the final punch line of the Harper advertisement intrudes an ominous note (Will we still be here tomorrow?), the copy for the advertisement by which *Life* directs an appeal to new subscribers in May 24, 1917, circles even closer to the fact that the war in Europe was no longer at a safe remove from America.

> Sons and Daughters of Uncle Sam, Don't Worry!—If you are poor, you will be able to make more money than ever before, so that doesn't matter. If you are rich, one of two things is certain: either you are depressed over the war or you feel happy about it. If you feel happy about it, there is no cause for worry. If you feel depressed, then one of two things is certain: either you are not a subscriber to LIFE or you don't even buy it on the newsstand. . . . If you become a subscriber, one of two things is certain: either you feel that you are doing your duty or you are as cheerful as anyone can be who is filled to the brim once a week with the spirit of Uncle Sam. In either case, there is no cause to worry.

With these odd little attempts to whistle its way through the graveyard of wartime, *Life* continued to resist worry, war, and weaponry's destructive powers well into 1917. In 1918 a changing of the guard took place in the editorial offices of *Life* that marked the coming to the end of its long-held pacifist stance. Two back-of-the-book advertisements give evidence for the shift from a periodical that for thirty-five years had been under the benign eye of John Ames Mitchell to a journal whose more abrasive editorial position was now fully under the control of Edward S. Martin, who was appointed head editor after Mitchell's death in June 1918.[8] The following advertisements promote books authored by Mitchell and Martin which reflect opposing views—old and new—on how *Life*'s readers should face a world at war.

Under the heading "Getting Away from War," an advertisement that ran in January 10, 1918, singles out the main reason potential buyers would want to read Mitchell's newest (and last) novel. The copy details the pleasures of Mitchell's airy touch—the same touch he had applied, oh so lightly, upon the magazine since its founding in January 1883.

> One of the most interesting human touches that have come to us from the western front is the observation of a soldier who declared the other day that he derived more genuine pleasure in the trenches from the perusal of Jane Austen's works than from any other source. He explained it by saying that the intense strain of modern warfare continued over a period of time, created a kind of passion for idyllic quietness, for the serenity of domestic life.
>
> ... Books are rare that can perform this invaluable service for us. To be able to lose one's self in a good story, which transports us on the wings of fancy to remote regions, which deals with foolish love, and treats with rare humor and nature vivacity those things which invigorate our spirits—surely this is more than worth while at the present moment; it is essential.

In June 1918, the same month Mitchell died, another advertisement appeared in *Life* announcing a collection of war essays to be published by Doubleday, Page and Company that came from Edward Martin's editorial desk. The advertisement excerpts a passage from the editorial Martin had recently addressed to Henry Ford, in which he repudiates Ford's pacifist activities.

> You help to make life pleasant, but war, Henry, helps to make it noble, and if it is not noble it does not matter a damn, Henry, whether it is pleasant or not. That is the old lesson of Calvary repeated at Mons and Ypres, and Liege and Namur. Whether there are more people in the world or less—whether there are Fords, or oxen, makes no vital difference, but whether men shall be willing to die for

what they believe in makes all the difference between a pigsty and paradise. Not by bread alone, Henry, shall men live.

Thirty-five years had passed since *Life*'s initial allegiance to the credo of pleasure and joy, an editorial position that, with marked consistency, had resisted (in ways both frivolous and serious) the myths of war's flamboyance and the moral glory of global expansion. *Life* was now ready to speak in the front of the book to the necessity and/or nobility of war. The reasons for this about-face are many and complex, not to be sorted out in this essay. "Periodicals Back (Advertisers) to Front (Editors)" has simply tried to demonstrate that when we look hard at what appears in print and picture, whether as editorial commentary or as patent marketing ploy, we get a glimpse at how national values are promoted, centaur fashion—with the godhead at the fore and the devil taking the hindmost. Or is it the other way around?

Notes

1. Between November 1902 and September 1903, Smith & Wesson offered other "spirited Indian pictures" by Dan Smith: *Through the Line* and *Outnumbered*. Decades after the close of the Indian wars, Smith & Wesson continues to privilege those moments from the past that authenticate the revolver's usefulness in modern matters of "life and death" requiring "a perfect defense."

2. The turn of the century gave advertisers the opportunity to market "race anxiety," as exampled by *Everybody's Magazine* promotion of the serialization of a new novel by Honoré Willsie, captioned "What Has Became of the Anglo-Saxon in America?" (*Life*, December 3, 1914). How better to justify expansionist moves abroad than to agitate the nerves of "sturdy old Plymouth Rock stock" by telling its members that they have lost their place, "crowded out of their old homes."

3. This Kodak advertisement features a Frederic Remington sketch of *The Correspondent*, a manly figure looking out over a battlefield. It would seem as though Remington's art aided the promotion of whatever kind of "shooting" was required by America's expansionist enterprises: with Smith & Wesson Revolvers or the Kodak Camera.

4. Some manufacturing companies attempted quite a stretch in associating their products with America's claims to military glory. An advertisement of September 15, 1898, for Waltham Watches tried hard to bring this off:

"The men behind the guns have made the American Navy respected the world over and American mechanics at Waltham, Mass., have made the world acknowledge that American watches are the best." Notice the forcefulness of the coercive use of the verb "have made."

5. For further analysis of the dizzying back-and-forth movements between illustration and printed text for which Thackeray was responsible, see Robert P. Fletcher, "Visual Thinking and the Picture Story in *The History of Henry Esmond*," *PMLA* 113 (May 1998): 379–94.

6. Judith L. Fisher, "Image versus Text in the Illustrated Novels of William Makepeace Thackeray," in Carol Christ and John Jordan, eds., *Victorian Literature and the Victorian Visual Imagination* (Berkeley: University of California Press, 1995), 60–87. This and the following quotations are from pp. 63, 65–66.

7. In another odd twist that demonstrates the affinities between the editorial and the advertisement, on June 8, 1905, the Lord and Thomas Agency ran a full-page spread in the back section of *Life* that "editorialized" the sales power of product advertising. How easily *Life*'s editorials could "advertise" and advertisements could "editorialize."

8. Edward Martin took over the weekly task of writing editorials early in *Life*'s career, leaving Mitchell to devote his attention to the magazine's art work and general genial tone—a sweetly childlike nature that seems to have created the special flavor for which *Life* was best known. Martin's natural asperity was held in check to some extent during Mitchell's lifetime, but tracking his editorials makes it clear that his mood grew increasingly militant during the ten years prior to the First World War.

Politics and the Writer's Career: Two Cases
Michael T. Gilmore

1.

I want to advance a simple proposition in this essay. My thesis, stated as broadly as possible, is that politics influences the writer's career. Politics can operate as a limit, a check on what can be said, and how it is said; and as a limit on what can be heard, and how it is heard. At times politics can even function as a restraint on what can be thought. But the political ferment of a given historical epoch can also operate as inspiration and possibility. It can start writers into speech; it can enable them to find their voices; it can embolden them with the assurance of a sympathetic hearing. And politics can effect these conflicting results within the career of a single author, stirring him or her to bursts of productivity and then stunting the very talent it has liberated, driving the writer to silence or to the protracted suicide of drink and despair.

Self-evident assertions, some might say. Yet they have not been conspicuous in the best-known treatments of the American writer's career. The marketplace, the rise of domestic ideology, the institutionalized culture of letters—we have all read, indeed, many of us have written, studies that specify *these* factors as having been instrumental in shaping major artists. While I have no desire to deny the impact of such formations on authorial development, I do want to note that the current interpretations share a certain impatience with the epiphenomenal, or what is perceived as the epiphenomenal, a tendency to treat as superficial the ordinary political changes through which every American has passed since the Republic's inception. Politics is seldom granted the weight of systemic consequence. Its very nature is assumed to be reactive, not causative. It has small power to shape, we think, because it is itself the product of other forces.[1]

"Political changes" are meant here to encompass a variety of events, from long-term decreases in the tolerance, say, of radical ideas, to convulsive occurrences like the election or defeat of a particular candidate for the presidency or, what is familiar to us all today, the capture of the Congress by a party long out of power. Even the most rabid New Historicists, with their method of analogizing between social and literary states of affairs, tend to shy away from this level of political specificity. Ronald Reagan's second term as somehow germinative of Toni Morrison's *Beloved* (1986), or Newt Gingrich as the muse behind John Updike's portrayal of America in *The Beauty of the Lilies* (1996), seems a fantastic and trivializing coupling, guilty of attributing effectual power to surface disturbances, of mistaking responses for determinations.

But I submit that we have been too quick to dismiss the cutaneous as inconsequential. If recent history teaches us anything, it is that political phenomena which appear trifling in the greater scheme of things, like mid-term electoral results, can have far-reaching cultural reverberations. The scope of public debate may be sharply narrowed, new voices thrust into prominence, others caused to disappear. It would be curious if such discursive aftershocks did *not* make an impression on politically sensitive writers like Morrison and Updike.

To illustrate my thesis, I propose briefly to investigate a pair of literary careers, drawn not from the present but from the early and middle years of this century. My examples are the African American novelist, poet, songwriter, diplomat, and political activist James Weldon Johnson and the critic and textual scholar whom we honor at this conference, William Charvat. Two books will stand at the center of my analysis: Johnson's anonymously published *The Autobiography of an Ex-Coloured Man,* which first appeared in 1912, and Charvat's posthumous collection of essays, *The Profession of Authorship in America, 1800–1870* (1968).

Politics left deep imprints on both men's lives and works. Johnson composed his highly equivocal novel at a moment when he dreamed of transcending America's racial categories. The color-blind opportunity that seemed possible under Presidents Roosevelt and Taft energized his imagination, though it did so at the price of what was then called "race loyalty" and what, from our current perspective, looks uncomfortably like collusion with imperialism. When the apparent openness of governmental service evaporated under Woodrow Wilson, Johnson abandoned fiction writing for political organizing.

Political retrenchment had a less immediate but more damaging effect on Charvat's creativity. It may seem curious, in view of his high standing today, that a colloquium formally acknowledging his legacy had to wait until thirty years after his death. The reasons for the delay lie partly outside the academy, and they are inextricable from the thwarting of Charvat's academic ambitions. Although no single event was decisive here, the electoral outcome of 1948 can be taken as a turning point: it brought an escalation of the Cold War bipolarism that consigned left-wing ideas to marginality. The long resistance, or perhaps indifference, to Charvat's brand of economics-oriented scholarship was rooted in that attitudinal shift, which contributed to the frustrations of his final years and to his tragic failure to complete his masterpiece.

2.

"Will we permit the Soviet Union to put a second Cuba, a second Libya, right on the doorsteps of the United States? . . . Could there be any greater tragedy than for us to sit back and permit this cancer to spread?" The words are Ronald Reagan's, the subject the Sandinista regime in Managua, but the sentiments have a long history in American imperial politics.[2] For a hundred and fifty years, Washington has not hesitated to impose its will on the people of Nicaragua, either through direct military intervention or through the deployment of surrogates like Reagan's secretly financed Contras. American possessiveness antedates the Civil War and was implicated from its origin in the problem of race. Interference began in 1855 when the filibuster William Walker—the term derives from the Spanish *filibustero* and means pirate or adventurer—invaded the country at the head of an army of mercenaries and overthrew the native government. Walker rallied to his side several hundred would-be planters, who were fired by the dream of establishing a southern empire in Central America. In 1856, having installed himself as president, he cancelled Nicaragua's emancipation law and issued a proclamation relegalizing slavery. Walker was ousted a few months later when the Pierce administration, anxious to calm sectional passions, withdrew diplomatic recognition.[3]

Nicaragua declared itself a republic in 1857, and for the next half-century enjoyed the relative peace of rigged elections and *coups d'etat*, engineered with implicit or direct approval from North America. A justification commonly advanced for United States involvement, especially after the occupation of Cuba and the Philippines in 1898, was that superior nations, like superior races, had the right to rule their inferiors. In this instance, I am paraphrasing from Charles W. Chesnutt's novel *The Marrow of Tradition,* in which white supremacist sentiments are said to be gaining ground as the country hurtles toward "colossal wealth and world-dominion." Chesnutt's book is a fictionalized account of the 1898 "race riot" in Wilmington, North Carolina, where armed whites went on a murderous rampage to intimidate the black majority and reclaim political control. One of the plotters, a Confederate veteran named General Belmont, invokes Nicaragua as his model for the conspiracy against black rights. "Down in the American tropics, they have a way of doing things," the general says, explaining that the lesson of insurgent success is to strike when the "negroes are not expecting trouble."[4]

What does all this have to do with James Williams Johnson, as he was christened, and *The Autobiography of an Ex-Coloured Man?* A good deal, as it happens, beginning with the fact that Johnson completed his novel in 1912 while serving as United States consul in Corinto, Nicaragua, a post to which he had been appointed by President Roosevelt. Johnson was in office when rebels launched an attack against the government of General José Santos Zelaya, a dictator known for "his hostile and tricky attitude toward American concessionaires." The State Department threw its support behind the rebels, who had given assurances of protecting "lawful American interests," and Johnson, as he relates in his actual autobiography, *Along This Way* (1933), did his best to assist the insurrection. Further upheavals followed, and eventually United States Marines had to be dispatched to ensure a sympathetic regime. Though in his memoirs Johnson is defensive about American imperialism, at the time he was thoroughly involved with the invading force: four hundred troops were billeted in Corinto, at a site revealingly called Camp Dixie, and the consulate doubled as Marine headquarters, with machine guns guarding its front. As usual in these interventions, the fighting took a heavy toll on the natives, while American casualties were light. A full twenty years elapsed before the Marines departed Nicaragua for good.[5]

Johnson's entanglement in the occupation bristles with contradictions. He had played a central part in crushing national sovereignty in a land where antebellum adventurism revoked emancipation, yet at the very same time he also wrote his famous poem on the fiftieth anniversary of Lincoln's signing of the American Emancipation Proclamation. According to *Along This Way*, the poem, which was printed with great fanfare in the *New York Times* on January 1, 1913, was crafted while heavily armed Marines from Camp Dixie slept in the consulate. Johnson later regretted the stanza proclaiming "the superiority in the absolute of so-called white civilization over so-called primitive civilization,"[6] but this was just one glaring example of how his willingness to identify with official policy suspended his awareness of the racism infecting that policy. The Johnson of Nicaragua and the foreign service resembled the subject of another poem he composed on American imperialism, punningly titled "The Color Sergeant (On an Incident at the Battle of San Juan Hill)." A soldier of the "sable Tenth" who perishes in Roosevelt's famous charge is celebrated for patriotic selflessness in rising above the military's bigotry: "Despised of men for his humble race, / Yet true, in death, to his duty."[7]

In actuality, Johnson differed from the fallen trooper as much as he resembled him: they parted company over their equanimity at being despised. The light-skinned, college-educated, and cosmopolitan diplomat, who married the even lighter-skinned Grace Nail while stationed in Corinto, had no intention of suffering the kind of humiliations common to African American men in the post-Reconstruction United States. He had of course been exposed to racism while growing up in Florida, and as a member of the songwriting team of Cole and Johnson Brothers, he had cherished trips abroad, above all to Paris, because of the relative lack of color prejudice in Europe.[8] The diplomatic corps, which he entered shortly after the musical trio disbanded, attracted him for its promise of a career based on merit. Johnson always prided himself on having inherited his father's practical side, and he hoped to find in the consular service the economic security and social acceptance unavailable in a racially divided America.⁹

Teddy Roosevelt, the hero of San Juan Hill, was a crucial figure in his decision. Roosevelt has taken his lumps in recent scholarship, and although there's no doubt that his record on race was uneven, to contemporaries he appeared far more enlightened than most national politicians. Roosevelt had appointed a number of blacks to government offices, and as a patron of Booker T. Washington, he invited the Tuskegee educator to dine at the White House in defiance of the Southern press. Johnson, like the great majority of American blacks, belonged to the party of Lincoln, and he helped get out the vote for Roosevelt's re-election through the Colored Republican Club of New York. The President returned the favor by naming Johnson to a diplomatic post in Venezuela and then promoting him in 1909 to be the new consul in Nicaragua.¹⁰

This was the background to his writing the fictional life of a refined black musician with Caucasian features who elects to pass. Johnson produced his narrative out of the belief that for him, at least, America's racial boundaries were fluid and the benefits of whiteness within reach. He was as invested as his protagonist in the act of passing. The novel's concluding utterance—"I have sold my birthright for a mess of pottage"—might be cited against this identification. But the lament reads like an afterthought and strikes a rare maudlin note in a novel that otherwise prizes the matter-of-fact. The words are not so much a heartfelt confession of the "ex-coloured" man's guilt as they are a proleptic exposure of the sentimentalism of identity politics.¹¹

The optimism bred by Republican control of the White House encouraged Johnson to view race as less integral to personhood than class and cultivation. Repeatedly in *The Autobiography of an Ex-Coloured Man*, Johnson's narrator challenges the essentialist ideology of "one-droppism," a legacy of the segregation ruling in *Plessy v. Ferguson*, with the greater possibility for self-making implied by social condition. Noting that "there are in this country three or four million people with the blood of both races in their veins," he ridicules the idea of an "impassable gulf" between white and black and the equally untenable notion of an instinctive bond between members of the same race (189). The social characteristics dividing African Americans by class are tirelessly documented, and we are told that "refined coloured people get no more pleasure out of riding with offensive Negroes than anybody else would get" (81). Just as he emphasizes class stratification within race, so the "ex-coloured" man highlights class affinity across race. "When one has seen something of the world and human nature," he writes, "one must conclude ... that between people in like stations of life there is very little difference the world over" (85).

The narrator's position is the democratic, quintessentially American one that individuals have the right to pursue their happiness and create of themselves whatever they can. If his story has a bedrock principle, it is social mobility and not race. Even color prejudice among African Americans is attributable to "economic necessity," he contends. Since a light skin confers benefits, blacks understandably put a premium on complexion and try to "marry up" racially in order to provide advantages for their children (154–55). In deciding to pass so that he can enjoy the full measure of those advantages himself, the narrator argues that forsaking one's race to better one's situation is "no less worthy an action than to forsake one's country for the same purpose." The "ex-coloured" man may be vain, he may be disloyal, but what American in this society of "ex's"—ex-Russians or ex-Koreans, ex-New Yorkers, ex-Hoosiers, and ex-Catholics—can deny the legitimacy of his reasoning? Certainly not the author who imagined him. The narrator vows to change his name and "let the world take me for what it would" (190). Johnson changed his own name shortly after publishing his novel. He dropped the "Williams" for what he considered the more literary "Weldon," and what one cannot help but notice is a more aristocratic and less black-sounding name.

But the temptation of passing didn't last; Johnson's buoyancy about meritocratic advancement in the consular service was swiftly deflated. Roosevelt's successor, William Howard Taft, had chipped away at diplomatic opportunity but generally maintained Republican tolerance for blacks. Then, in 1912, with Roosevelt campaigning as an independent, both men were defeated in their bid for re-election by the Virginia-born Democrat Woodrow Wilson. The new President's minions set out immediately to segregate all branches of the federal government, on the spurious ground that rigid separation would spare African Americans the hurt of white disapproval. Johnson, who expected another promotion on the basis of his performance in Nicaragua, encountered instead the hostility of the freshly appointed Secretary of State, William Jennings Bryan. The author of *The Autobiography of an Ex-Coloured Man* resigned his office and returned to the United States.

Johnson never wrote fiction again, and he never again entertained the illusion of being an ex-African American. If he were to prosper at all, he realized, it would have to be in his increasingly color-conscious homeland, and he would have to embrace rather than disavow his racial identity. The about-face toward activism was not so abrupt as it might seem. Johnson had always been torn between race betterment and race desertion; his novel, in which the protagonist emigrates across the color line only reluctantly, reflected that division. As early as 1900, Johnson had composed "Lift Every Voice and Sing," the stirring poem that came to be known as the "Negro National Anthem." And he had served his people as principal of a black grammar school in Jacksonville before fleeing the South for a career as a songwriter for the New York stage.

What Johnson lost in novelistic inspiration in 1913, with the unambiguous acceptance of his blackness, he made up for in resolve to combat social injustice. As it was politics that shut down possibilities for him, so it was to politics that he now turned his energies with the aim of improving the lot of all African Americans. First through his editorials for the black newspaper *New York Age,* and then through his activism as field secretary for the NAACP, Johnson labored to expose the hypocrisy of a nation that professed equal liberty but devoted itself to sweeping away a half century of African American progress. No politician aroused his indignation so much as the Southerner sitting in the Oval Office. "Mr Wilson," he declared in a representative piece from 1914, "bears the discreditable distinction of being the first President of the United States, since Emancipation, who openly condoned and vindicated prejudice against the Negro." The self-styled advocate of "The New Freedom" had done everything in his power to humiliate ten million citizens and stamp them with the "official government badge of inferiority."[12]

One other noteworthy change accompanied Johnson's intensified commitment to civil rights. The diplomat who had defended United States intervention in Central America evolved into an outspoken foe of imperialism, which he came to see as thoroughly compromised by anti-black prejudice. In 1920, he traveled to Haiti on behalf of the NAACP to investigate abuses under the American military occupation, begun in 1915 and destined to continue until 1934.

In articles published in the *Nation* and the *Crisis,* Johnson deplored the violation of Haitian sovereignty—"the first of the American Republics, after the United States, to gain its independence"—condemned "Government of, by, and for the National City Bank" of New York, and pointed out how deeply American policy was entwined with racist contempt. Washington justified military action by belittling the Haitian people, with their supposed "savagery," and President Wilson staffed the occupying forces with Southern white men, turning the country into "a veritable promised land of 'jobs for deserving Democrats.'"[13] The implications of an American outpost in Nicaragua named "Camp Dixie" were no longer lost on Johnson in the era of government-sponsored segregation.

3.

Anyone studying American literature in the late sixties or early seventies would have heard of William Charvat. Perhaps the person would have read several of Charvat's essays, been struck by their originality, and wondered why their author had ceased developing his own interpretations and shifted his efforts to textual scholarship. But that would probably have been the extent of it. Charvat's work was admired some thirty years ago, but it wasn't exactly central to the critical enterprise. It lacked the audacity of the grand synthetic overviews then popular—the studies of F. O. Matthiessen, Henry Nash Smith, Richard Chase, R. W. B. Lewis, Leo Marx, and others. Nor did it focus on the autonomous text, as mandated by the New Criticism, and it didn't pay a lot of attention to the myths and symbols thought to be constitutive of American writing's uniqueness.

I bring up this imaginary scenario not for the purpose of congratulating ourselves on better appreciating the value of Charvat's achievement, but in order to remind us of how peripheral he seemed until his rediscovery in the late seventies and early eighties. There were many reasons for his relative obscurity, including the decline in his output and his theoretical circumspection. He had a tendency to wrap himself, as it were, in the antiquarian aspects of his scholarship. But the main reason for marginalization, as I've suggested, is that the critical fashion had moved away from Charvat's interest in the commercial side of art, the unglamorous details of literary manufacture, promotion, and distribution. And this change in cultural emphasis cannot be understood apart from the political mutations that accompanied and produced it.

The most important such event was the Cold War, and the attendant recoil against the radical ideas of the thirties and forties. Charvat belonged to a generation whose thinking was shaped by leftist ferment. He had entered graduate school at the University of Pennsylvania in 1929, the year of the stock-market crash and the beginning of the Great Depression. Two years later he landed a position as an instructor at New York University, and although he himself was insulated from unemployment, no academic person living and working in New York during that season of crisis could have failed to imbibe the interrogations of capitalism current among intellectuals. Charvat did in fact became knowledgeable about Marxism and may even have briefly flirted with the Communist Party. His groundbreaking essay of 1937, "American Romanticism and the Depression of 1837," first appeared in *Science and Society*, then a new magazine with the subtitle "A Marxian Quarterly."[14]

Charvat also familiarized himself with indigenous sources of social radicalism. In the same year he published in *Science and Society*, he gave a radio interview on Edward Bellamy's utopian work of fiction, *Looking Backward* (1888). The discussion showed his regard for Bellamy's critique of the unregulated market but sharply distinguished the novelist's program from that installed in Soviet Russia: "Radical as he was, Bellamy was completely American in point of view, and he would have wanted us to work out a system based on our own traditions. Bellamy may have read Marx, but I doubt that communistic theory had much to do with his utopia."[15]

A similar refusal of orthodoxy marked Charvat's nuanced analyses of literary culture—he had little patience, for example, for the sentimental leftist notion that commercialization invariably degrades art—but such subtleties were not always respected in the Cold War climate of intimidation. The political temper altered for the worse shortly after he relocated with his family to Columbus in the mid 1940s. Alarm over Communist advances in Asia and Eastern Europe, combined with mounting domestic intolerance for "subversive" ideas, came to an early head in the election of 1948. The campaign was in part a referendum on the growing anti-Communist militancy of the Truman administration, which had initiated loyalty oaths for government employees a year earlier. A breakaway Democrat, Henry Wallace, ran for the White House on a coalition Progressive ticket.

Wallace, whose candidacy Charvat supported, had been Franklin Roosevelt's Vice-President as recently as 1944; he went down to crushing defeat, winning not a single electoral vote in a four-way contest in which the conservative Dixiecrat Strom Thurmond garnered thirty-nine.

Leftist sympathizers were fair game after that. Joe McCarthy, elected to the Senate after having wrested his party's nomination from the old-time liberal, Robert M. La Follette, Jr., erupted into national prominence in 1950 with charges that the State Department was infiltrated with Communists. College professors, movie actors, and low-level government officials fell victim to McCarthyite assaults. Charvat's son, Ted, remembers his parents being distressed at the height of the anti-Red witch-hunts because a faculty neighbor had been harried by the FBI. Ted's frightened mother "said that WC [William Charvat] had many years earlier published in a Marxist poetry journal. She told Ted not to talk about it anymore."[16]

Charvat was hardly the only former radical to feel menaced in the fifties, but he was one of the few in the academic literary establishment not to join the rush to American exceptionalism. Many of his generation's critical landmarks—Matthiessen's *American Renaissance* (1941), Smith's *Virgin Land* (1950), Chase's *The American Novel and Its Tradition* (1957)—have come under attack in recent years for overselling the singularity of American culture (in which socialism failed to take root) and for unwittingly replicating the ideological biases of the Cold War.[17] One does not have to add one's voice to these often patronizing rebukes to note the obvious fact that Charvat followed a different and far less crowded path. He almost uniquely carried into scholarship, and never wavered in his focus on, the kind of materialist issues that had engaged many people both inside and outside the profession in the 1930s but that had since fallen out of favor.

His great subject, of course, was the economics of authorship. At a time when leftists and even liberals ran the risk of political ostracism and, in extreme cases, of being fired from their jobs, Charvat dealt with subjects that appeared vaguely heretical and tinged with Marxism. He explored the class status of the writer, the artist's alienation in a democracy, the filiations between culture and the marketplace. Consider what it must have been like to encounter the titles of some of the papers collected in *The Profession of Authorship in America:* the already mentioned "American Romanticism and the

Depression of 1837," "Longfellow's Income from His Writings, 1842–1852," published in 1944, "Literary Economics and Literary History," from 1950. What did such matters have to do with the unsourced American Adam or with the culture's standard disembodied chronicle of maturation and independence? Dozens of scholars, inspired by Leo Marx, expatiated on the threat posed by technology, and particularly by the railroad, to the American wilderness and imagination. Charvat, in stark contrast, wrote of how the primitive condition of transportation retarded the growth of an indigenous literature, and he detailed the importance of the railroad to the publishing boom of the 1840s and 1850s.

None of this should be construed to mean that politics alone silenced Charvat, eventually causing him to abandon his projected study of nineteenth-century authorship and the book trade. He himself complained that his labors were impeded by "the lack of adequate research tools," such as a complete bibliography of American imprints.[18] And no doubt heavy drinking, his wife's illness, and his inability to attract an offer from the East Coast, where he dreamed of returning, were all factors in his unhappy last years. My point has been that political constriction, no less than scholarly obstacles and personal circumstances, lay behind Charvat's increasing sense of isolation. The change in what was politically acceptable, in what could be said without being misunderstood or summarily dismissed as obsolete, added to his feeling that the profession had passed him by and that he could not be certain of finding the responsive audience any author longs for. So William Charvat effectively gave up, producing less and less of his own writing and throwing himself into editing the Centenary Edition of the Works of Nathaniel Hawthorne, the massive textual enterprise on which he worked from the early 1960s until his death in 1966.

In a sense Charvat's greatest tragedy was posthumous. James Weldon Johnson lived to see the political winds shift again and to enjoy the plaudits of his contemporaries. *The Autobiography of an Ex-Coloured Man* was reissued under his own name in 1927, during the Harlem Renaissance. Five years later Teddy Roosevelt's distant cousin Franklin was elected President in a landslide victory that inaugurated the mass exodus of black voters to the Democratic Party. Johnson, by then settled at Fisk University as writer-in-residence, brought out his autobiography of a coloured man, *Along This Way*, in 1933; the book, arguably his best, has never been out of print. He had fulfilled the early ambition of his novel's protagonist "to be a great man, a great coloured man, to reflect credit on the race and gain fame for myself" (46). Charvat was considerably less fortunate. Though he was anything but a New Historicist—he would have balked at today's more extreme conflations of the writer with the marketplace—he anticipated the current reassessment of the literary as embedded in and permeated by the social. Dispirited in his mid-fifties, dead at sixty-one, Charvat was deprived of the chance to see the reconfiguration of critical attitudes that his own pioneering scholarship helped to make possible.

Notes

1. I do not mean to suggest that there have been *no* recent studies of the effect of politics upon American literature. What seems undeniable, however, is that such discussions have not set the agenda for the profession. Two examples would be Carolyn L. Karcher, *Shadow over the Promised Land: Slavery, Race, and Violence in Melville's America* (Baton Rouge: Louisiana State University Press, 1980); and Len Gougeon, *Virtue's Hero: Emerson, Antislavery, and Reform* (Athens: University of Georgia Press, 1990).

2. Reagan is quoted (from a speech of 1986) in Michael Paul Rogin, *Ronald Reagan, the Movie, and Other Episodes in Political Demonology* (Berkeley and Los Angeles: University of California Press, 1987), xiv–xv.

3. For information on Walker, see James M. McPherson, *Battle Cry of Freedom: The Civil War Era* (New York: Ballantine Books, 1989), 110–15.

4. *The Marrow of Tradition* (1901; rpt. New York: Penguin Books, 1993), 238, 249–50.

5. *Along This Way* (1933; rpt. New York: Penguin Books, 1990), 255–90; quotations from page 260. On American involvement in Nicaragua, also see Robert A. Pastor, *Condemned to Repetition: The United States and Nicaragua* (Princeton: Princeton University Press, 1987), esp. 3–25.

6. Johnson, *Along This Way*, 290–92.

7. The poem, from *Fifty Years and Other Poems* (1917), is reprinted in *The Selected Writings of James Weldon Johnson*, vol. 2: *Social, Political, Literary Essays*, ed. Sondra Kathryn Wilson (New York: Oxford University Press, 1995), 365.

8. Johnson, *Along This Way*, 203, 209.

9. Johnson's biographer, Eugene Levy, remarks on the "racially neutral fantasy of a merit-based career in the foreign service." See *James Weldon Johnson: Black Leader, Black Voice* (Chicago: University of Chicago Press, 1973), 124.

10. See Levy, *James Weldon Johnson*, 109–13. Roosevelt's mixed record (with emphasis on the negative side) is discussed by Kenneth O'Reilly, *Nixon's Piano: Presidents and Racial Politics from Washington to Clinton* (New York: Free Press, 1995), 63–77. A particularly unflattering assessment is Amy Kaplan, "Black and Blue on San Juan Hill," in Kaplan and Donald E. Pease, eds., *Cultures of United States Imperialism* (Durham, North Carolina: Duke University Press, 1993), 219–36.

11. *The Autobiography of an Ex-Coloured Man* (New York: Vintage Books, 1989), 211; future quotations are from this edition and will be included parenthetically in the text. For a forceful critique of the essentialism inherent in identity politics, with brief reference to Johnson's book, see Walter Benn Michaels, *Our America: Nativism, Modernism, and Pluralism* (Durham, N.C.: Duke University Press, 1995), esp. 116–18.

12. This and other relevant editorials are reprinted in *The Selected Writings of James Weldon Johnson*, vol. 1: *The New York Age Editorials, 1914–1923*, ed. Sondra Kathryn Wilson (New York: Oxford University Press, 1995). The quotations are from 182–83. See also *Along This Way*, 297–326.

13. See *The Selected Writings of James Weldon Johnson*, vol. 2: *Social, Political, Literary Essays*, 244, 218, 227, 251.

14. For information on Charvat's life, I am indebted to his daughter, Judith C. Watkins. The source for his 1937 essay is given in *The Profession of Authorship in America, 1800–1870: The Papers of William Charvat*, ed. Matthew J. Bruccoli (Columbus: Ohio State University Press, 1968), 317.

15. A typescript of the radio broadcast is in the Houghton Library at Harvard University.

16. Books on the Cold War are legion. Some relevant titles for this and the previous paragraph are Richard J. Walton, *Henry Wallace, Harry Truman and the Cold War* (New York: Viking, 1976); Michael Paul Rogin, *The Intellectuals and McCarthy: The Radical Specter* (Cambridge: MIT Press, 1967); and Richard Fried, *Nightmare in Red: The McCarthy Era in Perspective* (New York: Oxford University Press, 1990).

17. A single attack, one of the earliest, will have to stand for many. See Donald E. Pease, "*Moby-Dick* and the Cold War," in Walter Benn Michaels and Donald E. Pease, eds., *The American Renaissance Reconsidered: Selected Papers from the English Institute, 1982–83* (Baltimore: Johns Hopkins University Press, 1985), 113–55.

18. Charvat, *Literary Publishing in America: 1790–1850* (Philadelphia: University of Pennsylvania Press, 1959), 9.

CONTRIBUTORS

MARTHA BANTA, Professor Emeritus of the University of California, Los Angeles, is past president of the American Studies Association, current editor of *PMLA*, a Guggenheim Fellow, and the author of several books, including *Imaging American Women: Idea and Ideals in Cultural History* and *Taylored Lives: Narrative Production in the Age of Taylor, Veblen, and Ford.*

LAWRENCE BUELL is John P. Marquand Professor of and Chair of English at Harvard University and author of several books and articles on U.S. literary and cultural history, including nineteenth-century print culture, such as *New England Literary Culture* and *The Environmental Imagination.*

STEVEN FINK, Associate Professor of English at The Ohio State University, is the author of *Prophet in the Marketplace: Thoreau's Development as a Professional Writer.* He is currently writing a book on the careers of several antebellum women periodical editors.

FRANCES SMITH FOSTER is Charles Howard Candler Professor of English and Women's Studies at Emory University. She is the author of several studies of nineteenth-century African American literature and co-editor of *The Norton Anthology of African American Literature* and *The Oxford Companion to African American Literature.* She is writing a book on the influence of the African American church upon African American literature.

MICHAEL T. GILMORE, Professor of English at Brandeis University, is the author of several works on American literature and culture, including

American Romanticism and the Marketplace. His most recent book is *Differences in the Dark: American Movies and English Theater*.

JAY GROSSMAN teaches American literature, poetry, and gay studies in the English Department at Boston University. He is co-editor of the essay collection *Breaking Bounds: Whitman and American Cultural Studies,* and he is completing a book manuscript entitled "Emerson, Whitman, and the Politics of Representation."

JULIAN MARKELS is Professor Emeritus of English at The Ohio State University. He is the author of *Melville and the Politics of Identity* and is currently writing about the representation of class in the novel.

MEREDITH L. MCGILL is Assistant Professor of English at Rutgers University. She has published essays on handwriting and mass production, American copyright law, Edgar Allan Poe, and James Russell Lowell and Robert Lowell. She is currently completing a book on the emergence of a mass market for books in America, titled "American Literature and the Culture of Reprinting, 1837–1854."

GRANTLAND S. RICE is the author of *The Transformation of Authorship in America* and several articles on American literature and culture. He has held fellowships from the National Endowment for the Humanities, the American Council of Learned Societies, and the Institute of United States Studies at the University of London. He is currently working on a sequel to *Transformation* entitled "The Velvet Prison: The Fate of Political Writing in America."

SUSAN S. WILLIAMS is Associate Professor of English at The Ohio State University. She is the author of *Confounding Images: Photography and Portraiture in Antebellum American Fiction* as well as of numerous essays on nineteenth-century American writers. She is currently at work on a book on women writers and publishing culture in nineteenth-century America.

MICHAEL WINSHIP, Professor of English at the University of Texas at Austin, is the author of *American Literary Publishing in the Mid-Nineteenth Century: The Business of Ticknor and Fields*. He is currently co-editing volume 3, *The Industrial Book*, of the American Antiquarian Society's *History of the Book in America*.

INDEX

Adams, John Quincy, 86–87
advertisements: in *Freedom's Journal*, 32; and *Leaves of Grass*, 80, 175; in *Life* magazine, 173–75, 182–97; in the *Missionary Record*, 34; and transatlantic book trade, 103; for *Woman in the Nineteenth Century*, 67–68
Afric-American Female Intelligence Society, 25
African Union Society, 25
Alcott, Amos Bronson, 48
Alexander's Messenger, 42
Allen, Bishop Richard, 26, 32
Along This Way (Johnson), 202–3, 210
AME Book Concern, 26
AME (African Methodist Episcopal) Church, 27–28, 29, 31, 34 n. 5
A.M.E. Review, 29
"American Literature" (Fuller), 70
American Magazine of Useful and Entertaining Knowledge, The, 40
American Monthly Magazine, 56, 58–59, 69
"American Scholar, The" (Emerson), 91–92
AME Zion Church, 5, 30, 34 n. 5; Publishing House, 26
Andrews, William, 34
anthologies: and African American literature, 31; of Civil War poetry, 126; Nathaniel Hawthorne's work in, 43; Mark Twain's work in, 143; Walt Whitman's work in, 128–30
Appeal to the Colored Citizens of the World (Walker), 33–34
Appeal to the Females of the African Methodist Episcopal Church, An (Still), 27–28
Atkinson's Casket, 43
Atlantic Monthly, 124, 151, 164
Attwood, F. G., 175, 178, 182
Auden, W. H., 49
Autobiography of an ex-Coloured Man, The (Johnson), 9, 204–7, 210–11
Autobiography of Rev. Thomas James, The, 30

Bancroft, George, 57
Banneker, Benjamin, 25
Barlow, Joel, 56
"Battle Hymn of the Republic" (Howe), 124
Battle-Pieces (Melville), 7, 125, 127, 132–33
Baym, Nina, 40
Bell, Michael Davitt, 164
Bellamy, Edward, 208
Benét, Stephen Vincent, 124, 135
Benjamin, Park, 58
Benjamin, Walter, 15
Bentley, Richard (publisher), 104–5
Bercovitch, Sacvan, 15
Billy Budd (Melville), 125, 147, 150 n. 12

INDEX

Bird, M. B., 126
Bohn, H. G. (publisher), 105
Boker, James, 126–27
books, coffee table, 126, 182
Boston Daily Advertiser, 57
Bridge, Horatio, 40
Brother Jonathan, 42, 65
Brownell, Henry Howard, 126–27
Browning, Elizabeth Barrett, 106
Bruccoli, Matthew J., 1
Buell, Lawrence, 55–56
Bunce and Huntington (publishers), 127
Burns, Ken, 123, 135
Byron, George Gordon, Lord, 59

Caine, Hall, 162
cartoons, in *Life* magazine, 175–77, 178–79, 189–90
Channing, William Ellery, 64
Channing, William Henry, 61, 67
Chapman and Hall (publishers), 106–7
Chapters from a Life (Phelps), 152, 157, 158, 160, 162
Charvat, William, 1–4, 9, 10, 13–15, 21, 22, 36–38, 50–51, 75–76, 83, 91, 93, 98, 107, 124, 139–40, 151, 200–201, 207–11
Chesnutt, Charles, 202
Christian Recorder (AME), 5, 28, 29
Civil War, poetry of, 123–35
Clarke, James Freeman, 59, 60
Cleaver, Eldridge, 34
Coffin, Charles M., 129
Colacurcio, Michael, 42
Cold War, influence of on William Charvat, 208–9
Coleridge, Samuel Taylor, 15
Collier's Weekly, 182–83, 185
Colored American, The, 32
Colored Reading Society of Philadelphia, 25
"Color Sergeant, The" (Johnson), 203
Colt's Patent Fire Arms Manufacturing Company, 184–85, 188–89
"Come Up From the Fields, Father" (Whitman), 128–29, 131, 134
commodity: definitions of, 7, 124–25, 128, 131–32; literature as, 57, 58; magazine as saleable, 64–65, 173, 191, 194
Confession of John Joyce, 26
copyright, 6, 14, 26, 56, 65, 101–2, 105–6

Cornish, Samuel, 32
Coultrap-McQuin, Susan, 161
Cowley, Malcolm, 79
Crèvecoeur, J. Hector St. John de, 4, 16–22
Crummell, Reverend Alexander, 31

Darnton, Robert, 2–3, 4, 9, 16
Davidson, Cathy N., 2
"David Swan" (Hawthorne), 42, 43, 49
Delany, Martin, 5, 29, 34
Democratic Review (*United States Magazine and Democratic Review*), 42, 60
Detter, Reverend Thomas, 31
Dial, The, 48, 56, 61–67, 69
Dickens, Charles, 105–7
Douglass, Frederick, 5, 29–31
Drum-Taps (Whitman), 7, 125–28
Duyckinck, Evert, 69–70

"Eighteenth Presidency!, The" (Whitman), 88, 90–91
Emerson, Ralph Waldo: as agent for Margaret Fuller, 65–67, 71; and the canon, 130; and the *Dial*, 61–64; relation to public, 86–93; theory of language, 87; and Ticknor and Fields, 105; Twain and, 141, 144; and Whitman, 75–84, 93. Works: "The American Scholar," 91–92; "The Rhodora," 89
Evening Star, The, 29
Everybody's Magazine, 183, 186, 197 n. 2

Fay, Theodore S., 48
Fields, James T., 38, 161. *See also* Ticknor and Fields (publisher)
Fisher, Judith L., 189–91
Foote, Shelby, 123
Freedom's Journal, 31–33
Friendly Society of St. Thomas's African Church, 25
Fuller, Margaret: and audience, 57, 61–63, 67–69; Conversations, 56, 60–61; and the *Dial*, 56, 61–66; and the New York *Tribune*, 56, 67–69; and periodical publication, 56–60; and publishers, 56, 66–71. Works: "American Literature," 70; "Defense of Brutus," 57–58; "The Great Lawsuit," 63, 67; "Modern British Poets," 58; *Papers on Literature and Art*, 56; "A Short Essay on Critics," 62;

Summer on the Lakes, in 1843, 56, 66–67; *Woman in the Nineteenth Century,* 56, 63, 67–68

Ganyard, A. O., 126
Garnet, Reverend Henry Highland, 31, 34
Garrison, William Lloyd, 5, 30
Gibson, Charles Dana, 175–77, 179
Gilmore, Michael T., 43
Glazener, Nancy, 168
Godey's Lady's Book, 44
Goethe, Johann Wolfgang von, 15, 59, 63
Goodrich, Samuel, 56
Graham's Magazine, 44
"Great Lawsuit, The" (Fuller), 63, 67
Greeley, Horace, 6, 56, 67–69
Greeley and McElrath (publishers), 56, 67
Griswold, Rufus Wilmot, 43
Grossman, Allen, 87–89, 91
Gustafson, Thomas, 93

Hale, Sarah Josepha, 48
Hall, Prince, 25
Hammon, Jupiter, 25
Hampden Washingtonian, The, 42
Harper, Frances E. W., 29
Harper's Magazine, 126–27, 132–33, 167
Harris, Sharon, 167
Hawthorne, Nathaniel: Poe's reviews of, 43–51; publication of early fiction, 37, 40–44, 56, 60; self-representation, 38–44; and Wiley and Putnam, 69. Works: *American Magazine of Useful and Entertaining Knowledge* (editor), 40; "David Swan," 42–43, 49; "Footprints on the Sea-Shore," 43, 49; *The House of Seven Gables,* 38, 43; *Mosses from an Old Manse,* 44, 46; *The Scarlet Letter,* 38–39, 43; "Sights from a Steeple," 42–43, 49; *Twice-Told Tales,* 38–40, 42–43, 45; "The Wives of the Dead" ("The Two Widows"), 42, 49
Haynes, Lemuel, 26
Hazlitt, William, 45
Hedge, Frederick Henry, 61
Hedrick, Joan, 161
Herron, George Davis, 156
History Book Club, 123

Holmes, Oliver Wendell, Sr., 104, 126, 141, 144, 165
Homer, Winslow, 130
Hooper, Ellen, 64
Hopkins, Gerard Manley, 129
Horton, George Moses, 33
Houghton, Henry Oscar, 158
House of Seven Gables, The (Hawthorne), 38, 43
Howe, Julia Ward, 124
Howells, William Dean, 8, 141, 148, 163–65, 167
Huckleberry Finn (Twain), 8, 139–49
Hugo, Victor, 162
Hunt, Leigh, 45

Irving, Washington, 45, 46, 49

Jackson, Andrew, 91–92, 96 nn. 29, 32
James, Henry, 161–62, 164
James, Thomas, 30–31
Jehlen, Myra, 15
John Brown's Body (Benét), 124
Johnson, James Weldon, 9, 200–207, 210–11. Works: *Along This Way,* 202–3, 210; *The Autobiography of an ex-Coloured Man,* 204–7, 210–11; "The Color Sergeant," 203; "Lift Every Voice and Sing," 206
Jones, Absalom, 25

Kaplan, Justin, 93
Kelley, Mary, 55, 152
Kodak camera, 189

Lakoff, George, 14
Lamb, Charles, 45
Lang, Amy Schrager, 166
Leaves of Grass (Whitman), 6, 76, 78–84, 90, 93, 125, 128, 130–31, 175
Letters from an American Farmer (Crèvecoeur), 4, 16–22
Liberator, The, 30
Lienesch, Michael, 15
Life magazine, 8, 174–97
"Lift Every Voice and Sing" (Johnson), 206
Lincoln, Abraham, 77, 123, 130–31
Little, Brown (publishers), 56, 66–67
Living Way, The, 29
Locke, John, 14, 19

Longfellow, Henry Wadsworth, 56, 104, 130, 141, 144, 210
Lowell, James Russell, 126–27

magazines: and advertising, 103, 173–75, 182–97; African American periodicals, 27–30; British imports, 108; Margaret Fuller and, 58–65, 69; Hawthorne and, 38, 40–45, 48; as material objects, 8–9, 173–74; as publishing outlets, 4, 6–7, 56, 60, 63–65. *See also under individual titles*
"March to the Sea, The" (Melville), 127, 132–33
marketplace, literary, 2–3, 5–7, 9, 16, 33–38, 41, 43–45, 48, 55–72, 125–27, 132–34, 160–61, 191–94, 199, 209–11
Martin, Edward S., 196, 198 n. 8
Marx, Karl, 18
Marx, Leo, 210
Masson, Tom, 179–80, 182
Matthews, Cornelius, 70
Matthiessen, F. O., 75–76, 86
McCarthy, Joseph, 209
McClure's Magazine, 151, 182–83
Melville, Herman: 7, 125–27, 132–33. Works: *Battle-Pieces*, 7, 125, 127, 132–33; *Billy Budd*, 125, 147, 150 n. 12; *The Confidence Man*, 132; "The March to the Sea," 127, 132–33; *Moby-Dick*, 8, 139, 142, 143, 145, 147, 148; *Redburn*, 7, 142–43, 145–48; *White Jacket*, 150 n. 12
Missionary Record, 34
Mitchell, John Ames, 196, 198 n. 8
Moby-Dick (Melville), 8, 139, 142, 143, 145, 147, 148
Moore, Frank: *Rebellion Record*, 126, 132
Morrison, Toni, 200
Mosses from an Old Manse (Hawthorne), 44, 46
Munroe, James (publisher), 66–67
Mystery (newspaper), 5, 29

Narrative of the Life of Frederick Douglass (Douglass), 30
Newfield, Christopher, 87, 89
newspapers: African American, 24–25, 28–29, 31–34; Margaret Fuller and, 68–69, 71; Hawthorne reprinted in, 38, 42–43; imported, 105; and literary marketplace, 56–57. *See also under individual titles*
Nicaragua, American intervention in, 201–3
Nichols, Major George Ward: *Story of the Great March*, 127, 133, 137 n. 32
Nissenbaum, Stephen, 39
North American Review, 48, 57
North Star, 29, 31

"O Captain! My Captain!" (Whitman), 128, 130–31
Oration, Commemorative of the Abolition of the Slave Trade, An (Sidney), 26

Papers on Literature and Art (Fuller), 56, 69–70
Parrington, Vernon, 167
Payne, Bishop Daniel, 25
Peabody, Elizabeth Palmer, 58, 60
Phelps, Austin, 159, 161, 169 n. 10
Phelps, Elizabeth Stuart: and authorship, 153, 159–68; marriage of, 160; and notions of realism, 152–53, 161–66; relation to father, 159, 161; relation to mother, 152, 161; stage fright of, 151–53, 165–66. Works: *Chapters from a Life*, 152, 157, 158, 160, 162; *Doctor Zay*, 164; *Friends: A Duet*, 164, 165; *The Gates Ajar*, 151; "A Plea for Immortality," 162; *The Silent Partner*, 157, 166; *A Singular Life*, 153–60, 165; *The Story of Avis*, 157; *The Whole Family*, 166, 171 n. 33
Philosophical and Political History of the Settlements and Trade of the Europeans in the East and West Indies (Raynal), 16–18
Pillsbury, Parker, 30
Planet (Georgetown), 34
Plessy v. Ferguson, 204
Poe, Edgar Allan: review of Fuller, 68; reviews of Hawthorne, 38, 44–50; and Wiley and Putnam, 69. Works: "The Philosophy of Composition," 48, 50; "The Raven," 50
Prose Writers of America, The (Griswold), 43
Publisher's Circular, 103

Raynal, Abbé Guillaume Thomas François, 16–18
Read, Thomas Buchanan, 126
reader response, 139–43

readers: African American, 33; and Crève-coeur, 20–21; and the *Dial*, 61–63; and Fuller, 67–69; and Hawthorne, 39, 44, 46–47, 49–50; imagined, 139–40, 145, 147; in literary marketplace, 2, 3–5, 7–8, 10; of Melville, 133; of Whitman, 86, 131–32
Reagan, Ronald, 200, 201
realism, literary, 152–53, 161–68
Redburn (Melville), 7, 142–43, 145–48
"Religion and the Pure Principles of Morality" (Stewart), 33
Remington, Frederic, 184, 187, 197 n. 3
Reni, Guido, 157
Repository of Religion and Literature and Science and Art, 29–30
Repplier, Agnes, 177–79
Reynolds, David, 77, 131, 134
Reynolds, Larry J., 61
Rights of All, 32
Riis, Jacob, 154
Ripley, George, 59, 62
Rogers, W. A., 175–77
Roosevelt, Theodore, 9, 181, 183, 184, 186, 201–5, 210
Roughing It (Twain), 7, 142–45

Scarlet Letter, The (Hawthorne), 38–39, 43
Scientific American, 34
Sedgwick, Catherine Maria, 48
Sherman, William T., 124, 133
"Short Essay on Critics, A" (Fuller), 62
Sidney, Joseph, 26
"Sights from a Steeple" (Hawthorne), 42–43, 49
Sigourney, Lydia, 48
Silent Partner, The (Phelps), 157, 166
Singular Life, A (Phelps), 8, 153–60, 165
Smith, Adam, 14
Smith, Dan, 183, 197 n. 1
Smith, Henry Nash, 140–41, 148
"Song of Myself" (Whitman), 84, 90–91
Spectator, The, 45, 49
Stead, William T., 156
Stewart, Maria W., 33
Still, Mary, 27–28
Story, William Wetmore, 64
Stowe, Harriet Beecher, 163, 165, 167
Sturgis, Caroline, 64
Summer on the Lakes, in 1843 (Fuller), 56, 66–67

Taft, William Howard, 201, 205
Tennyson, Alfred, 105–6, 127
Thackeray, William Makepeace, 105, 189–90
Thoreau, Henry David, 64, 130
Ticknor and Fields (publishers), 6–7, 41, 50, 56, 103–8, 126–27
Token, The, 42
Tribune (New York), 6, 56, 67–69, 71, 80
Trübner, Nicolas, 103–5
Twain, Mark, 139–42; in *Life* magazine, 183, 195; readers of, 139–41, 145; rhetorical self-consciousness of, 142; use of frame narrative by, 141. Works: *Huckleberry Finn*, 139–49; *Roughing It*, 7, 142–45; "A 'War Prayer,'" 183
Twice-Told Tales (Hawthorne), 38–40, 42–43, 45, 50

Updike, John, 200
United States Magazine and Democratic Review (*Democratic Review*), 42, 60

Van Anglen, Kevin, 87

Walker, David, 33–34
Walker, William: *Life* cartoonist, 175, 178; Nicaraguan filibuster, 201–2
Wallace, Henry, 208–9
Walpole, Horace, 105
war, conflicting views of in *Life* magazine, 8, 174–97. *See also* Civil War; Cold War
Ward, Herbert, 160
Ward, Mrs. Humphrey, 156
Ward, Samuel, 64
Warner, Michael, 92
Washington, Booker T., 204
Watkins, Reverend William, 25
Watson, Harry L., 91
Weekly Advocate, The, 32
Wells-Barnett, Ida B., 29
Western Messenger, 59
Wheatley, Phillis, 25–26, 33
Whitman, Walt: and Emerson's letter, 75–83, 93; and fan letters, 131; lectures of, 130; in literary anthologies, 128–30; persona of, 130; relation to public, 88–93. Works: "Come Up From the Fields, Father," 128–29, 131, 134; *Drum-Taps*, 7, 125–28; *Leaves of Grass*, 6, 76, 78–84, 88, 90, 125, 128, 130–31, 175; "The

Whitman, Walt (*continued*)
Eighteenth Presidency!" 88, 90–91; "O Captain! My Captain!" 128, 130–31; "The Return of the Heroes," 130; "Song of Myself," 84, 90–91; *Two Rivulets*, 130

Whittier, John Greenleaf, 126–27, 135, 141, 152, 165. Works: *In War Time and Other Poems*, 127; *National Lyrics*, 127; *Snow-Bound*, 127

Wiley and Putnam (publishers), 56, 69–70

Williams, Raymond, 5, 55–56, 64, 68

Willis, Nathaniel Parker, 56

Wilson, Clint, 27

Wilson, Woodrow, 9, 201, 205–7

Woman in the Nineteenth Century (Fuller), 56, 63, 67–68

www.ingramcontent.com/pod-product-compliance
Lightning Source LLC
Chambersburg PA
CBHW030136240426
43672CB00005B/154